Build Applications

Full stack development

Dobrin Ganev

BIRMINGHAM - MUMBAI

Build Applications with Meteor

Copyright © 2017 Packt Publishing

First published: May 2017

Production reference: 1260517

Published by Packt Publishing Ltd.
Livery Place
35 Livery Street
Birmingham
B3 2PB, UK.
ISBN 978-1-78712-988-7

www.packtpub.com

Credits

Author
Dobrin Ganev

Reviewer
Olivier Pons

Commissioning Editor
Ashwin Nair

Acquisition Editor
Shweta Pant

Content Development Editor
Roshan Kumar

Technical Editor
Murtaza Tinwala

Copy Editor
Shaila Kusanale

Project Coordinator
Devanshi Doshi

Proofreader
Safis Editing

Indexer
Rekha Nair

Graphics
Jason Monteiro

Production Coordinator
Shraddha Falebhai

About the Author

Dobrin Ganev is a Calgary-based software developer with years of experience in various domains, from large-scale distributed applications to frontend web development with the latest JavaScript frameworks. In recent years, he has been focusing on architecting and prototyping solutions in various subjects, such as enterprise search, GIS, predictive analytics, and real-time distributed systems.

I would like to thank Packt for giving me the opportunity to work on this exciting book and for their great support from the initialization of the idea through the publishing stage.

About the Reviewer

Olivier Pons is a highly-skilled developer who's been building websites for many years. He's a teacher in France at the IUT (University of Sciences) in Aix-en-Provence, CESI (Centre d'Études Supérieures en Informatique), ISEN (Institut Supérieur de l'Électronique et du Numérique), G4 Marseille, and École d'Ingénieurs des Mines de Gardanne, where he teaches state-of-the-art web techniques: Django/Python, Node.js, Big Data / NoSQL, MVC fundamentals, PHP for experts, WordPress for experts, Symfony, jQuery, Apache, nginx and Apache advanced configuration, Linux basics, and advanced VIM techniques. He has already done some technical reviews, including the PacktLib books *Learning ExtJS, Building Modern JavaScript Applications, jQuery hotshots, jQuery Mobile Web Development Essentials*, and *Wordpress Complete*, among others. In 2011, he left a full-time job as a Delphi developer and PHP expert to concentrate on his own company, HQF Development (http://hqf.fr). He currently runs a number of websites, including http://www.cogofly.com, http://www.kry stallopolis.com, http://www.papdevis.fr, and http://olivierpons.fr, his own web development blog. He's currently making a Unity mcq mobile application, which works along with a Django website.

He works as teacher, highly-skilled developer and project manager, and also helps big companies' CTOs make the best choices for their web projects.

www.PacktPub.com

For support files and downloads related to your book, please visit www.PacktPub.com.

Did you know that Packt offers eBook versions of every book published, with PDF and ePub files available? You can upgrade to the eBook version at www.PacktPub.com and as a print book customer, you are entitled to a discount on the eBook copy. Get in touch with us at service@packtpub.com for more details.

At www.PacktPub.com, you can also read a collection of free technical articles, sign up for a range of free newsletters and receive exclusive discounts and offers on Packt books and eBooks.

https://www.packtpub.com/mapt

Get the most in-demand software skills with Mapt. Mapt gives you full access to all Packt books and video courses, as well as industry-leading tools to help you plan your personal development and advance your career.

Why subscribe?

- Fully searchable across every book published by Packt
- Copy and paste, print, and bookmark content
- On demand and accessible via a web browser

Customer Feedback

Thanks for purchasing this Packt book. At Packt, quality is at the heart of our editorial process. To help us improve, please leave us an honest review on this book's Amazon page at `https://www.amazon.com/dp/1787129888/`.

If you'd like to join our team of regular reviewers, you can e-mail us at `customerreviews@packtpub.com`. We award our regular reviewers with free eBooks and videos in exchange for their valuable feedback. Help us be relentless in improving our products!

Table of Contents

Preface   1

Chapter 1: Foundation of Meteor   7

  Foundation of Meteor   7

  Setting up the development environment   8

  Building a Meteor app   11

  The frontend with React   12

    The React's state   16

      Adding state to a stateless function component   16

    Inheritance versus composition   18

    Adding a state to a component   19

    Meteor with React   22

      Adding and removing atmosphere packages in Meteor   22

      Integrating React with Meteor's reactive data system   26

      Explore MongoDB in the Meteor shell   27

      Publishing and Subscribing   27

        Improvements in the current code   30

  Summary   32

Chapter 2: Building a Shopping Cart   33

  Creating the project structure   33

  On the server   36

  Building the application components   39

    The ProductsContainer   40

      PropTypes   44

    The CartContainer   44

  Adding router to the application   50

    App.js   54

    ProductComponent.js   54

    The data containers   55

      BooksContainer.js   56

      MusicContainer.js   56

  Meteor methods   58

    Removing item from the cart   59

    Updating the quantity of an item in the cart   60

    Let's create another method that will calculate the cart's total price   60

  Considerations for scalability   63

Basic validations on the server	63
Defining a schema	64
Defaults	66
Summary	68

Chapter 3: Style Your React Components with Bootstrap and Material Design 69

Mobile first	70
Making it mobile friendly!	74
Modular CSS with LESS	74
Test it out!	78
Modular CSS with Syntactically Awesome StyleSheets	78
Bootstrap and Meteor	80
Using CSS modules with Meteor	82
Meteor and webpack styling the shopping cart	86
Test it out!	91
Test it out!	101
Styling the shopping cart with Material Design Lite	101
The grid	103
Summary	108

Chapter 4: Real-Time Twitter Streaming 109

Twitter streaming	109
The application structure	112
Meteor with Redux	114
Redux and pure functions	114
The Redux parts	116
Why do we need Redux when we have Minimongo on the client?	117
Building the App	118
Folder structure client	120
Getting the data from the collection	125
Async actions in Redux	126
Creating the App components	129
Connecting the Redux store with the React components	129
The containers and the components of the App	132
The Filter components	133
Tweets component	138
The Sentiment component	139
On the Server	142
Test it out and improve it!	144

Summary	145
Chapter 5: Developing Kanban Project Management Tool	147
Drag and drop in React	148
Test it out!	158
Building the App	158
The reducer function	167
Building the Modal	173
Test it out!	186
Higher-Order Components	187
Test it out!	191
Summary	191
Chapter 6: Building a Real-Time Search Application	193
Importing the data	194
Index a text field	195
Try it out!	204
Building the app	204
Test it Out!	232
Summary	233
Chapter 7: Real-Time Maps	235
Building the App	240
The server side	264
Test it out!	270
Summary	270
Chapter 8: Build a Chatbot with Facebook's Messenger Platform	271
Test it out!	283
Building the app	284
Training the bot	301
Moving the chatbot to the Meteor app	311
Test it out and improve it!	316
Adding Cassandra to our stack	317
Adding GraphQL to the stack	322
Summary	331
Chapter 9: Build Internet of Things Platform	333
Introduction	333
What is gRPC?	335
Test it out!	346
Building the apps	346

Test it out!   356
Test it out!   363
Test it and improve it!   368
Summary   369
Index   371

Preface

This book will help you explore the basics of Meteor, right from its core components to understanding how the platform works for building a variety of applications. This book will also help in familiarizing you with a variety of modern-day applications. It will also give an introduction to various systems, such as Redux and React, and explore how to launch an app idea in a very short period of time.

What this book covers

Chapter 1, *Foundation of Meteor*, walks you through the installation of Meteor and getting to grips with the core concepts of the framework.

Chapter 2, *Building a Shopping Cart*, teaches you to build a CRUD shopping cart application using React as a view layer. Also, we will cover client-side routing and Meteor methods.

Chapter 3, *Style Your React Components with Bootstrap and Material Design*, provides an overview of the responsive web design by building a mobile first CSS grid from scratch using SASS and LESS; then we will move on to exploring the two most popular CSS frameworks: Bootstrap and Material Design. By styling the shopping cart application from the last chapter, we will go over the challenges of building scalable CSS and concepts such as CSS modules and React inline styles.

Chapter 4, *Real-Time Twitter Streaming*, introduces a frontend state management container, called Redux. We will also become familiar with Twitter's Streaming API by building an application that will parse tweets by user and location, perform a simple sentiment analysis, and ingest them into MongoDB.

Chapter 5, *Developing Kanban Project Management Tool*, outlines the steps for building a Kanban app by implementing the React DnD library; we will also learn how we can enhance our React components using a pattern called Higher-Order Components.

Chapter 6, *Building a Real-Time Search Application*, explores adding a full-text search on MongoDB collection to our Meteor application. Calling the async functions in Meteor Methods with Fibers and Promises, and adding the native Node.js MongoDB, driver will also be covered.

Chapter 7, *Real-Time Maps*, covers adding user accounts into our Meteor app, client-side routing, and real-time geo functionality with React-Leaflet components.

Chapter 8, *Build a Chatbot with Facebook's Messenger Platform*, gets you started with using Angular 2 for your view layer. We will also add a distributed database, Cassandra, and with GraphQL we will be able to query both the MongoDB and Cassandra databases in a single trip to the server. Using the Wit.ai API, we will build a chatbot prototype that will mock up an online flower store.

Chapter 9, *Build Internet of Things Platform*, explores another data transport layer, gRPC from Google, by implementing a server-to-server data transport without human intervention.

What you need for this book

For this book, you will need a text editor and OS X, Windows, or a Linux box.

Who this book is for

If you are a developer who is looking forward to taking your application development skills with Meteor to the next level by getting your hands on different projects, this book is for you.

Conventions

In this book, you will find a number of text styles that distinguish between different kinds of information. Here are some examples of these styles and an explanation of their meaning.

Code words in text, database table names, folder names, filenames, file extensions, pathnames, dummy URLs, user input, and Twitter handles are shown as follows: "All native npm packages' metadata is in the `package.json` file."

A block of code is set as follows:

```
function Greeting({ hello }) {
    return <div>{hello}</div>;
}
```

When we wish to draw your attention to a particular part of a code block, the relevant lines or items are set in bold:

```
server.addProtoService(messages_proto.Messages.service, {
    sendMessage: sendMessage,
    clientStream: clientStream
});
```

Any command-line input or output is written as follows:

```
>> sudo apt-get update
```

New terms and **important words** are shown in bold. Words that you see on the screen, for example, in menus or dialog boxes, appear in the text like this: "Here, we added an inner grid with two full-size columns; one for the **Price** of an item and the other will wrap up the **Quantity** component."

Warnings or important notes appear in a box like this.

Tips and tricks appear like this.

Reader feedback

Feedback from our readers is always welcome. Let us know what you think about this book-what you liked or disliked. Reader feedback is important for us as it helps us develop titles that you will really get the most out of.

To send us general feedback, simply e-mail feedback@packtpub.com, and mention the book's title in the subject of your message.

If there is a topic that you have expertise in and you are interested in either writing or contributing to a book, see our author guide at www.packtpub.com/authors.

Customer support

Now that you are the proud owner of a Packt book, we have a number of things to help you to get the most from your purchase.

Downloading the example code

You can download the example code files for this book from your account at http://www.packtpub.com. If you purchased this book elsewhere, you can visit http://www.packtpub.com/support and register to have the files e-mailed directly to you.

You can download the code files by following these steps:

1. Log in or register to our website using your e-mail address and password.
2. Hover the mouse pointer on the **SUPPORT** tab at the top.
3. Click on **Code Downloads & Errata**.
4. Enter the name of the book in the **Search** box.
5. Select the book for which you're looking to download the code files.
6. Choose from the drop-down menu where you purchased this book from.
7. Click on **Code Download**.

Once the file is downloaded, please make sure that you unzip or extract the folder using the latest version of:

- WinRAR / 7-Zip for Windows
- Zipeg / iZip / UnRarX for Mac
- 7-Zip / PeaZip for Linux

The code bundle for the book is also hosted on GitHub at `https://github.com/PacktPubl ishing/Build-Applications-with-Meteor`. We also have other code bundles from our rich catalog of books and videos available at `https://github.com/PacktPublishing/`. Check them out!

Downloading the color images of this book

We also provide you with a PDF file that has color images of the screenshots/diagrams used in this book. The color images will help you better understand the changes in the output. You can download this file from `https://www.packtpub.com/sites/default/files/down loads/BuildApplicationswithMeteor_ColorImages.pdf`.

Errata

Although we have taken every care to ensure the accuracy of our content, mistakes do happen. If you find a mistake in one of our books-maybe a mistake in the text or the code- we would be grateful if you could report this to us. By doing so, you can save other readers from frustration and help us improve subsequent versions of this book. If you find any errata, please report them by visiting `http://www.packtpub.com/submit-errata`, selecting your book, clicking on the **Errata Submission Form** link, and entering the details of your errata. Once your errata are verified, your submission will be accepted and the errata will be uploaded to our website or added to any list of existing errata under the Errata section of that title.

To view the previously submitted errata, go to https://www.packtpub.com/books/content/support and enter the name of the book in the search field. The required information will appear under the **Errata** section.

Piracy

Piracy of copyrighted material on the Internet is an ongoing problem across all media. At Packt, we take the protection of our copyright and licenses very seriously. If you come across any illegal copies of our works in any form on the Internet, please provide us with the location address or website name immediately so that we can pursue a remedy.

Please contact us at copyright@packtpub.com with a link to the suspected pirated material.

We appreciate your help in protecting our authors and our ability to bring you valuable content.

Questions

If you have a problem with any aspect of this book, you can contact us at questions@packtpub.com, and we will do our best to address the problem.

1
Foundation of Meteor

Foundation of Meteor

Meteor is an open source web and mobile development platform, simplifying the process of building applications using only one programming language--JavaScript.

What is included in Meteor?

- **Server**: As a full-stack platform needs a web server, Meteor runs on top of Node.js, and we get all the benefits of using the Node, such as non-blocking I/O event driven architecture, an enormous amount of open source packages via NPM, plus we don't need to switch the language from the backend to the frontend.
- **Database(s)**: Meteor comes with MongoDB in a universal way. We get a light copy of MongoDB on the browser called Minimongo. Both the databases are in sync in real-time out of the box, which means that the UI can be updated even before the data reaches the server, and that is one of the most compelling features of the platform.
- **Communication**: How do the client and server talk to each other? The communication is done via **DDP (Distributed Data Protocol)**, which is an RPC (Remote Procedure Call) protocol built on top of WebSockets instead of HTTP. Due to the bidirectional communication nature of the web sockets, Meteor is a real-time platform by default.
- **Frontend UI frameworks**: Meteor was using Blaze as its primary template engine, which is Meteor's implementation of Handlebars; however, it also ships with support for Angular and React currently.

Now you must be wondering how all these technologies are glued together. On a very high level, the way Meteor works is that the server publishes channels and the client subscribes to those channels, then all updates from the client can update the server in real time and the other way around--updates on the server can update the client.

Now, let's look at what else is included in Meteor:

- There is also a native for Meteor package management, called **Atmosphere**, where you can find tons of useful packages. Note that all Atmosphere packages will be moved to NPM in the future.
- ECMAScript 6 or ES6 is the major upgrade of JavaScript language, and you can code in ES6 in any of your js files. There is no need for configuring anything like babel, webpack plugins, dev servers, and task runners.
- Any changes on the server or the client create a build automatically for you, and there is no need for browser refresh or manual server restarts.
- Throughout the book, we will be using React expect for Chapter 8, *Build a Chatbot with Facebook's Messenger Platform*, where we will use Angular 2. With Meteor, there is zero effort to start writing React apps. There is no need for any babel presets or anything else. The support for JSX extension comes with the default **ecmascript** package.

In this chapter, we'll be looking at the following topics:

- Downloading and installing Meteor
- Installing packages with NPM and Meteor
- Overview of React's API
- Creating an example application with React and Meteor

Setting up the development environment

Installing and running Meteor is extremely easy.

For Linux and iOS, all you need is the terminal and cURL. cURL is basically a command-line tool that we can use to move data with URL syntax, such as a GET, POST, and more, all directly from the terminal.

For Windows users, Meteor comes with an installer. You can download it from `https://www.meteor.com/install">https://www.meteor.com/install`. All the commands in the book are executed in a Linux terminal; just skip the `sudo` command and execute the commands as administrator if you are on Windows.

If you don't have cURL installed, open your terminal and install it with the following commands:

1. Run update as a superuser:

   ```
   >> sudo apt-get update
   ```

2. Install cURL:

   ```
   >> sudo apt-get install curl
   ```

3. Verify the installation:

   ```
   >> curl --version
   ```

4. Once you have cURL installed, installing Meteor is easy as it's a one line command:

   ```
   >> curl https://install.meteor.com/ | sh
   ```

This will download the latest version of Meteor, and it will install it globally on your machine. Node.js, NPM, MongoDB, and all other default packages will be inside the `.meteor` directory.

The final installation looks like this:

```
Meteor 1.4.4.2 has been installed in your home directory (~/.meteor).
Writing a launcher script to /usr/local/bin/meteor for your convenience.
This may prompt for your password.
```

In *Chapter 9*, *Build Internet of Things Platform*, we will build Node.js apps connecting to a Meteor app. If you don't have Node.js and MongoDB and you want to run them outside Meteor, here's a list of commands and installing scripts that you might find useful:

Install Node.js with cURL	curl -sL https://deb.nodesource.com/setup_7.x | sudo -E bash - sudo apt-get install -y nodejs
Uninstall Node.js	sudo rm /usr/local/bin/{node,npm}
Update node with NPM	sudo npm cache clean -f sudo npm install -g n sudo n stable
Update to specific version with NPM	sudo n 4.4.4

Check the version of Node.js	`node -v or node --version`
Check the version of NPM	`npm -v or npm --version`

Install cURL and check its version	`sudo apt-get update`
	`sudo apt-get install curl`
	`curl --versionc`

Uninstall cURL	`sudo apt-get remove --auto-remove curl`
Purging cURL config data	`sudo apt-get purge --auto-remove curl`
MongoDB install(Ubuntu)	`sudo apt-get update` `sudo apt-get install -y mongodb-org`
MongoDB version	`mongod --version`
Stop MongoDB	`sudo service mongod stop`
Restart MongoDB	`sudo service mongod restart`
Remove MongoDB	`sudo apt-get purge mongodb-org*`
Remove Data Directories	`sudo rm -r /var/log/mongodb` `sudo rm -r /var/lib/mongodb`

The following are the Meteor scripts:

Install Meteor	`curl https://install.meteor.com/ | sh`
Check the Meteor version	`meteor --version`
Update Meteor to the latest version	`meteor update`
Check the Node.js version in Meteor	`meteor node -v`
Create a Meteor App	`meteor create app_name`
Add an Atmosphere package to a Meteor app	`meteor add package_name`
Remove Atmosphere package	`meteor remove package_name`
List all the Atmosphere packages	`meteor list`
Install an npm package	`meteor npm install package_name --save`
List all the npm packages	`npm list`

Run a Meteor app on a specific port; the default is `3000`	`meteor --port 2000`
Launch the MongoDB shell in a meteor app	in the app directory execute `meteor mongo`
Show all databases from the MongoDB shell	`show dbs`
Switch to a database	`use database_name`
Show all collections in a database	`show collections`
Reset Meteor app	`meteor reset`

Building a Meteor app

The steps for creating a meteor app are as simple as the installation:

1. Open your terminal and change your directory to where you want to have your app installed. With the meteor **command line interface** (**CLI**), we can create an app with just one command:

```
>> meteor create <appname>
```

You can name it as anything you want; I am naming mine `timerapp`. We'll go through the steps of creating a basic timer, updating the time from the server side to the client in real time:

```
>> meteor create timerapp
```

The `meteor create appname` command installed all packages and libraries specified in the `.meteor` folder in the app directory. In Meteor, the packages can be installed from Atmosphere and NPM, and there are two places where you can see what is installed by default.

Atmosphere packages are specified in `./meteor/packages`. All native npm packages' metadata is in the `package.json` file.

Folders: If you go into your app directory, you will note that Meteor created three folders and two files: `client`, `server`, `.meteor`, `package.json`, and `.gitignore`:

- `client`: This is for all client-side code.

- `server`: This is for all server-side code.
- `.meteor`: This refers to all the core functionality of meteor: packages, databases, and many more.
- `package.json`: This includes all NPM installed and saved packages.
- `.gitignore`: This will ignore before the commit the specified files.

2. `cd` to that app directory:

```
>> cd timerapp
```

To start the server, run the following command:

```
>> meteor
```

After some installation logs in the terminal, you'll see something like this:

```
=> Started proxy.
=> Started MongoDB.
=> Started your app.
=> App running at: http://localhost:3000/
```

 You can also start the app with `npm start`. This will execute the start script from `package.json`. `"scripts": {"start": "meteor run"}`. You can start meteor in another port by passing port as argument, for example, `$ meteor --port 2000` . in case you have the 3000 port in use.

3. Open the project in any text editor of your choice.

In my setup, I am using Atom `https://atom.io/` with the Facebook package Nuclide `https://nuclide.io/`. There are other very good editors, such as Sublime Text, Visual Studio Code, WebStorm, Brackets, and many more.

The app skeleton, created by default, is nice and minimal. In the client and server folders, there is a startup JS `main.js` file. All this comes by default, and you do not need to create additional configs, specify entry points of the application in different environments, dev servers, plugins, and so on.

The frontend with React

The best way to start with React is by modifying and extending a Hello World example. There is a basic template available in the Facebook documentation.

For simplicity, you don't need a server to get started with React; you can load it and explore it as an HTML document by opening it in your browser.

Create a basic HTML page and place the scripts into the `head` tag:

```
<head>
<meta charset="UTF-8" />
<title>Hello World</title>
  <script

src="https://unpkg.com/react@latest/dist/react.js">
  </script>
  <script

src="https://unpkg.com/react-dom@latest/dist/
  react-dom.js"></script>
  <script

src="https://unpkg.com/babel-standalone@6.15.0/
  babel.min.js"></script>
</head>
```

With the preceding scripts, we loaded `react` and `react-dom` and the third script--babel--will make (transpile) our ES6 and JSX scripts compatible with the browsers.

Also, we can render our first component in the `body` tag:

```
<body>
<div id="root"></div>
<script

type="text/babel"> //this will make ES6 code and React Jsx compatible with
the browser.

ReactDOM.render(<h1>Hello, world!</h1>,
   document.getElementById('root'))
</script>
</body>
```

There are two ways to define components in React: as plain JavaScript functions or as an ES6 class that extends from `React.Component`.

Let's look at a basic ES6 class component:

```
class Greeting extends React.Component

{
   render() {
```

```
    return <h1>Hello, {this.props.name}</h1>;
  }
}
```

In the preceding code, we have an ES6 class Greeting that extends from React Component class; then we defined a *render* method that returns HTML tags. HTML tags in JavaScript is the special thing that comes with React. In essence, it is **JavaScript XML (JSX)** that Facebook added to React to make it more descriptive, and it also saves typing.

You can use plain JavaScript but many developers, including myself, find it actually easier to write HTML into the JavaScript.

Next, paste the Greeting component just above the ReactDOM.render line:

```
class Greeting extends React.Component {
render() {
    return <h1>Hello,

{this.props.name}</h1>;
  }
}
ReactDOM.render(
  <h1>Hello, world!

</h1>,document.getElementById('root')
)
```

If you save your file and refresh your browser, you'll see that nothing changed. To render a component, you need to attach it to an actual DOM element or add it to a parent component that can render it.

The idea of React is that we can build components or blocks and put them together to assemble complex user interfaces. Another thing you may find different is that the data flow between components is not that well prescribed like other frameworks. React itself has no actual strict pattern on how that should be done.

However, the intention is to have the data always flowing from top to bottom in one direction, or unidirectionally as many refer to it, like a waterfall. Top-level components can pass data to their child components in one direction; if you want to update the data of a child component, you'll need to update it in the parent and pass it down again. Let's see how this works.

Here's how we can render the Greeting component that we created:

```
ReactDOM.render(


<Greeting name="Joe"/>,document.getElementById('root')
);
```

We added the Greeting component as a <Greeting/> element, and we also passed a parameter, called name, with the value Joe.

Save the document, refresh the browser, and see what it does.

The properties or the props in the components are the way we pass data to components and the parameter name is accessible from the Greeting component as this.props.name.

If we want to render many instances of the Greeting component, for example, we need a parent component that can render multiple child Greeting components:

```
class App extends React.Component {
  constructor(props) {
  super

(props);
  console.log(props); // array of three children components
}
render() {


return (
    <div>
      {this.props.children} // render the children components


</div>)
  }
}
const Greeting = ({ name}) => (
  <div>{name}


</div>
)
```

Here the parent `App` component wraps and renders many children `Greeting` components:

```
ReactDOM.render(
  <App>
      <Greeting

name="Joe"/>
      <Greeting name="Tony"/>
      <Greeting name="Harry"/>


  </App>,document.getElementById('root'))
```

The React's state

Besides the flexibility of decoupling your development with reusable components, another powerful feature of React is in its component state. Every React component comes with an internal state.

If the state of a component changes, the render method will fire and re-render the component. One thing that's very different from other frameworks is that React will re-render only the changes and nothing else.

Also, it does so in a very efficient way, and it doesn't have to touch the DOM for searching before making any changes. What is happening in the back is that JSX actually represents the DOM in JavaScript, and all the updates are happening on the script site in memory first; then it will do some checks, then batch the changes and, finally, it will commit them to the DOM.

Adding state to a stateless function component

What is a state in React's components?

Components can be declared as pure JavaScript functions, and they are called Stateless, such as this one:

```
function Greeting({ hello }) {
    return <div>{hello}</div>;
}
```

Alternatively, you can write the preceding code as an ES6 arrow function:

```
const Greeting = ({ hello }) => (
    <div>{hello}</div>
)
```

Every component can hold internal encapsulated data, and we call this a state of the component. If you want to add a state to a stateless component, you should define it as an ES6 class.

Before adding an ES6 constructor and super methods to the stateless components, we can overview what an ES6 constructor is and what the super method does in ES6 classes.

In ES6, we can create a class, such as the following:

```
class Component {
constructor(props){
    this.props = props;
  }
}
```

The names of the parameters and methods are named as React's once. This is not from the React library source.

We can add a method called `render`, as mentioned in the following code:

```
class Component {
    constructor(props){
    this.props = props;
},

render() {
    return this.props;
  }
}
```

In an ES6 classical way, we can extend the base/parent class `Component`:

```
class Greeting extends Component{
constructor(name){
    super(name) // passing the value to the parent class which gets
    assigned to the props
    console.log(super.render()) // with the super method we can call the
functions from the parent class
    console.log(this.render()) // or directly as this.render
  }
}
```

In a classical way, we can create a `new` instance of the `Greeting` class, like this:

```
let greet = new Greeting('Joe');
console.log(greet.render()) // have an access to the parent method render
```

We can create a `render()` method with the same name in the child class:

```
class Greeting extends Component{
    constructor(name){
    super(name)
    this.name = name;
    console.log(super.render())
}
 render() {
   return 'Hi ' + this.name;
   }
}
let greet = new Greeting('Harry');
console.log(greet.render()) // child overrides the parent
```

Inheritance versus composition

Facebook and the React community encourage the use of composition over classical inheritance. It can be said that any other pattern to reuse code is considered anti-pattern in React. A lot more can be said about that, but React has been heavily used in production at Facebook without using inheritance for sure. In such a large-scale application, the advantage of building independent pieces and combining them to form a complex functionally is what made React so popular. Components can be moved around, organized by common functionality; they can be well tested and refactored without much of a risk of breaking other parts of the system.

Extending from the `React.Component`:

```
class Greeting extends

React.Component {
  constructor(props){ // ES6 class constructor
  super(props) // ES6
 }
  render() {
   return <h1>Hello, {this.props.name}</h1>; //local
  }
}
```

Instead of creating a new `Greeting` instance, we are adding it as a `<Greeting/>` tag:

```
ReactDOM.render(
<Greeting name="Johny"/>, document.getElementById('root'))
```

Some components can be strictly presentational; others may not know who can be their children components in advance. Many namings later came from the community, Smart and Dumb components, Containers and Components, functional and classical.

How React is used it's all up to the developers, the team, and the organization. It's a very powerful and unopinionated library and can be used along with other frameworks.

Adding a state to a component

One can say that React barely has any API. It has about 9-10 methods and that is all we get.

The `State` is one of the main APIs in React. The best place to define the initial state of a component is in the class constructor.

Create a class component and initialize its state:

```
class Button extends React.Component

{
    constructor(props){
    super(props)
this.state = {text: 'OFF'}
    this.handleClick = this.handleClick.bind(this)
}
  handleClick(){
this.state.text === 'OFF' ? this.setState({text: 'ON'}) :
this.setState({text: 'OFF'})
}
 render() {
  return (
    <button type="button" onClick={this.handleClick}>
  {this.state.text}</button>)
  }
}
```

This is an example of an internal state of a button that changes its text on user click (it toggles between ON and OFF).

A few things are required for that component to maintain a `state`:

- We defined the state in the class constructor method. This is the first entry of the class that will be executed. We can think of that definition as the default state of the component.
- We created a `handleClick()` method and bound it to the `this` class in the class constructor. It will fire when the user clicks on the button.
- In the `handleClick` method, we used one of the React's APIs--`this.setState`-- and based on the comparison of the current state, we set our new state.

 React is built with functional purity in mind, and if you set the state directly as `this.state.text = 'OFF'`, the component will not re-render.

- In the button, we added a simple JavaScript event--`onClick`. Here, React has a slightly different syntax on events; it uses camel case. `onClick` becomes `onClick`.

The second form of the `setState()` method is passing a function in the state instead of an object; in the callback, we get the previous state:

```
this.setState
(function(prevState) {
return {
   text: prevState.text === 'OFF' ? 'ON' : 'OFF'
   };
});
```

Alternatively, an arrow ES6 function can be used:

```
this.setState((prevState) => ({
   text: prevState.text === 'OFF' ? 'ON' : 'OFF'
}));
```

Other React methods.

A few other important React APIs are the component life cycles methods:

```
class Greeting extends React.Component {
    constructor(props) {
    super(props);
    console.log('constructor');
}
componentDidMount() {
```

```
      console.log('componentDidMount');
  }
  componentWillUnmount() {
      console.log('componentWillUnmount');
  }
  render() {
      return (
      <div>
          <p>{this.props.name}</p>
          {this.props.children}
      </div>)
  }
}
```

Let's test these life cycle methods by adding a simple button to the body of the HTML:

```
<button onclick="umountComponent()">Unmount</button>
```

Also, we can define that function in the JavaScript tag, as follows:

```
function umountComponent(){
ReactDOM.unmountComponentAtNode(document.getElementById('root'))
}
```

When the app is loaded, the order of the events is as follows:

1. Constructor method is called.
2. componentDidMount() is called when the component is mounted to a parent or directly to the DOM.
3. componentWillUnmount() is called just before the component will unmount from the DOM.

A simple use of these events can be as shown:

1. Constructor: Initialize the component's default state in the constructor.
2. componentDidMount(): The component is ready. You can perform any actions at that point.
3. componentWillUnmount(): The component will be detached from the DOM; here, you can clear any resources that may cause memory leaks.

Meteor with React

Starting from the client, let's create our simple app:

1. Delete all the content of the client folder.
2. Create the `index.html` file with the following content:

```html
<head>
    <title>Timer</title>
</head>
<body>
  <div id="root"></div>
</body>
```

3. Meteor will take care of the missing HTML tags. It will compile it as a template rather than serve it as an HTML document.
4. It will throw an error if you try to add the `<!DOCTYPE html>` and `html>` tags:

```
While processing files with <cdpcomment data-comment-id="2521"
data-comment-text="Sounds incomplete. ">">templating-compiler
(for target web.browser):

client/index.html:1: Expected one of: <body>, <head>, <template>.
```

Since we are using only React, we don't need to have the `blaze-html-templates` package installed.

Adding and removing atmosphere packages in Meteor

There are two ways to add and remove atmosphere packages in Meteor: directly add it in `.meteor/packages` or use the `meteor add` or `meteor remove` commands.

We will remove `blaze` and `jquery` for this example:

```
>> meteor remove blaze-html-templates
```

This will result in the following terminal:

```
blaze-html-templates removed from your project
caching-compiler removed from your project
caching-html-compiler removed from your project
templating removed from your project
templating-compiler removed from your project
templating-runtime removed from your project
templating-tools removed from your project
```

Now if you run your app, you will note that nothing is loaded. You'll need to install the `html-static` package to let Meteor load a static HTML file.

You can install it with the following command:

```
>> meteor add static-html
```

It will add all the needed dependencies:

```
caching-compiler added, version 1.1.8
caching-html-compiler added, version 1.0.7
static-html added, version 1.1.13
templating-tools added, version 1.0.5
Remove Jquery by deleting it in the package file (.meteor/packages)
jquery@1.11.10 # Helpful client-side library
```

You can add and remove packages even if the server is running. Meteor will restart it automatically when a package is removed or added.

The next step is directories and files:

- Create `index.js` in the root of the `client` folder. This will be our start up file where we can import and render the rest of the components.
- Create the `components` folder. For a small demo app like this, we can keep the components in a `folder` components.
- In `folder` components, create a `Timer.js` file, you can use and also `Timer.jsx`; Meteor will transpile JSX into JavaScript by default. Both ways are fine.

Install `react` and `react-dom` with npm:

```
>> npm install react --save
>> npm install react-dom --save
```

In the `Timer.js` file, let's define our component:

```
import React from 'react';
import ReactDOM from 'react-dom';
class Timer extends React.Component {
  constructor(props) {
  super(props);
}
render() {
  return (<div>
          <p>Timer</p>
          </div> )
  }
```

```
    }
    export default Timer;
```

It is a `class` component that will display the *time* pushed in real time from the server. The only difference between preceding examples and this one, is that we **exported** that component to use it in other components.

Now, let's import and render it in the `index.js` file:

```
import React from 'react';
import {render} from 'react-dom';
import Timer from './components/Timer'
render(<Timer/>, document.getElementById('root'))
```

First, let's create the functionality of the app on the client; then we can start pushing the data from the server.

Initialize the state in the constructor and set a new state every second:

```
constructor(props) {
    super(props);
    this.state = {time: 0};
}
    componentDidMount() {
    setInterval(() => this.setState({time: new Date().toLocaleString()}),
    1000);
}
```

Also, we have the following code in the `render()` method:

```
render() {
    return (<div>Time :
    {this.state.time}</div>)
    }
```

When the component mounts, we set a new state every second. This will force the component to re-render and display the latest state.

To exercise the idea of the state and the props, we can now create a child component that the `Timer` component will render and pass its state as prop.

Create a child component in the components folder, called `TimerDisplay`:

```
class TimerDisplay
extends React.Component {
    constructor(props) {
      super(props);
```

```
    }
  render() {
    return
    (
        <div>Time : {this.props.time}</div>
    )
    }
}
export default TimerDisplay;
```

The TimerDisplay will receive and render the data through the props.time. It can be a stateless presentational component, and it can be defined as a function instead of a class:

```
import TimerDisplay from './TimerDisplay';
class Timer extends React.Component {
    constructor() {
    super();
this.state = {time: new Date().toLocaleString()};
}
    componentDidMount() {
setInterval(() => this.setState({time: new Date().toLocaleString()}),
1000);
    }
  render()
{
    return (
    <div>
    <TimerDisplay time={this.state.time}/>
</div>)
    }
}
export default Timer;
```

Here, the parent component, Timer, re-renders every time its state changes, and then renders the child component, TimerDisplay, by passing its state as props.

What will happen if we add another TimerDisplay, but this time with a static value:

```
render()
{
  return (
    <div>
      <TimerDisplay time={this.state.time}/>
      <TimerDisplay time='today'/>
    </div>)
}
```

To see the power of React in action, open the console in Chrome and press the *Esc* key then go to **Rendering** and click on the checkbox **Paint Flashing**. You will note that even if we rendered both `TimerDisplay`, only the one that has its value changed is re-rendering.

Integrating React with Meteor's reactive data system

In the preceding example, the data passed to the child component via props was generated in the parent component itself in the `setInterval` function. In order to render React components on Meteor's data change, we need to create a component container.

The steps are as follows:

1. Add `react-meteor-data` and `react-addons-pure-render-mixin` npm packages using the following command:

```
>> npm install react-meteor-data --save
>> npm install react-addons-pure-render-mixin --save
```

2. Import `createContainer` into the `Timer.js` component:

```
import React from 'react';
import TimerDisplay from './TimerDisplay';
import { createContainer } from 'react-meteor-data';
```

3. Export the container function instead of the component:

```
export default createContainer(() => {
return {
   time: Time.find().fetch()
  };
},
Timer);
```

The first parameter is a `callback` function that returns the result as an object named `time`, and the second parameter is the `Timer` component. The way it works is that on any changes in the browser database Minimongo, the data will be fetched and passed to the component as props (time in our case).

To break this down, refer to this:

1. We defined `Time` as a MongoDB collection.
2. `find()` is a MongoDB method to query records (records are called documents in MongoDB) from the collection. If there is no query specified, will return cursor for the first 20 records by default.

3. Adding the `fetch()` method will return the documents as an array.

Meteor allows us to create a collection directly in the code:

```
Time = new Mongo.Collection('time');
```

Explore MongoDB in the Meteor shell

You can access all the application data with the Meteor MongoDB shell.

Open another terminal, `cd` to the app directory, and start the MongoDB shell.

 The app should be running at the same time.

`>> meteor mongo`

Show all the databases in MongoDB:

`>> show dbs`

The default database for the app is named `meteor`; switch to the `meteor` database:

`>> use meteor`

Display all collections in the database:

`>>show collections`

The `show collections` command will not return any results.

The reason is that we created a collection on the client side only. This collection exists in Minimongo, and it is in the browser's memory. If we refresh the page, the collection and the data will be gone.

In order to create the same collection and persist data into MongoDB, we have to execute the exact same `Time = new Mongo.Collection('time');` on the server. As soon as we do that, both the collections will be in sync and the data will be persisted into the database.

For now, we don't want to save the timer data on the server; we only want to take advantage of the Meteor server to client real-time communication.

Publishing and Subscribing

The way we can get real-time updates from the server is through the Publishing and Subscribing messaging pattern of Meteor.

The server publishes an event and on the other side, the client subscribes to that event and listens to data changes.

On the server, in our case in the `server/main.js` file, we can publish an event in a very simple way:

```
import { Meteor } from 'meteor/meteor';
Meteor.startup(() => {
   // code to run on server at startup
 Meteor.publish('time', function() {
    ...
   });
});
```

The publish function takes two arguments: name of the collection and a callback function that will be executed on each subscription from the client.

On the client, we can subscribe to it as shown here:

```
Meteor.subscribe('time');
```

All updates from the server will push an update to Minimongo collection on the client. The subscriber can also pass a parameter as a second argument and/or have subscription handlers as callback functions:

```
Meteor.subscribe('time', id);
```

Also, the subscription handlers look like this:

```
Meteor.subscribe('time', {

  //called when data is availble in  Minimongo
   onReady: function() {
   },
   // called on error
   onError: function() {
   },
   // called when the subcription is stopped.
   onStop: function () {
   }
});
```

Here's the server-side code of the subscription:

```
import { Meteor } from 'meteor/meteor';
import { Random } from 'meteor/random';

Meteor.startup(() => {
// code to run on server

at startup
Meteor.publish('time', function() {
    let self = this;
    const newTime = () => {
    let

id = Random.id();
    let time = {
     time: new Date().toString()
  }
    self.added

('time', id, time);
}
Meteor.setInterval(function() {
    newTime();
  }, 1000);
});
```

What we did is covered in the following points:

1. We created a publisher with a collection called `time`.
2. We used one of the Meteor's timer functions, `setInteval()`, to call a `newTime()` function every 1000 milliseconds or one second.
3. In the `newTime()` function, we created an ID of the document and the document as the current time.
4. We then called the `added` method, which will notify the subscriber that we added a new document to the `time` collection.

The client-side code is as follows:

```
Time = new Mongo.Collection('time');
class Timer extends React.Component {
    constructor(props)

{
    super(props);
    Meteor.subscribe('time');
```

```
  }
render() {
    return

  <TimerDisplay time={this.props.time}/>;
    }
  }
export default createContainer(() => {
  return

  {

      time: Time.find().fetch()
    };
  }, Timer);
```

This is what we did here:

1. We created a collection called `time`. The collection is created locally in Minimongo. If we don't create the same collection on the server, it will be only in the browser's memory.

2. In the class constructor, we subscribed to the dataset time published on the server.

3. In the `render` method, we rendered the `TimerDisplay` component as we passed `time` as `props`.

4. At the end, we created a Meteor React container that listens to data changes, fetches the latest data from the collection, and passes it down to the component as `props`.

Improvements in the current code

In both the server and the client, we didn't provide an unsubscribing mechanism. For example, if you close the browser, the server will continue calling the `newTime()` function indefinitely.

`Meteor.publish()` provides some other useful APIs. When the client is subscribed for the first time, we can send a notification that the initial dataset was sent using `this.ready()`. This will call the `onReady` callback on the client.

We can also unsubscribe the client with `this.stop()` or listen whether the client subscription is stopped.

The publisher on the server:

```
Meteor.publish('time', function() {
   let self = this;
   self.added('time', id, time); // notify if record is added to the
collection time
  let interval = Meteor.setInterval(function() {
      newTime();
  }, 1000);
 this.ready(); //

notify that the initial dataset was sent
   self.onStop(function () {
   self.stop()
   console.log('stopped called')
   Meteor.clearInterval(interval); // clear the interval if the the client
unsubscribed
  });
});
```

The subscriber on the client:

```
const handle = Meteor.subscribe("time", {
   onReady: function() {
// fires when this.ready() called on the server.
  }
});
 handle.stop() // will call onStop(callback) on the server.
 handle.ready() // returns true if the server called ready()
```

The clientTimer component:

```
Time = new Mongo.Collection('time');
const handle = Meteor.subscribe('time');
class Timer extends React.Component {
    constructor(props) {
    super(props);
 }
 shouldComponentUpdate() {
    return this.props.handle.ready() && this.props.time.length > 0;
 }
 componentWillUnmount() {
   this.props.handle.stop();
 }
 render() {
    return <TimerDisplay time = { this.props.time }/>;
 }
}
```

```
export default createContainer(() => {
  return {
    time: Time.find().fetch(), handle: handle
  };
}, Timer);
```

Here, we passed the subscriber's handle as a prop to the component and in `shouldComponentUpdate`, we check whether the publisher sent the first dataset and whether it has any records. If yes, it will render the `imerDisplay` component.

When we unmount the component, we send a notification to the that we stopped the subscription.

Summary

We went over the foundation of Meteor and overviewed its core components. High-level databases, servers, package managers, and its communication protocol (Distributed Data Protocol). On a high level, we now understand how the platform works.

We installed Meteor and created a sample app with the Meteor CLI. Then, we went over the default app skeleton and some of the included Atmosphere and NPM packages.

On the frontend, we overviewed the basics of React, its data flow, and component architecture. Then, we created a sample real-time server to client communication app and got familiar with the core functionality of the Meteor Publish and Subscribing API.

In the next chapter, we will get more familiar with the Meteor Methods, Schema, and validation by building a simple shopping cart app, and we will continue exploring data handling and reactive rendering with React on the frontend.

2
Building a Shopping Cart

In this chapter, we will build a simple **create, read, update, and delete** (CRUD) application that will allow the user to add items to a shopping cart, remove them, update the quantity of each item, and track the total price of all added items. This is not, by any means, an e-commerce app but a brief overview of data handling with Meteor. For the frontend view layer, we will use React; also, we will take advantage of Meteor's reactive data package **react-meteor-data** to handle all the data changes and the dynamic rendering.

First, we will start with a very basic CRUD implementation and, moving forward, we'll refactor the app with the introduction of more concepts.

Here's what this chapter covers:

- An overview of basic project structures and installation of the required packages
- An overview of the application architecture
- Inserting sample data in MongoDB
- Implementation of a client-side routing with React-Router
- Refactoring the app from client database edits to Meteor's Methods
- Adding database Schemas to Meteor collections and validations on Methods

Creating the project structure

Ctrl + *Alt* + *T* will open the terminal, change the directory to the desired location, create a shopping cart app with the meteor CLI, and install all the required packages.

Copy the following commands serially to create the app and install the packages:

```
>> meteor create shopping_cart
>> npm install
```

```
>> npm install react --save
>> npm install react-dom --save
>> meteor add react-meteor-data
>> npm install --save react react-addons-pure-render-mixin
```

Starting from the client side, let's delete all the default folders and create the following files and folders:

How to structure your app is completely up to you. For quick prototypes, you can use the defaults and just add more into the directories or, if you have a favorite open source project and you like its setup, you can copy the design from it. However, in real life, how the app is architected can depend on many factors. Often, we work on a mixture of new and legacy code and sometimes even different frameworks into one big application.

Personally, I always try to ensure that I can easily remove or add new components without touching other parts of the system; that is always a challenge:

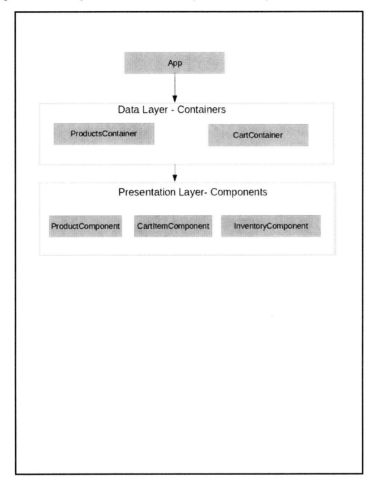

The first step is to break down the app into core components.

This is a common way of splitting the components into two main categories in the app tree: a Container and Presentational components. The parent component `App` renders the **container components** that will render the **presentational components**.

The main idea of this splitting is that the containers are responsible for the data handling, and they are usually at the top level; each time changes in the data occur, they will pass the new data down to their children as props that will force React to re-render the new changes. React's philosophy is that we should keep in mind that the data should always flow from top to bottom in one direction:

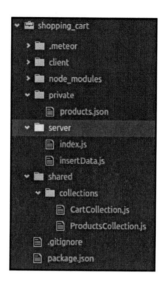

On the server

On the server-side, we have two files: `index.js` and `insertData.js`. There is also a private folder where we can define sample data that we can work with. Meteor will treat the private folder as an assets folder and will not bundle it with the rest of the execution code, which makes it a perfect place to have the test data.

In the private folder in file, `products.json` will have the following fields:

```json
[{
  "id": 1,
  "title": "JavaScript: The Good Parts",
  "price": 24.54,
  "inventory": 2,
  "department": "books"
}, {
  "id": 2,
  "title": "Secrets of the JavaScript Ninja",
  "price": 49.24,
  "inventory": 10,
  "department": "books"
}, {
  "id": 3,
  "title": "Mastering JavaScript Design Patterns
  "price": 51.68,
  "inventory": 5,
  "department": "books"
}, {

  "id": 4,
  "title": "Hardwired…To Self-Destruct (Deluxe)",
  "price": 15.97,
  "inventory": 45,
  "department": "music"
}, {
  "id": 5,
  "title": "Nevermind (Vinyl)",
  "price": 30.00,
  "inventory": 100,
  "department": "music"
}, {
```

private/products.json

The fields of the `Products` collection are as follows:

`id`: This is the product ID.

`title`: This refers to a product title.

`price`: This is the price per unit.

`inventory`: This is the currently available product inventory in the store.

`department`: This refers to the department ID the product belongs to.

In the root of the application tree, we also have a shared folder where we can have modules used by both the client and the server.

In there, we define the two Collections that we will be using: `Products` and `Cart`:

```
export const ProductsCollection = new Mongo.Collection('products');
export const CartCollection = new Mongo.Collection('cart');
```

The simplest way to insert the data is through a looping in the JSON file and call the `collection.insert()` query on each iteration:

```
export default function() {
  if (ProductsCollection.find().count() > 0) {
     return;
  }
const products = JSON.parse(Assets.getText('products.json'));
     _.each(products, function(product) {
        ProductsCollection.insert(product);
  });
}
```

When we boot the server, this script will run and insert the data from the `products.json`. We insert data only if the `Products` collection is empty.

In the `server/index.js`, the code is as follows:

```
import insertData from './insertData';
  Meteor.startup(() => {
  insertData()
...
```

Building the application components

Let's start building the application from top to bottom. The first two entries in the app are the `index.html` and `index.js` files. You can name them `main.js` or `app.js` or anything you want. I have a preference of naming index (starting with lowercase) as the first entry of any directory in my apps. That said, all React components should be capitalized when you import them; otherwise, React will thread them as HTML tags. To keep it intuitive, you can have the component names and their files' names capitalized.

In the `index.html` file, we can have our root DOM element:

```
<head>
  <title>Shopping Cart</title>
  </head>
 <body>
 <div id="root"></div>
</body>
```

We have a pretty simple HTML with only the `<head>` and `<body>` tags, and one `<div>` that will be the root of the parent top-level component, `App`.

In HTML, we don't have to specify anything else; Meteor will load it and add all the necessary scripts for us:

You can investigate what Meteor added to the app in the browser's console.

Next is the `index.js`--the first entry point on the client:

```
import React from 'react';
import { Meteor } from 'meteor/meteor';
import { render } from 'react-dom';
import App from './containers/App';
  Meteor.startup(() => {
     render(<App />, document.getElementById('root'));
});
```

We import the `App` component, then on `Meteor.startup()` execution, we mount it to the `<div>` tag with the `root` ID.

Moving to the containers directory, the first component we need to initialize is the `App`:

```
import React from 'react';
import Products from  './ProductsContainer';
import Cart from  './CartContainer';
class App extends React.Component {
render() {
   return (
      <div>
        <h2>Store</h2>
         <Products/>
         <Cart/>
      </div>
   )
  }
}
export default App;
```

The only thing this component will do is render the container components that will take care of the data and their children.

The ProductsContainer

In the following figure, we have a **ProductsContainer** as the top-level parent component connected to the data source:

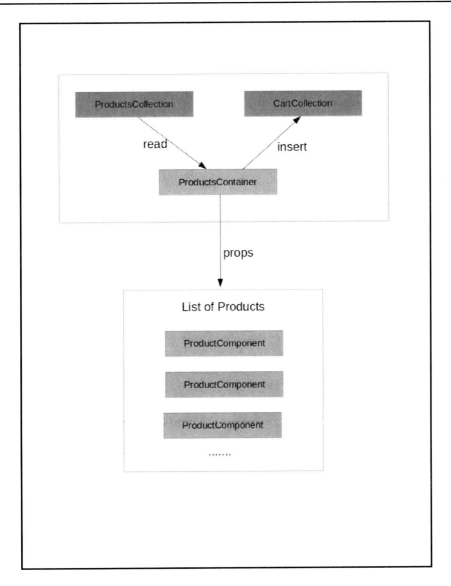

The functionality of the **ProductsContainer** is to load all the products from the
ProductsCollection and render a Product presentational component for each product item.
As always, we pass the data down as **props**.

To access the data, we need to import both the collections from the shared directory.

We will read the data from **ProductsCollection** and, on a user action, we will insert, update, or delete an item in the CartCollection:

```
import React from 'react';
import { createContainer } from 'meteor/react-meteor-data';
import {ProductsCollection} from
'../../shared/collections/ProductsCollection';
import {CartCollection} from '../../shared/collections/CartCollection';
import Product from  '../components/ProductComponent';
```

We also want to have a function for the user to add each product to the cart; the function is as follows:

```
class Products extends React.Component {
    constructor(props) {
    super(props);
this.onAddToCart = this.onAddToCart.bind(this);
}
```

Products is declared as a class component and, in its constructor method, we've added the onAddToCart function. The constructor is the best place where we can bind this event handler. Binding it there will bind it to this component's context. Anywhere in the component context, we can call it with this.onAddToCart.

When this function is called, we will insert the product passed as an argument to the CartCollection. Then, we simply alert the user that the product has been added to the cart. Note that the insert to the collection is synchronous:

```
onAddToCart (product) {
    CartCollection.insert({
      'title' : product.title,
      'price' : product.price,
      'inventory' : product.inventory,
      'quantity': 1
  });
    alert(product.title + ' added to your cart')
}
```

In the render() method, we render a child presentational component Product for each item in the array of products. We pass the data to each of the children as props so that each child can render it in the UI:

```
render() {
  const { products } = this.props
return (
<div>
  <h2>Product List</h2>
```

```
        {products.map(product =>
    <Product
        title={product.title}
        price={product.price}
        quantity={product.inventory}
        key={product._id}
    onAddToCart={() => this.onAddToCart(product)}
        />
    )}
        </div>
    )
    }
```

The `key={product._id}` is an important part of React. The key is how React identifies which component has changes in order to re-render it. It is not optional if the component was generated from a list and should be unique for each item. In our case, we are getting the ID from the database collection. Each document of a collection has a unique ID (`_id`).

```
onAddToCart={() => this.onAddToCart(product)}
```

Here, we passed a function to the child as a prop of type function. The presentational component is responsible for the user actions, such as clicking on a button, to add an item to the cart. The parent will take care of moving the data in and out of the database.

The separation of concerns in this example may seem like overkill, but it is important to understand how we can abstract components based on common functionality:

```
export default createContainer(() => {
return {
    products: ProductsCollection.find({}).fetch()
  };
}, Products);
```

At last, we export the `Products` component wrapped in a Meteor reactive container. Each time the data changes in the `ProductsCollection`, the `ProductsContainer` will re-render with the new prop's products.

All the `Product` component does is to display the data passed as props and render a button that has the `onClick` event. The `onAddToCart` function, which we also passed as a prop, will fire back each time users click on the button:

```
export default class Product extends React.Component {
  render() {
    const { price, inventory, title, onAddToCart } = this.props;
     return (
    <div>
    <span> {title} - ${price} {inventory ? `Current inventory
```

```
      ${inventory}` : null} </span>
        <button onClick={onAddToCart}>
          Add To Cart
      </button>
    </div>)
    }
  }
  Product.propTypes = {
    price: PropTypes.number,
    inventory: PropTypes.number,
    title: PropTypes.string,
    onAddToCart: PropTypes.func.isRequired
  }
```

PropTypes

React comes with one very useful feature--PropTypes. PropTypes are a type checking mechanism on received props. It's a good practice to include these checks in every component. You can skip this part if you are using other tools, such as TypeScript or Facebook's Flow.

It works pretty well. For example, if we change the onAddToCart type from PropTypes.func to a PropTypes.string, it will throw an error. You can also add isRequired to each prop that can catch missing props that you may want to be necessary to the component.

This improves component reusability and readability, and it can also serve as a code documentation.

The CartContainer

The CartContainer reads data from the CartCollection, then it renders a list of presentational components, which display the item information and the numbers of available products (inventory) in a dropdown for each item.

The functionality of the cart is that users can remove added items and update the quantity per item in the cart, using the following two functions:

```
import {CartCollection} from '../../shared/collections/CartCollection';
  class Cart extends React.Component {
    constructor(props) {
    super(props);
  this.onRemoveItem = this.onRemoveItem.bind(this);
```

```
      this.onChangeQuanity = this.onChangeQuanity.bind(this);
  }
```

In the constructor, we bind two event handlers: `onRemove`, the item from the cart, and `onChange`, the quantity of the item in the cart. Here's how it looks:

```
onChangeQuanity(id, event) {
  CartCollection.update({
    _id: id
    }, {
    $set: {
      quantity: parseInt(event.target.value)
    }
    });
  }
  onRemoveItem(product, event){
    CartCollection.remove({_id:product._id });
  }
```

The two methods are pretty simple. On changing the quantity, we update the cart collection with the new value. On removing an item, we remove it from the collection.

To get all items in the cart and listen for changes, we wrap the `Cart` in a Meteor reactive container:

```
export default createContainer(() => {
  return {
    products: CartCollection.find({}).fetch()
  };
}, Cart);
```

Then, we can render them in the `render()` method, as shown:

```
{products.map(product =>
<div key={product._id}>
  <CartItem
      title={product.title}
      price={product.price}
      key={`cartItem_${product._id}`}
    onRemoveItem={() => this.onRemoveItem(product)}
/>
  <Inventory
      inventory={product.inventory}
      quantity={product.quantity}
      key={`inventory_${product._id}`}
      onChangeQuanity={(event) => this.onChangeQuanity(product._id, event)}
      _id = {product._id}/>
  </div>
```

```
) }
```

Here, we loop through all the products in the cart and render the two presentational components: `cartItem` and the `Inventory`. We pass down some of the values of the products as props and the event methods. For every child in the render, we have to provide a unique ID for the `key` prop.

For the `<div>` wrapper, I have the `product._id` from the `<div key={product._id}>` collection, and for the two child components you can just prefix the IDs as `key={`cartItem_${product._id}`}` for the `cartItem` component and `key={`inventory_${product._id}`}` for the `Inventory` component.

It doesn't really matter how you generate your IDs for every child; the only rule is that, in dynamic rendering like this (a list of components), you have to provide a unique key for each child. Another important thing about the keys is that they should be stable and predefined. `Math.random()` for a key will force recreation of the component. It will unmount it and then mount it again.

One little extra feature we want to have is the total number of the items in the cart. We can easily do that by calculating it on every render call:

```
render() {
 const { products } = this.props;
  let total = 0;
    _.each(products, function(product) {
      total += parseInt(product.quantity * product.price);
});
 return (
  <div>
  ......

 <span>
    Total: {total}
 </span>
 </div>
```

It is not very sophisticated or exciting, but it does the work for now:

```
import React, { Component, PropTypes } from 'react'

export default class CartItem extends Component {
  render() {
    const { title, price, onRemoveItem } = this.props
      return (
      <div>
        <span>{title}</span>
        <span>Price: {price}</span>
        <button onClick={onRemoveItem}>
          Remove
        </button>
      </div>
    )
  }
}

CartItem.propTypes = {
  title: PropTypes.string,
  price: PropTypes.number,
  onRemoveItem : PropTypes.func

}
```

The `cartItem` component is pretty simple. It can be easily written as a functional component instead of a class component if you wish:

```
1  import React, { Component, PropTypes } from 'react'
2
3  export default class Inventory extends Component {
4    constructor(props) {
5    super(props);
6    this.changeHandler = this.changeHandler.bind(this);
7  }
8
9  changeHandler(event) {
10   this.props.onChangeQuanity(event);
11 }
12
13   render() {
14     const { inventory, quantity, _id } = this.props;
15     let options = [];
16       for (let i = 1; i < inventory + 1; i++) {
17         options.push(<option key={`inventory_${i}_${_id}`} value={i}>{i}</option>);
18       }
19      return (
20      <div>
21        <span>Quantity</span>
22        <select onChange={this.changeHandler} defaultValue={quantity} required>
23          {options}
24        </select>
25      </div>
26      )
27   }
28 }
29
30 Inventory.propTypes = {
31   inventory: PropTypes.number,
32   _id: PropTypes.string,
33   quantity:  PropTypes.number,
34   onChangeQuanity : PropTypes.func
35 }
```

The inventory component has a little bit more logic on the generation and rendering of the dropdown.

To break this down, each time this component is rendered, we loop through the size of the inventory and create a new `<option>` tag with a unique ID for the `key` prop and a value of the `<option>`.

For example, if the current inventory of a product is 20 in stock, we generate a dropdown with **20** items:

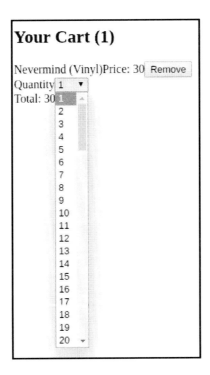

```
<select onChange={this.changeHandler} defaultValue={quantity} required>
    {optons}
</select>
```

In the JSX section, we can render the array of `<option>` tags with this syntax `{optons}`.

Again, we bound an event handler--`changeHandler`--to the component context in the constructor:

```
this.changeHandler = this.changeHandler.bind(this);
```

When `onChange` fires in the `<select>`, we call the local to the component `changeHandler` method, and then we call the parent, `onChangeQuanity(event)`, by passing the event:

```
changeHandler(event) {
this.props.onChangeQuanity(event); //passed as a prop
}
```

 Test it out: Try adding and removing items and updating the quantity in the cart.

Adding router to the application

In our sample data, we have specified two departments: music and books. Currently, our App parent component renders the `products` and the `cart` into a single page.

In **Single Page Applications (SPA)**, most of the time we want to give the user the best user experience by separating parts of the app into pages. The advantages of client site routing are that the user can navigate through different URLs without loading and reloading/refreshing the pages. This great user experience comes with a price. One of the challenges for client routing is the amount of code that the application initially needs to load for all pages. This problem can be solved by splitting the code by pages/routes and lazy loading only those parts of the code for the pages that a user visits.

For this example, we'll use the **react-router** library to manage the client-side routing:

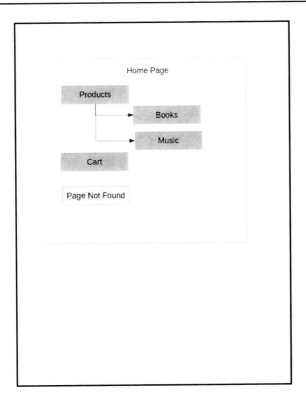

In total, we have six pages:

- **Home**: The main page that will contain links (navigation) to the **Products** and **Cart** pages.
- **Products**: This page will have two links to the **Books** and **Music** subpages, for each of the departments that we have in the Products collection.
- **Cart**: This page will contain only the shopping cart.
- **Page Not Found**: In case if the user types a non-existing URL in the browser, we will render Not Found Page. This page will have a link to the main page so that the user can navigate back to the home page.

The first step is to install the react-router module:

```
>> npm install react-router --save
```

That's all we need for routing. It comes with all the necessary APIs for handling links navigation and browser history.

The changes on the client are as follows:

In the root of the client directory, create routes.js. In the routes, we will import and render all the pages/components:

```
export const renderRoutes = () => (
  <Router history={browserHistory}>
    <Route path="/" component={App}>
      <Route path="cart" component={CartContainer}/>
      <Route path="products" component={Products}>
        <Route path="books" component={BooksContainer}/>
        <Route path="music" component={MusicContainer}/>
      </Route>
    </Route>
    <Route path="*" component={PageNotFound} />
  </Router>
);
```

```
import { Router, Route, browserHistory } from 'react-router';
```

The imported `Router` and `Route` are React components, and for their prop component, we pass our components `App`, `CartContainers`, `Products`, and the rest:

```
<Router history={browserHistory}>
<Route ...List of child components Route with props component and path.
 .....
</Router>
```

`Router` is the parent component that takes prop history and wraps all children `Routes`.

The `browserHistory` module has an access to the browser's history, and it's required by the `Router` component.

The `path` attribute in the Route is the browser URL. For example, the URL to the **Cart** page, if you run the app on localhost, will be `http://localhost:3000/cart`:

```
<Route path="cart" component={CartContainer}/> //renders the CartContainer
```

Books and music pages are children of the **Products** Route. Their URLs are as follows:

- `http://localhost:3000/products/books`
- `http://localhost:3000/products/music`

The way we can nest Routes is by wrapping the children `Routes` with a parent `Route`:

```
<Route>
    <Route></Route>
</Route>
```

To render all of them in our `index.js` page, we import the router and call it in the `render` method:

```
import { renderRoutes } from './routes';
 Meteor.startup(() => {
     render(renderRoutes(), document.getElementById('root'));
});
```

App.js

Here, we refactored the App component to render two Link components that will become HTML links to the two containers: ProductsContainer and CartContainer:

```
import React from 'react';
import { Link } from 'react-router'

export default class App extends React.Component {
  constructor(props) {
    super(props);
  }
  render() {
    return (
      <div>
        <h1>Store</h1>
        <ul>
          <li><Link to="/products">Products</Link></li>
          <li><Link to="/cart">Cart</Link></li>
        </ul>
        {this.props.children}
      </div>
    )
  }
}
```

When rendered in the DOM, it becomes just a `<a>` link with `href`:

```
<a href="/cart">Cart</a>
```

The App component is on the top of the tree, but it doesn't know which would be its children components and for that reason, we need to add {this.props.children}. This is required in order to render all its children. They will be rendered exactly there after the </ul> tag.

ProductComponent.js

Here, we are defining the Products component; very similar to the App component, it will play the role of a menu on the **Products** page:

```
import React from 'react';
import { createContainer } from 'meteor/react-meteor-data';
import {ProductsCollection} from '../../shared/collections/ProductsCollection';
import Product from '../components/ProductComponent';
import { Link } from 'react-router';


export default class Products extends React.Component {
    constructor(props) {
    super(props);
  }
  render() {
    return (
      <div>
        <h2> Available Products</h2>
        <ul>
          <li><Link to="/products/books">Books</Link></li>
          <li><Link to="/products/music">Music</Link></li>
        </ul>
        {this.props.children}
      </div>
    )
  }
}
```

The next step is to create two containers: one for the `music` department and one for the
`books` department. For the sake of simplicity, they will be the exact same thing with a few
small differences.

The data containers

We'll now look at two types of data containers:

- BooksContainer.js
- MusicContainer.js

BooksContainer.js

To get the books from the `product` collection, we query the collection by `department id`
books:

```
import React from 'react';
import { createContainer } from 'meteor/react-meteor-data';
import {ProductsCollection} from '../../shared/collections/ProductsCollection';
import {CartCollection} from '../../shared/collections/CartCollection';
import Product from '../components/ProductComponent';

class Books extends React.Component {
  constructor(props) {
    super(props);
    this.onAddToCart = this.onAddToCart.bind(this);
  }
  onAddToCart(product){
    CartCollection.insert({
      'title' : product.title,
      'price' : product.price,
      'inventory' : product.inventory,
      'quantity': 1
    });
    alert(product.title + ' added to your cart')
  }
  render() {
    const { products } = this.props
    return (
      <div>
        <h2>Books</h2>
        {products.map(product =>
          <Product
            title={product.title}
            price={product.price}
            inventory={product.inventory}
            key={product._id}
            onAddToCart={() => this.onAddToCart(product)}
          />
        )}
      </div>
    )
  }
}
export default createContainer(() => {
  return {
    products: ProductsCollection.find({department: 'books'}).fetch()
  };
}, Books);
```

```
export default createContainer(() => {
  return {
    products: ProductsCollection.find({department: 'books'}).fetch()
  };
}, Books);
```

MusicContainer.js

The `MusicContainer` component is the same as the `Books`, but we just queried the
`ProductsCollection` by department `music`:

```
products: ProductsCollection.find({department: 'music'}).fetch()
```

```
import React from 'react';
import { createContainer } from 'meteor/react-meteor-data';
import {ProductsCollection} from '../../shared/collections/ProductsCollection';
import Product from '../components/ProductComponent';
import {CartCollection} from '../../shared/collections/CartCollection';

class Music extends React.Component {
    constructor(props) {
    super(props);
    this.onAddToCart = this.onAddToCart.bind(this);
  }
  onAddToCart(product){
    CartCollection.insert({
        'title' : product.title,
        'price' : product.price,
        'inventory' : product.inventory,
        'quantity': 1
    });
    alert(product.title + ' added to your cart')
  }
  render() {
    const { products } = this.props
    return (
      <div>
        <h2>Music</h2>
        {products.map(product =>
          <Product
            title={product.title}
            price={product.price}
            inventory={product.inventory}
            key={product._id}
            onAddToCart={() => this.onAddToCart(product)}
          />
        )}
      </div>
    )
  }
}
export default createContainer(() => {
  return {
    products: ProductsCollection.find({department: 'music'}).fetch()
  };
}, Music);
```

So far so good, but there is a problem. What if we open the browser's console and start adding data directly by just typing it in the console. Of course, you need to hit a breakpoint when the CartCollection is defined, but it's pretty easy to find it in the source code:

```
Elements   Console   Sources   Network   Timeline   Profiles   Application   Security   Audits

top                              ▼  ☐ Preserve log

CartCollection.insert({
      'title' : 'fake title',
      'price' : product.price,
      'inventory' : product.inventory,
      'quantity': 1
});
"JWMCWXLnsmAeyW9XQ"
```

As soon as we insert data into the client database (Minimongo), the data will be synced back to the MongoDB and our shopping cart will contain bad data:

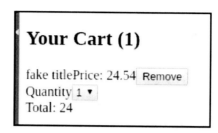

That is a serious security issue and the way we solve it is with Meteor's `Methods`. From the client, we call methods that are defined on the server, pass our data and, on the server side, we can authenticate the user, sanitize the data, validate it against the collection schema, or do anything we wish before we modify the data in the collections.

Using client inserts, updates, and deletes are fine during a prototype stage or in an early development and are available by default when we initialize the app with the Meteor CLI. The default package is called **insecure**.

If we remove it using the following code, the user will not be able to insert, delete, or update:

```
> meteor remove insecure
```

Meteor methods

To make our app work with methods, we need to create tree methods and move all the edits from the client to the server.

Let's place all the methods in a folder called `api` on the root of the `client`. The concept of `Methods` is very similar to Ajax calls to the server:

On the server, we can define them when on the startup:

```
    Meteor.startup(() => {
….. Methods definition
});
 Meteor.methods({
cartInsert: function(product) {
        CartCollection.insert({
          'title' : product.title,
          'price' : product.price,
          'inventory' : product.inventory,
          'quantity': 1
});
},
```

In `Meteor.methods`, we can define all the methods.

Let's start by adding the `product` method in the cart.

The `cartInsert` method is the name of the method and, in the `body` function, we can just copy exactly the same code that we had on the client.

To call that method on the client, we do it with `Meteor.call('cartInsert',`
`product);`.

On the client, in the `api/index.js`, we create all the methods and export them as functions:

```
export const addToCart = (product) => {
    Meteor.call('cartInsert', product);
};
```

Removing item from the cart

On the server:

```
cartRemove: function(id) {
  CartCollection.remove({
    _id: id
  });
},
```

On the client:

```
export const removeFromCart = (id) => {
  Meteor.call('cartRemove', id);
};
```

Updating the quantity of an item in the cart

On the server:

```
cartUpdate: function(id, value) {
  CartCollection.update({_id: id},
    { $set: {
      quantity: value
    }
  });
},
```

On the client:

```
export const quantityUpdate = (id, value) => {
Meteor.call('cartUpdate', id, value)
};
```

Let's create another method that will calculate the cart's total price

On the server:

```
cartTotal: function() {
  let total = CartCollection.aggregate([
    { $project: {"priceByquantity":{ $multiply: [ "$price", "$quantity"
] } }},
    { $group: { "_id": "null", "totalPrice": { $sum: "$priceByquantity"
```

```
} } }
        ]);
    return total;
  }
```

Instead of looping in the items, we can use the MongoDB aggregates. With aggregates, we can group multiple documents, perform calculations, and return a result.

To use aggregates with Meteor, we need to install a package to add support for it. I am using meteorhacks:aggregate, which is available in Atmosphere:

```
>> meteor add meteorhacks:aggregate
```

We use $project: to generate the priceByquantity key with a value multiplication of the price and quantity documents, then we group all the documents and sum them.

The way we group all documents in the collection is by assigning the _id with null.

To get the cart total, we use the following code on the client:

```
export const getCartTotal = () => {
  return new Promise((resolve, reject) => {
  Meteor.call('cartTotal', (error, data) => {
      if (error) {
          reject(error)
      }
      if(!data[0]){
         resolve(0)
      }
       resolve(data[0].totalPrice)
    })
  });
};
```

Here, we use Promise to resolve or reject the result when it is returned from Meteor.

One interesting thing about how Meteor handles the edits on the client is that updates are re-rendered on the client even before they reach the server. This makes the response look and feel instant. With a normal Ajax call, we will update the UI on the response from the server. Usually, we will have some UI indication that data is processing.

Where can we call the getCartTotal method?

We can't call it in the `createContainer()` because it is an `async` method and all the methods that we can call in there should be synchronous. The places where we want to have the total price of the cart checked is when the component receives new props and at the beginning, when the component is mounted for the first time:

```
componentDidMount() {
  let self = this;
  getCartTotal().then(result => {
    self.setState({
      totalPrice: result
    })
  }).catch(error => {
    alert('error')
  });
}

componentWillReceiveProps(){
  let self = this;
  getCartTotal().then(result => {
    self.setState({ totalPrice: result })
  }).catch(error => {
    alert('error')
  });
}
```

Here, we will set the total price as a Component's `state` instead of a prop.

In the preceding constructor, we define our `totalPrice` state with the initial price of zero:

```
this.state = {
  totalPrice:0
}
```

When adding and removing new items or changing the quantity, the cart will receive new props, and it will update the state.

In the `render` method, we can display the cart total as follows:

```
<span>
 Total: {this.state.totalPrice}
</span>
```

Considerations for scalability

There are two things we can improve if we'd like to scale this application. The first one is passing event handlers to a child component and listening for the child to fire back with data. That itself may work well for such a small example but, in real life, it can become very difficult to track down such a workflow. The child can be a grandchild or even further down the tree, and we have to pass that prop event through all of them, even if they don't need it. To solve this, we can implement a different approach. A child who needs to fire an event back with the data (props) to the parent; we can dispatch an action to a common function that can modify the data on the top level above the parent and pass the data down again. You can say that we are doing something like that by calling the Meteor Methods from the Parent, and the reactive container will pass the props down again. This is pretty close, but we can do better. This need of a child to parent data passing led to the development of the Flux architecture and that influenced the development of other similar approaches. Redux, with its simplicity, quickly become one of the most popular ones.

The second way to improve our app is to preserve the state of each action the user does. Right now, we can get the previous state and the new state, and also the next props and the current props, which is great. The component state is internal and the props are passed from parent to child, and there is no way to go back in time and check all the actions that the user did. Here, Redux or similar libraries come to help again. With Redux, we can manage all the states that you may need to persist for the application.

With Meteor, we get a database on the client. Can we just save all application states in there and just query the data we need? You can create local collections and store stuff you need, or have global session variables to manage your state, but that can lead to difficulties managing which local collection got overwritten, and global variables are probably not the best approach to store an application's state.

Basic validations on the server

On the server, we can run type checks with the given package:

```
import { check } from 'meteor/check';
```

Each time a method is called, we can check the type and the structure of the arguments passed to it. It is very similar to what we did on the frontend with the `ReactProps`:

```
cartInsert: function(product) {
  check(product.title, String);
  check(product.price, Number);
  check(product.inventory, Number);
  CartCollection.insert({
      'title' : product.title,
      'price' : product.price,
      'inventory' : product.inventory,
      'quantity': 1
  });
},
```

On the method call, before inserting the data into the collection, we can verify if the types are correct. If any of the checks fail, the data won't be inserted. The client will receive a generic `Error Match Failed`, and the error will be logged on the server.

These types of check are fine, but they are not really useful if you want to keep the integrity of the collection. MongoDB is a schema-less database, and you can change it on each document that freedom can lead to very inconsistent documents in the collections.

Defining a schema

On the server, in `index.js`, assign the schema to our imported `CartCollection` using `SimpleSchema` from Meteor, and validate each method call against it:

```
CartCollection.schema = new SimpleSchema({
    _id: {
        type: String,
        optional: false
    },
    id: {
        type: Number,
        optional: true
    },
    title: {
        type: String
    },
    price: {
        type: Number,
        decimal: true
    },
    inventory: {
        type: Number
    },
    department: {
        type: String,
        optional: true
    }
});
```

The package you need is this:

```
> meteor add aldeed:simple-schema
```

```
cartInsert: function(product) {
    CartCollection.schema.validate(product);
    check(product.title, String);
    check(product.price, Number);
    check(product.inventory, Number);
    CartCollection.insert({
        'title' : product.title,
        'price' : product.price,
        'inventory' : product.inventory,
        'quantity': 1
    });
},
```

```
CartCollection.schema.validate(product);
```

To test what it actually does, try changing the price in the schema. Consider that you set the price to be an integer, as follows:

```
price: {
  type: Number,
  decimal: false
},
```

You will get an error in the browser's console:

```
Error invoking Method 'cartInsert': Price must be an integer [validation-
error]
```

From the client, we are sending the entire product object that contains the department, even if we don't insert it in the `Collection`.

If you comment out the `department` field from the schema, you will also get an error:

```
// department: {
// type: String,
// optional: false
// }
Error invoking Method 'cartInsert': department is not allowed by the schema
[validation-error]
```

The client is passing more fields that are specified in the collection schema, and the schema validation prevents it from going further and inserts it into the database.

Defaults

Every time we insert a new item, we set the quantity to one manually, which is what we need when a user adds one product to the cart.

We can specify defaults in the schema and let it take care of it:

```
quantity: {
  type: Number,
  defaultValue: 1,
  optional: false
},
```

In the `cartInsert` method, we can `clean` the document before inserting it:

```
cartInsert: function(product) {
CartCollection.schema.clean(product);
```

This will add the `quantity` field to the product document, which was not passed by the client.

Checks with the Schema:

```
cartInsert: function(product) {
check( product, CartCollection.schema);
```

The way we've added the Schema is by importing the collection and then assigning the schema to it. Another, cleaner, way is to attach a schema to all our collections during their initialization.

For that, we need a package wrapper for the `SimpleSchema`:

```
> meteor add aldeed:collection2
```

In our collection definition, we can attach the schema in the following way:

```
import { Mongo } from 'meteor/mongo';

CartCollection = new Mongo.Collection('cart');

let CartSchema = new SimpleSchema({
  _id: {
    type: String,
    optional: false
  },
  id: {
    type: Number,
    optional: true
  },
  title: {
    type: String
  },
  price: {
    type: Number,
    decimal: true
  },
  inventory: {
    type: Number
  },
  quantity: {
    type: Number,
    defaultValue: 1,
    optional: true
  },
  department: {
    type: String,
    optional: true
  }
});

CartCollection.attachSchema(CartSchema);
export default CartCollection
```

In the methods, our checks become as illustrated:

```
check( product, CartCollection.simpleSchema());
```

Another important thing the package offers is that it will perform data cleaning before every insert, delete, or update by default. You don't need to do that:
CartCollection.simpleSchema().clean(product);.

Summary

In this chapter, we built a simple CRUD implementation of a shopping cart application. On the frontend, we started building the application with a very basic one-page implementation and, through refactoring, we implemented client-side routing with the react-router module. We continued exploring the data patterns of React and its implementation with Meteor's reactive container.

On the server with the second refactoring, we moved the client side of the data modifications to the server with the implementation of the Meteor Methods. We also got familiar with the common pitfalls of the schema-less architecture of MongoDB, and we learned the basics of type checks on incoming documents and validations against predefined schemas.

3
Style Your React Components with Bootstrap and Material Design

We often need to quickly prototype ideas for a company's internal R&D or for demonstrations for potential clients or investors. Most of the time, the audience is not technical at all and to increase the success of a demo, a visually appealing solution is quite important.

Years ago, expectations were lower and usually, the salesperson would build a powerpoint presentation and would pitch how the software should work, its benefits, and so on.

With so many open source technologies and cloud services (which are often free for a basic app deployment) available, expectations are now way higher. To make a successful demo to a nontechnical audience, the app should be visually appealing. If you build a presentation for developers, and it's not about how to style applications, unstyled apps actually work better. In many cases, styles can be distractive if you want to learn other concepts not related to it.

In this chapter, we will go over the two most popular **Cascading Style Sheets** (CSS) frameworks and apply styles to the shopping cart app from Chapter 2, *Building a Shopping Cart*. Frameworks are great for fast prototyping and extremely helpful for developers who don't want to spend time building something from scratch. The main goal of the chapter is to help non-designer developers to gain skills to make reasonably good-looking apps.

We will start with the most popular CSS framework, Bootstrap. Initially developed by Twitter in 2011 and open sourced later, it has over 800 contributors at the time of this writing. Then, we will move to another, newer, and also very popular framework from Google--Material Design. Developed in 2014 as a design language for Android mobile, it has now become the visual signature of Google devices and web apps. Google released design guidelines describing in great detail the best practices of how you should design your interfaces. Later on, a CSS framework called Material Design Lite was introduced for the web.

Here's what the chapter covers:

- An overview of Bootstrap
- Building a basic responsive grid from scratch and exploring variables, mixins, media queries, and loops
- Installation of Bootstrap in Meteor
- An overview of CSS Modules
- Using Meteor with Webpack
- Common folder styles structure in React Apps
- Styling the shopping cart app using CSS Modules, inline styles, and Sass
- Exploring the classnames module

Mobile first

In my opinion, one of the worst user experiences is when you browse a website/app and you see only one big logo and nothing else. Then, you'll have to pan with your fingers horizontally and vertically to navigate and find the content of the page. Maybe it's a great functional app but with bad user experience; users will leave your site and may never come back. Well over 50% of the web is accessed daily from mobile devices. 85% of Twitter users are spending time on a mobile rather than the desktop version.

The least we can do for our users is to design our apps for mobile devices first and then for bigger screens, such as desktop monitors.

However, before we jump right into Bootstrap and start adding classes to the HTML tags, let's explore what responsive design means and how it works.

We will build a very simple grid with vanilla (plain) CSS, and then we will add responsiveness to it.

This simple grid consists of three main parts:

- **Container**: This is the wrapper of the grid, similar to the `<table>` tag in HTML
- **Rows**: This is similar to the table rows, `<tr>`
- **Columns**: This is kind of similar to the table header, `<th>`

For simplicity, we will use Bootstrap's class names for our classes--a **container**, **row**, and **col** with 12 columns in size.

First, let's start with a basic HTML file and, to keep it simple, we will include the CSS right into the HTML:

```
<!DOCTYPE html>
 <html>
<head>
<meta charset="UTF-8">
 <title>Grid</title>
 <style>
     .. all css
</style>
 </head>
 <body>

 </body>
</html>
```

Define the grid container as a `<div>`:

```
<body>
      <div class="container"></div>
</body>
```

Then add the corresponding CSS class **container**:

```
.container {
  width: 100%;
  max-width: 1200px;
  /*only for visual test*/
  background-color: LightBlue;
}
```

We defined the container class with a `max-width` of 1200px and a default `width` of 100%.

The next step is the `row` class:

```
.row:before,
.row:after {
    content: "";
    display: block;
    clear: both;
}
```

In this declaration, we are saying--**before** and **after** this element, the content of the element should be empty, with a display of type block. When we clear both (the left and right), the next element will be pushed down, and this will create an *illusion* of a row instead of a column.

For testing purposes, let's have some type of box container so that we can visually track the changes we make:

```
.box {
    float: left;
    height: 100px;
    width: 100px;
    border-style: solid;
    content: "";
    margin: 10px;
}
```

It's a simple class with name `.box` that floats `left` with a fixed `width` and `height`:

```
<body>
<div class="container">
 <div class="row">
     <div class="box"></div>
 </div>
  <div class="row">
     <div class="box"></div>
  </div>
  <div class="row">
      <div class="box"></div>
  </div>
</div>
</body>
```

If you open the file with your browser, you'll see three rows with three boxes. If you comment out or remove the `clear: both;` property, the rows become columns. This is pretty much how we create rows in a grid.

The next step is to create the columns of the grid.

Like in Bootstrap, we'll name the classes col-1, col-2, and col-3 up to col-12 for a 12-column grid:

```css
.col-1 {
  float: left;
}
.col-2 {
  float: left;
}

...

<div class="container">
<div class="row">
  <div class="col-1">
      <div class="box"></div>
  </div>
  <div class="col-2">
    <div class="box"></div>
  </div>
</div>
</div>
</div>
```

Since we didn't specify the width of the columns, they will inherit the width of the box and line up one after another. This is not what we want from a grid.

We need each column to occupy a certain percentage of the width space of the grid.

The col-6 column should occupy exactly 50% of the width of the container since we have a 12-column grid.

To find out the exact width of each column, we simply need to divide the column number by the number of the total columns.

The col-1 column will be with width = **1** divided by 12 and then multiplied by 100 = 8.333333333 %

The col-2 column will be with width = **2** divided by 12 and then multiplied by 100 = 16.666666667 %

...

And the col-6 column will be with width = **6** divided by 12 and then multiplied by 100 = 50%

And here's how they look in our CSS:

```
.col-1 {
  float: left;
  width: 8.333333%;
}
.col-2 {
  float: left;
  width: 16.66666%;
}
...
```

To test it, remove the width of the test box class, and you'll see the size of each column.

Making it mobile friendly!

How can we make this grid responsive to different screen sizes?

This is a pretty simple thing to do using media queries:

```
@media screen and (max-width: 600px) {
  [class*="col-"] {
    width: 100%;
  }
}
```

With this definition, we are saying that when screen (mobile or tablet) and browser **window** are at max-width of 600px, all class names that contain col- in their name set their width to 100%. To test it, manually resize the browser, and you'll see that when the size of the window is 600px, the query will hit a breakpoint and set all the columns' width to 100% dynamically.

Modular CSS with LESS

All class names and IDs in CSS are global, which makes it extremely difficult to maintain in large-scale projects. No matter how well you specify your naming conventions, vanilla CSS is a pretty messy language to work with.

Some of the ways we can solve that problem, or at least minimize it, is by implementing CSS preprocessor frameworks, such as Sass and LESS. Both of them are allowing us to separate the style sheets into logical modules (files), create variables, mix in classes, and generate CSS with loops and conditions. At the end of the development cycle, we can compile all the files into one or many plain CSS files before moving the styles to production.

Let's set up a simple Meteor app and implement the same grid with LESS.

In the terminal, run the following command:

```
>> meteor create less_app;
```

We need to add the `less` package, as follows, to allow Meteor to compile the LESS files into CSS:

```
>> meteor add less;
```

Here's a screenshot of the folders and files that we need in our app:

From the preceding screenshot, let's perform these steps:

1. Rename `main.css` to `main.less`.
2. Create the `variables.less` file. In that file, we will declare the variables needed for the grid.
3. You can also remove `main.js`; we don't need it.

For now, we can define variables as shown in the `main.less` file:

```
@grid-columns: 12;
@grid-container-width: 100%;
@grid-container-max-width: 1200px;
@background-color:LightBlue;
```

Then, we can assign the container's properties to the variables, as shown:

```
.container {
  width: @grid-container-width;
  max-width: @grid-container-max-width;
  background-color: @background-color;
}
```

The row can stay the same. You can have its properties as a variable too if you like:

```
.row:after,
 .row:before {
  content: "";
  display: block;
  clear: both;
}
```

Next is the interesting part of the preprocessor that saves us repetitive typing, which can lead to errors and bugs. Previously in the vanilla CSS version, we calculated the width of each column manually.

With LESS, we can use loops to generate the columns:

```
.createColumns(@index) when (@index > 0) {
... do something
  .createColumns(@index - 1);
}
```

The loops in LESS are basically LESS mixins (functions) that will call themselves (recursively) until they meet a specified condition.

Here, we can call this mixin and pass the `grid-columns` variable as a parameter:

```
.createColumns(@grid-columns);
```

We can generate the `col` classes in the body of the mixin, as follows:

```
.col-@{index} {
  width: percentage(@index/@grid-columns);
  float: left;
}
```

LESS also comes with useful `round()`, `ceil()`, `floor()`, and `percentage()` Math functions.

The entire mixin looks like this:

```
.createColumns(@index) when (@index > 0) {
   .col-@{index} {
   width: percentage(@index/@grid-columns);
   float: left;
 }
 .createColumns(@index - 1);
}
```

With only seven lines of code and without touching a calculator, we generated all the 12 column classes.

The way we can import one less module to another is with the `@import` keyword. You can move all the variables to the `variables.less` file and import them as shown:

```
@import 'variables';
```

For this example, they are in the same root folder, and there is no need to add `./` to the path.

However, this will also work:

```
@import './variables';
```

When the files grow, you can structure them in a way so that you can have one `main.less`/`index.less` file and import other root `index.less` files into it. You can group them by common functionality and each can have its own variables, custom mixins, and so on. The source code of Bootstrap is very well structured, and you can take a look at it and get ideas.

It is pretty simple to mix two classes with LESS:

```
.classA{
 width: 100%;
}
.classB{
   background-color: green;
}
```

Then you can mix both classes `classA` and `classB` like this:

```
.classA{
 .classB()
   width: 100%;
}
```

In the HTML we only need to add **classA** `<div class="`**`classA`**`"></div>`.

Test it out!

Try changing the variable values, generate a grid with different column sizes, and mix your classes:

```
@grid-columns: 6;
.createColumns(@index) when (@index > 0) {
   .col-@{index} {
   width: percentage(@index/@grid-columns);
   float: left;
 }
 .createColumns(@index - 1);
}
```

Modular CSS with Syntactically Awesome StyleSheets

Syntactically Awesome StyleSheets (Sass) is another popular preprocessor. It's very similar to LESS and offers all the features that you can find in LESS. Which one should you use? It's worth knowing both the frameworks. If you have to go with which has more stars on GitHub, then LESS, but that can change over time. The latest version of Bootstrap, Bootstrap 4, is written with Sass; the previous versions were with LESS and if you dig into the popularity numbers, it looks like Sass surpasses LESS. Also, Material Design Lite uses Sass too.

Let's write our grid with Sass this time.

In the terminal, run the following command:

```
>> meteor create sass_app;
```

Alternatively, you can modify your previous app if you don't want to create another app.

They are two required packages for Meteor in order to compile the `scss` files into `css`:

```
>> meteor add fourseven:scss
>> npm install node-sass
```

The file extension of Sass is `.scss`. In the previous versions, it was `.sass`. They both do the same thing underneath, but the syntaxes are different. `.scss` (**Sassy CSS**) is a superset of CSS3 and writing plain CSS into `.scss` is completely fine:

Rename `main.css` to `main.scss`, and create the `variables.scss` file.

Sass uses $ for identifying declared variables instead of @ in LESS:

```
$grid-columns: 12;
$grid-container-width: 100%;
$grid-container-max-width: 1200px;
$background-color:LightBlue;
$grid-container-break-point : 600px;
```

Importing modules works the same as with LESS:

```
@import 'variables';
```

Creating mixins in Sass is with the `@mixin` keyword:

```
@mixin createColumns($size) {
  .. body of the mixin
}
```

To call a mixin, Sass uses the `@include` keyword.

The loops in LESS were recursive functions; Sass has more JavaScript-like loops--`@for`, `@each`, and `@while`.

To generate the columns with the `@for` loop, the following is the code:

```
@for $index from 1 through $size{
.col-#{$index} {
 width: percentage($index/$size);
   float: left;
  }
 }
```

Also, the same thing can be done with `@while`:

```
 $index : 1;
@while $index <= $size {
.col-#{$index} {
   width: percentage($index/$size);
   float: left;
 }
  $index: $index + 1
 }
```

Mix-in the `box` class:

```
@mixin box-color(){
  background-color: green;
}
.box {
@include box-color();
  height: 100px;
  border-style: solid;
  content: "";
  margin: 10px;
}
```

Bootstrap and Meteor

To style our shopping cart app, we will use Bootstrap 4 with Sass.

Open the shopping cart project and install Bootstrap.

At the time of writing this, Bootstrap 4 is still in alpha:

```
>> npm install bootstrap@4.0.0-alpha.5
```

Import it in the `client/index.js` file like any JavaScript module:

```
import React from 'react';
import { Meteor } from 'meteor/meteor';
import { render } from 'react-dom';
import { renderRoutes } from './routes';
import 'bootstrap/dist/css/bootstrap.css';

Meteor.startup(() => {
    render(renderRoutes(), document.getElementById('root'));
});
```

Meteor will add it to the head, and the browser will reload automatically; you will immediately note a difference in the design. The fonts and links will be styled and the app will look a little better.

As I mentioned earlier, everything in CSS is global.For example, what will happen if we, accidentally, have the same class name defined twice with a different value for the same property:

```
.shopping-cart-btn{
   background-color: red;
}
```

In another CSS file we have the same class name but this time we have a blue for background-color:

```
.shopping-cart-btn{
   background-color: blue;
}
```

The overriding priority in CSS is what makes it really hard to work with and difficult to scale. In the preceding example, the `.shopping-cart-btn` class will have a blue background(if defined in that order), simply because of the order of the definition.

The order of priority is as follows:

1. Classes with the same names--the last defined takes priority.
2. IDs can override classes.
3. A class can only override ID with adding `!important`.
4. Inline styles can override classes and IDs.

In our style sheets, we have to track down what was defined and in what order it was compiled by the preprocessor. Bootstrap has over 600 global variables and all the SCSS files are compiled into one file. It is a very well-designed framework by many experienced developers who put an enormous amount of work. To stay on a safe side, the solution is to never write new classes or never override the Bootstrap classes? What if the app that we are working on has many pages, many developers, and designers across many teams, and it was started as a small project prototyped on top of Bootstrap.

How can we solve that problem, or at least minimize it?

First, we can start with a better naming of our CSS classes. To get all developers on the same page, some of the most experienced developers in the company can write a CSS style guide. You can also get ideas or adopt a guide from some of the open source projects. Airbnb has open sourced their style guides for React, ES5 and ES6, and CSS with Sass. I find them very well written.

We are using React and the whole idea behind it is to write very well decoupled reusable components. The components are maybe decoupled but their styles are not.All the styles in the app will be compiled in advance by the preprocessor into one or many files and even if you don't render your component the styles will be loaded in advance.

Another way to separate your CSS is to write a Modular CSS. Each component can have its own decoupled CSS file; when we load that component, we will load the CSS needed for that component. If the component is lazy loaded, the CSS will be lazy loaded too.

The third option was introduced and well described by Facebook engineer Christopher Chedeau in his talk.

```
https://speakerdeck.com/vjeux/react-css-in-js
```

With the use of React's inline styles, we can code the CSS in plain JavaScript objects and inline it with the component prop style:

```
<div className={someClass} style={styles.border}></div>
```

To make sense from all this, let's create a navigation bar in the shopping cart app and style it using all those methods.

Using CSS modules with Meteor

The first step is to install a package to support the CSS modules:

```
>> meteor add nathantreid:css-module.
```

In the components folder, create a `NavBar` subdirectory where we'll create the `NavBar` component.

In the `index.js` file , we will import and export the component:

```
import NavBar from './NavBar'
export default NavBar;
```

We will define the `NavBar` as a presentational component that will get an array of links as props and render them. As a presentational component, that is the only thing it will do:

```
import React from 'react'
import {Link} from 'react-router'
import styles from './style.css'
class NavBar extends React.Component {
   constructor(props) {
   super(props);
 }
 render() {
   const {links} = this.props;
   return (
     <nav className="navbar navbar-light bg-faded">
      <ul className="nav navbar-nav">
         {links.map((name, index) => {
           return <li className={'nav-item'} key={index}>{name}</li>;
         })}
      </ul>
    </nav>)
  }
}
export default NavBar;
```

We specify classes in React with the `className` attribute:

```
className="navbar navbar-light bg-faded"
```

Now, let's import it in the `App.js` component and render it:

```
import React from 'react';
import { Link } from 'react-router'
import NavBar from '../components/NavBar';
export default class App extends React.Component {
   constructor(props) {
   super(props);
 }
 render() {
 let links = [<Link className="nav-link" to="/products">Your Store</Link>,
    <Link className="nav-link" to="/cart">Cart</Link>]
```

```
    return (
      <div>
       <NavBar links={links}></NavBar>
          {this.props.children}
       </div>
    )
   }
 }
```

Here, we created the links as an array in the JSX and passed them as links props.

If you run the app, you'll note that Bootstrap wasn't loaded in an ordinary way; it was loaded as a CSS module.

`nathantreid:css-module` threads all CSS the same as CSS Modules. What it does, in fact, is prefix class names with a custom naming:

```
import bootstrap from 'bootstrap/dist/css/bootstrap.css';
console.log(bootstrap)
```

In the console, you can see Bootstrap as an object that has the actual Bootstrap class names for keys and a custom added one for the values:

```
btn:"_node_modules_bootstrap_dist_css__bootstrap__btn"
```

For example, that is how the `btn` class was converted. So, if you want to use this in your react components, you should simply do that.

First, import bootstrap as a module in your component:

```
import bootstrap from 'bootstrap/dist/css/bootstrap.css';
```

Then, import it in the JSX:

```
<button type="button" className={bootstrap.btn + ' ' + bootstrap['btn-
success']}>Default</button>
```

What problem does CSS Modules solve for us? It is the naming problem that we discussed previously. Each class is unique to the component directory name.

To test it, let's refactor the `NavBar` to use CSS Modules.

The same method will work with custom defined modules; create your own CSS class and override the Bootstrap navbar.

In the `NavBar` directory, create and add this class:

```
.navbarCustomBgColor {
  background-color: darkred;
}
```

Also, we can render our custom class in our NavBar component, as shown:

```
import React from react
import {Link} from react-router
import styles from ./style.css //import it as js module
import bootstrap from bootstrap/dist/css/bootstrap.css
class NavBar extends React.Component {
    constructor(props) {
    super(props);
}
render() {
   const {links} = this.props;
return (
   <nav className={bootstrap['navbar'] + ' ' + styles.navbarCustomBgColor}>
   <ul className={bootstrap['nav'] + ' ' + bootstrap['navbar-nav']}>
     {links.map((name, index) => {
       return <li className={bootstrap['nav-item']}
key={index}>{name}</li>;
     })}
   </ul>
</nav>)
  }
}
export default NavBar;
```

The compiled version of our class now has this name, which is unique to the component:

```
_client_components_NavBar__style__navbarCustomBgColor
```

Here's the drawback to this approach. Meteor scanned all directories for CSS files in the whole app and merged them into one file:

```
merged-stylesheets.css?hash=effc67a8fa0e529e9da522b51f53789ede9e64f8
```

Then, the file is appended to the `<head>` and loaded on the page load even if we didn't import and render the component.

Meteor and webpack styling the shopping cart

Webpack is basically the default build tool for React. It offers a lot that we can use in our development. It supports all the possible loaders: CSS, CSS Modules, Sass, LESS are just a few.

There is a great package offering zero-configuration integration for Meteor to work with Webpack called webpack:webpack:

```
https://atmospherejs.com/webpack/webpack.
```

The easiest way to start with it is to create an app from scratch and paste in our Shopping Cart App from Chapter 2, *Building a Shopping Cart*:

```
>> meteor create css_modules_webpack
>> cd css_modules_webpack
>> npm init
>> meteor remove ecmascript
>> meteor add webpack:webpack
>> meteor add webpack:react
>> meteor add webpack:sass
>> meteor add react-meteor-data
>> npm install
>> npm start
```

After the installs are completed, your `package.json` should look similar to this one:

```
1   {
2       "name": "css_modules_webpack",
3       "private": true,
4       "scripts": {
5           "start": "meteor run"
6       },
7       "dependencies": {
8           "babel-runtime": "6.18.0",
9           "font-awesome": "^4.7.0",
10          "meteor-node-stubs": "-0.2.0",
11          "node-sass": "^3.13.1",
12          "react": "^15.0.0",
13          "react-addons-pure-render-mixin": "^15.0.0",
14          "react-dom": "^15.0.0",
15          "react-fontawesome": "^1.5.0",
16          "tether": "^1.4.0"
17      },
18      "version": "1.0.0",
19      "main": "server/index.js",
20      "browser": "client/index.js",
21      "author": "Dobrin Ganev",
22      "license": "ISC",
23      "description": "",
24      "devDependencies": {
25          "babel": "^6.3.26",
26          "babel-core": "^6.3.26",
27          "babel-loader": "^6.2.0",
28          "babel-plugin-add-module-exports": "^0.1.2",
29          "babel-plugin-react-transform": "^2.0.0",
30          "babel-plugin-transform-decorators-legacy": "^1.3.2",
31          "babel-preset-es2015": "^6.3.13",
32          "babel-preset-react": "^6.3.13",
33          "babel-preset-stage-0": "^6.3.13",
34          "css-loader": "^0.23.0",
35          "expose-loader": "^0.7.1",
36          "extract-text-webpack-plugin": "^0.9.1",
37          "file-loader": "^0.8.5",
38          "font-awesome": "^4.7.0",
39          "json-loader": "^0.5.4",
40          "less": "^2.3.1",
41          "node-sass": "^3.4.2",
42          "react-transform-catch-errors": "^1.0.0",
43          "react-transform-hmr": "^1.0.1",
44          "redbox-react": "^1.2.0",
45          "sass-loader": "^3.1.2",
46          "style-loader": "^0.13.0",
47          "url-loader": "^0.5.7",
48          "webpack": "^1.13.0",
49          "webpack-hot-middleware": "^2.10.0"
50      }
51  }
52
```

Notice on line 19, we are providing a main entry file for the app. In our case it is the `server/index.js`.

In the next step, we will create 5 Presentational components that will help us render the whole app. The file structure that we will follow is like this:

The `index.js`, as in the preceding example, will import and export the Component, the rest are obvious.

What are the options we have, after all, that information?

Let's summarize the ways we can add styles to a React component:

- `className:btn`. A /global class called btn
- `className:{style.customClass}` A CSS imported module called customClass with a unique name in the global namespace
- `style:{style.border}` An inline style as vanilla JavaScript

With the current setup (Webpack and Meteor) we can use all of them in our projects. You can combine them and see what works for you the best.

In one of the preceding examples, we combined two classes using JavaScript string concatenation. That is fine but we can use better helper library to handle class names merging and so on:

```
>>npm install --save classnames
```

That is an excellent library that also handles conditional class names which you may use if the class names are bind to the state of the component or the class names are passed as props and we have specified defaults based on conditions.

Let's create a generic Bootstrap navbar component which has default classes, that can also be overridden by a passed props from the parent. That is a very common approach if you want to build your own toolbox of components that you can import and reuse across the app.

First, we will define the default classes as a vanilla JavaScript object with `key` class names and boolean for value:

```
let nav_bar_defaults = {
  light: this.props.flat || false,
  dark: this.props.dark || false,
  bgFaded: this.props.bgFaded || false,
  primary : this.props.primary || false
}
```

If any of those props are not passed from the Parent they will not be included in the combined class.

The second step is to build a class or classes based on the values of `nav_bar_defaults`:

```
import classNames from 'classnames'
let navClass = classNames('navbar', {
  'navbar-light': nav_bar_defaults.light,
  'navbar-dark': nav_bar_defaults.dark,
  'bg-primary': nav_bar_defaults.primary,
  'bg-inverse': nav_bar_defaults.inverse,
  'bg-faded': nav_bar_defaults.bgFaded
},this.props.className);
```

The `classnames` module will handle that for us in a very elegant way.

If no classes are passed as props, the result of `navClass` will be navbar. With `this.props.className` we can pass a custom class name from the parent.

For example, from the parent, we can Render the `NavBar` as:

```
<NavBar primary ></NavBar>
```

That will produce combined classes `navbar bg-primary` which are valid Bootstrap classes and, since we have Bootstrap globally, it will style the navbar accordingly.

With that in mind, you can completely build your own reusable components. Also, you can have those class definitions outside the component and, in that way, you can swap the CSS Framework without rewriting the components from scratch.

Here is the entire render method of the `NavBar`:

```
return (
<nav className={navClass} style={styles.border} >
    <ul className="nav navbar-nav">
     <li className="nav-item dropdown">
      <a className="nav-link dropdown-toggle"
        id="navbarDropdownMenuLink" data-toggle="dropdown"
        aria-haspopup="true" aria-expanded="false">
        <strong>Department</strong>
      </a>
    <div className="dropdown-menu" aria-labelledby="navbarDropdownMenuLink">
        {dropdown_links.map((name, index) => {
          return <div className={'dropdown-item'} key={index}>{name}</div>
        })}
    </div>
   </li>
      <li className={'nav-item float-lg-right'}><Link className={'nav-link'}
to="/cart"> Cart </Link> </li>
</ul>
</nav>)
```

We have conditionally build class names `{navClass}`, inlined a style as
`style={styles.border}`.

And the rest of it is directly from the Bootstrap globals `className="nav-item
dropdown"`.

For the inline styles, you could create a module where you can define them. You can call it
`NavBar.css.js` so you know it is a CSS JavaScript module:

```
export default {
 border: {
   "borderRadius": "0"
 }
}
```

Inline styles override the classes, so now the navbar will have a border radius set to zero:

```
<nav className={navClass} style={styles.border} >
```

The only thing you should remember is that all CSS properties should be camelCase. `border-radius` becomes `borderRadius`. It won't work and React will throw a warning otherwise:

```
Warning: Unsupported style property border-radius. Did you mean
borderRadius?
```

The last is the CSS Modules. The way we tell Webpack that those CSS classes are not global is by wrapping the class name in `:local()` class.

In `modulecss.css` file, add the following code:

```
:local(.bgCustom) {
   background-color: red;
}
```

When imported as a CSS Module will return as:

```
import cssModule from ./modulecss.css
Object {bgCustom: "_3SPoHdb3lirqavComX0D2T"}
```

You can also use it like this:

```
cssModule.bgCustom
```

Test it out!

Try passing classes as props; set different defaults and use all the styling possibilities that we covered. The only way to get comfortable with these approaches is by experimenting. React and especially styling it, is a pretty new form of development and there are not really any defined *best practices* for doing it. You have to figure out what works for you.

Moving forward, we will write the rest of the presentational components. For them, we will use plain `className` declarations of global Bootstrap. The idea is to get a grasp of how we can quickly prototype UIs and get the most of what Bootstrap can offer out of the box.

Create all these new 5 files and folders.

Start from the top with the Cart component as shown bellow:

And here is our Cart component:

```
import React from 'react'
import './style.scss'
class Cart extends React.Component {
    constructor(props) {
    super(props);
}
render() {
    return (
```

```
    <div className="row cart-bgcolor">
      {this.props.children}
    </div>)
  }
}
export default Cart;
```

A very simple grid row component with a custom `background-color` defined in `style.scss`.

In `style.scss`, add the following code:

```
@import variables;
  .cart-bgcolor {
    background-color: $cart-bgcolor;
}
```

And in the variables.scss, add the following line:

```
$cart-bgcolor:#F5F5F5;
```

The Cart component is not aware of its children in advance so we add `this.props.children` in the place where we want to render them.

Where will be this component rendered?

We import it in the container component `CartContaner`. The job of that component was to deal with all the data related to the shopping cart. Reading from the database, rendering all cart items and the inventory, also keeping the totals of the items and price.

In the `render` methods:

```
render() {
const {products} = this.props;
return (
<div>
  <CartComponent>
      <CartTotal products={products}
totalPrice={this.state.totalPrice}></CartTotal>
        {products.map(product =>
        <div key={product._id}>
      <CartItem title={product.title}
            price={product.price}
            key={`cartItem_${product._id}`}
            onRemoveItem={() => this.onRemoveItem(product)}>
        <Inventory
          inventory={product.inventory}
          quantity={product.quantity}
```

```
        key={`inventory_${product._id}`}
        onChangeQuanity={ (event) => this.onChangeQuanity(product._id,
  event)}
        _id = {product._id}/>
      </CartItem>
    </div>)}
  </CartComponent>
</div>)
  }
```

We are simply wrapping the entire Cart page with this component.

Next is the `CartTotal` component:

```
render() {
  const {products, totalPrice } = this.props
  return (
      <div className="container">
        <div className="row">
          <div className="col-xs-12 col-sm-12">
            <div className="card" style={style.cartTotal}>
              <div className="card-header text-xs-center">
                Shopping Cart ({products.length})
              </div>
              <div className="card-block text-xs-center">
                <h4 className="card-title"><strong>Subtotal ({products.length} {products.length > 1
                ? `items`
                : `item`}):</strong></h4>
                <p className="card-text">
                  <strong style={style.totalPriceStyle}>
                    USD&#36; {totalPrice.toFixed(2)}
                  </strong>
                </p>
              </div>
            </div>
          </div>
        </div>
      </div>
      )
}
```

For this one, we render a grid with one row and one column of size 12, which we know will be with 100% width.

There is a new class in Bootstrap 4, called **card**, which replaces the previous class **panel**. It is very similar to Google's Material Design signature **cards**.

For practice, we use an inline style for the total price number here:

```
<strong style={style.totalPriceStyle}>
```

And we define it in the *CartTotal.css.js* file like this:

```
export default {
  totalPriceStyle : {
  padding: 10,
  margin: 10,
  color: "#b12704"
},
  cartTotal:{
    marginTop: '20px'
  }
}
```

We can also do a simple conditional rendering. If the items are greater than one, display items instead of item.

Next is the `CartItem` component:

```
export default class CartItem extends Component {
  render() {
  const {title, onRemoveItem, price} = this.props
  return (<div>
   <div className="col-xs-4 col-sm-4">
   <div className="card">
     <div className="card-block">
        <h4 className="card-title">{title}</h4>
        <p className="card-text">Price ${price}</p>
        <a href="#" onClick={onRemoveItem}>Delete</a>
   </div>
   <div className="card-footer">
        {this.props.children}
   </div>
   </div>
  </div>
</div>)
  }
}
```

Here in the card-footer, we will render the `Inventory` component.

Everything else is pretty standard. We render it as column class with size 4. It means that we will have three items per row.

The next one is the `Inventory` component:

```
return (
<div className="row">
   <div className="col-sm-4">
     <span>Quantity</span>
```

```
    </div>
  <div className="col-sm-8">
      <select className="form-control" onChange={this.changeHandler}
defaultValue={quantity}    required>
    {options}
  </select>
  </div>
</div>)
```

There is very little change in this component. All we did is render it as a row that has two columns: one for Quantity span and the other for the `<select>`. Adding Bootstrap form-control will style the select pretty well by default.

If you run the app, the Cart page should look like this:

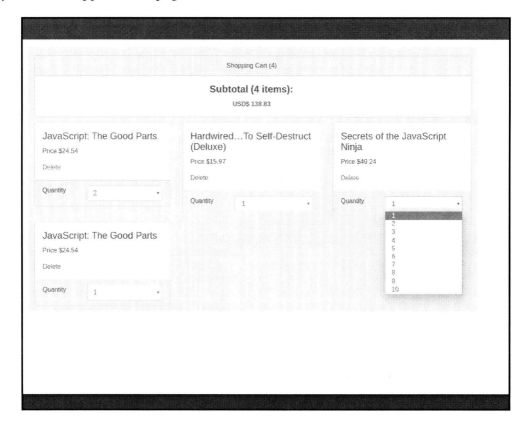

This is not bad with just using Bootstrap's defaults with a few of our own classes.

Moving to the Product pages, we have two pages--Music and Books--both of which are using the Product component to render the available products:

```
<div className="row">
<div className="col-xs-4 col-sm-4"></div>
    <div className="col-xs-4 col-sm-4">
    <div className="card">
    <div className="card-block">
<h4 className="card-title">{title}</h4>
  <p className="card-text">Price ${price}</p>
   <p className="card-text">{inventory
        ? `In Stock ${inventory}`
      : null}</p>
<div onClick={onAddToCart} className="btn" style={btnStyle}>
  <i className="fa fa-cart-plus" aria-hidden="true"></i> Add to Cart
   </div>
   </div>
   </div>
 </div>
 <div className="col-xs-4 col-sm-4"></div>
 </div>
```

In this page, we want to have the products positioned in the middle of the screen. There are two ways of doing that; we can add the .offset-md-4 offset class to the columns which, in this case, means moving 4 columns to the right. The other is by simply adding columns filling up space from the left and the right.

Here again, we are adding an inline style to the button:

```
let btnStyle = {
    background: 'linear-gradient(to bottom,#f7dfa5,#f0c14b)'
};
```

With the inline styles, we overrode the default button class from Bootstrap, with plain JavaScript:

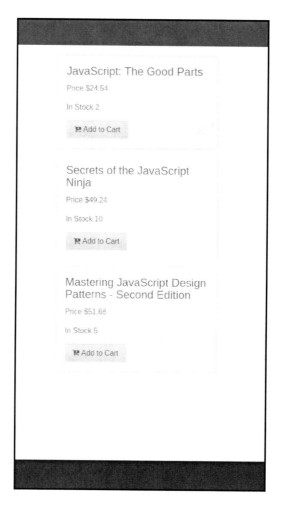

To add icons/fonts, you can install them and import them as any CSS files. A very popular collection of fonts is `font-awesome`:

```
>>npm install font-awesome --save
```

Then, in the `client/index.js`, you can import and make them available globally in the whole app:

```
import font-awesome/css/font-awesome.min.css
```

In the original unstyled shopping cart, we notified the user that he added an item to the cart with `alert()`. Alert is one of the three (alert, confirm, prompt) JavaScript native popups. You can't style them and, if you want to have a visual notification that is styled as the rest of your app, you have to either use what comes by default from Bootstrap or build your own.

To substitute the default alert, we will create a Snackbar notification with React, and then we will style it with Bootstrap classes.

We are defining the `Snackbar` just as we did with the other components:

In the render method, place the following code:

```
render() {
let {content, toast} = this.props
   let show = className("snackbar", {
     "show": this.state.toast,
     " alert alert-success": true
 })
return (
   <div className={show}>{content}</div>
 )
}
```

In the preceding code, we conditionally set the `show` class to **true** or **false** with the component state and, as in every React component, we set the initial state in the constructor:

```
class Snackbar extends React.Component {
   constructor(props) {
   super(props);
   this.state = {
     toast: false
   }
 }
}
```

The way our Snackbar should work is as follows:

- The user performs some action
- A toast message appears on the screen
- After a certain amount of time, the toast message disappears

One way to do it is by passing a prop from the parent component that we wish to display the toast; then we can change the state with timeOut, and the Snackbar component will re-render with the new state.

There are two important life cycle events that we should be careful with when setting the internal state.

If you try to set a state on unmounting or component will mount events, React will throw an error. When can this happen in our case?

A user adds an item to the cart, and then the parent will re-render the Snackbar. The Snackbar, in the meantime, will try to set a new state after some time in the timeOut function but, at the same time, the user leaves the page and goes somewhere else (to the cart page, for example). In other cases, the user can send Ajax requests to the server and leave before the response(s) are back.

The way we solve this in our case is shown here:

```
componentWillReceiveProps(nextProps) {
  let self = this;
    if (this.timeout) { //clear timeout
      clearTimeout(this.timeout);
  }
   this.setState({toast: nextProps.toast})
      this.timeout = setTimeout(() => {
      self.setState({toast: false})
      }, 5000);
  }
```

Each time the component receives new props, we set our state to the props values; then when the component is about to unmount, we clear the timeOut function:

```
componentWillUnmount() {
      clearTimeout(this.timeout);
  }
```

Rendering it from the parent is pretty simple:

```
<Snackbar content={this.state.productTitle}
toast={this.state.toast}></Snackbar>
```

And the initial state in the parent is as follows:

```
this.state = {
 productTitle: '',
 toast: false
 }
```

The style for this component with Sass is as follows:

```
@mixin centerer {
position: absolute;
  left: 50%;
  bottom: 60px;
  transform: translate(-50%, -50%);
}
.snackbar {
  @include centerer;
  visibility: hidden;
  min-width: 250px;
}
.snackbar.show {
  visibility: visible;
}
```

We position it in the center, closely 60px from the bottom, and it is hidden by default. Adding and removing class show will make appear and disappear. For the rest of the look, we use Bootstrap.

It looks way better and consistent with the rest of the App:

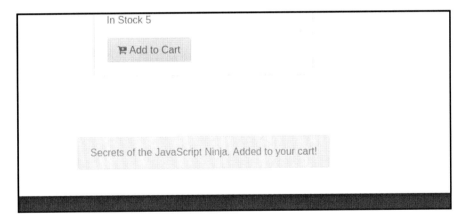

Test it out!

Try customizing the Snackbar to have defaults and also accept custom styles from the parent. For example, if the user deletes an item from the cart, the Bootstrap style can be set to danger or warning. The CSS classes are alert-warning and alert-danger.

Styling the shopping cart with Material Design Lite

The idea here is to swap Bootstrap with Material Design and swap Sass with LESS. We will again try to get as much as we can from what comes by default with **Material Design Lite** (**MDL**).

The first step is to install MDL with npm:

```
>> npm install material-design-lite --save
```

Next, we need to rename all the SCSS files to LESS and all variable declaration to start with $ to @.

Initially, a mobile framework/language, the navigation layouts in MDL are quite different from the Bootstrap defaults. The idea is to bring to the user a seamless transition between the native mobile apps and the web apps:

```
<div className="mdl-layout mdl-js-layout">
<header className="mdl-layout__header mdl-layout__header--scroll">
   <div className="mdl-layout__header-row">
    <span className="mdl-layout-title">Online Store</span>
    <div className="mdl-layout-spacer"></div>
    <nav className="mdl-navigation">
       <Link className="mdl-navigation__link" to="/cart"> Your Cart </Link>
     </nav>
   </div>
</header>
  <div className="mdl-layout__drawer">
   <span className="mdl-layout-title">Department</span>
     <nav className="mdl-navigation">
       {dropdown_links.map((name, index) => {
         return <div className={'mdl-navigation__link'}
key={index}>{name}</div>
     })}
   </nav>
 </div>
 {this.props.children}
</div>
```

The basic MDL layout consists of a few basic parts:

- Navigation
- Grid
- Footer

As with Android, MDL comes with a drawer; with the `mdl-layout__drawer` class, you can include a fully functional slider menu. The <header> with `mdl-layout__header` is what makes the `NavBar` similar to the Bootstrap `navbar` class.

To render it in the `App.js` render method, add the following code:

```
return (
<NavBar dropdown_links={dropdown_links}>
<main className="mdl-layout__content">
   <div className="page-content">
    {this.props.children}
  </div>
</main>
</NavBar>
)
```

Here, we again passed all the department links as pops; then all the content will be rendered inside the `page-content`.

The grid

MDL grid is very similar to the Bootstrap one--12 columns and responsive to many screen sizes, this should be an easy transition. The only and main difference is that MDL grid doesn't have a container and a row. Instead, you can define a grid with an inner <div> tag as cells:

```
<div className="mdl-grid">
<div className="mdl-cell mdl-cell--4-col">Content 1 </div>
  <div className="mdl-cell mdl-cell--4-col">Content 2 </div>
  <div className="mdl-cell mdl-cell--4-col">Content 3 </div>
</div>
```

Refactoring `Cart.js` in the `render` method can be done as follows:

```
render() {
   return (
     <div className="mdl-grid">
        {this.props.children}
     </div>)
}
```

In the Cart page, we will render all the added items as a grid with 3 columns of size 4.

The CartTotal component will be just another card styled differently:

```
<div className="mdl-cell mdl-cell--4-col">
<div className="mdl-card mdl-shadow--2dp mdl-card mdl-color--teal-500">
<div className="mdl-card__title">
<h2 className="mdl-card__title-text">Shopping Cart ({products.length})</h2>
</div>
    <div className="mdl-card__supporting-text mdl-color-text--blue-grey-50">
<h4>
<strong>Subtotal ({products.length} {products.length > 1
    ? 'items'
    : 'item'}):</strong>
</h4>
</div>
<div className="mdl-card__actions mdl-card--border">
<strong>Subtotal ({products.length} {products.length > 1
    ? 'items'
    : 'item'}):</strong>
 <strong style={style.totalPriceStyle}>
    USD$ {totalPrice.toFixed(2)}
 </strong>
</div>
</div>
</div>
```

If you take a closer look, we basically replaced the Bootstrap classes with MDL. Here, we also have a cart title and something like a footer that MDL has as a cart actions section.

Shadows (mdl-shadow--2dp) are a huge feature in Material Design's philosophy. You can specify the *elevation* by changing the dp unit. Another difference between Bootstrap and MDL is the colors. We can go through CSS source and just grab a color you like--mdl-color--teal-500; 500 is the amount of darkness. Usually, it goes from 50 to 900.

The CartItem component is as follows:

```
<div className="mdl-cell mdl-cell--4-col">
  <div className="mdl-card mdl-shadow--2dp">
  <div className="mdl-card__title">
 <h2 className="mdl-card__title-text">{title}</h2>
    </div>
<div className="mdl-grid">
  <div className="mdl-cell mdl-cell--12-col">
    <div className="mdl-card__supporting-text">Price ${price}</div>
    </div>
<div className="mdl-cell mdl-cell--12-col">
```

```
        {this.props.children}
    </div>
    </div>
    <div className="mdl-card__actions mdl-card--border">
<button onClick={onRemoveItem} className="mdl-button mdl-js-button mdl-
button--accent">
        Delete
</button>
</div>
</div>
</div>
```

Here, we added an inner grid with two full-size columns; one is for the **Price** of an item and the other will wrap up the **Quantity** component:

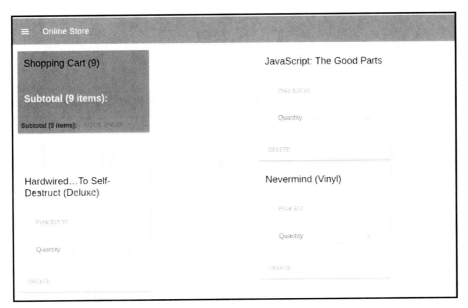

If you launch the app, the shopping cart should look like that. In Bootstrap, we have style for every single HTML element. MDL is way leaner and has only a few defaults.

For the `<select>`, we will have to style it ourselves in order for it to look similar to the rest of the components:

```
select {
    font-family: inherit;
    background-color: transparent;
    width: 100%;
    padding: 4px 0;
```

```
  font-size: 16px;
  color: rgba(0,0,0, 0.26);
  border: none;
  border-bottom: 1px solid rgba(0,0,0, 0.12);
}
select:focus {
  outline: none;
}
```

The `Product` component is straightforward:

```
return (
<div className="mdl-grid">
  <div className="mdl-cell mdl-cell--4-col"></div>
    <div className="mdl-cell mdl-cell--4-col">
    <div className="mdl-card mdl-shadow--2dp">
   <div className="mdl-card__title">
    <h2 className="mdl-card__title-text">{title}</h2>
  </div>
  <div className="mdl-grid">
 <div className="mdl-cell mdl-cell--12-col">
    <span className="mdl-card__title-text">Price ${price}</span>
 </div>
 <div className="mdl-cell mdl-cell--12-col">
    <span className="mdl-card__title-text">{inventory ? `In Stock
${inventory}` : null}</span>
 </div>
 </div>
 <div className="mdl-card__actions mdl-card--border">
 <button onClick={onAddToCart} className="mdl-button mdl-js-button mdl-
button--primary">Add to          Cart
</button>
 </div>
  </div>
 </div>
<div className="mdl-cell mdl-cell--4-col"></div>
</div>
```

We are placing it in the middle of the screen by adding two extra columns (cells) on both the sides.

This time, we'll leave the default buttons:

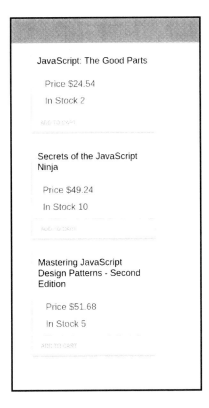

The last thing we have to do is change the `Snackbar` class to something more material.

Material Design has its own `Snackbar`; all we have to do is get its class and swap it with the Bootstrap one.

In the `Snackbar.js` component, add the following code:

```
let show = classNames("snackbar", {
 "show": this.state.toast,
 " mdl-snackbar": true
})
return (
<div className={show}>
 <div className="mdl-snackbar__text"> {content}</div>
</div>
```

If you add an item to the card, the snackbar should look something like this:

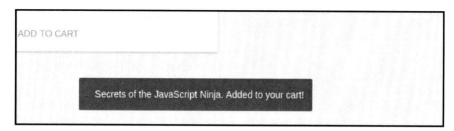

Summary

In this chapter, we covered the basics of Mobile First development with React. We started by building a simple grid with vanilla CSS; then we rewrote it using the two most popular preprocessors, Sass, and LESS. Moving forward, we discussed the challenges we face in writing scalable CSS in large-size apps. Global namespaces, CSS Modules, and the order of priorities in CSS class declarations are some of the topics covered. With the styling, the Shopping Cart from Chapter 2, *Building a Shopping Cart*, we applied the common ways of styling React. We also learned to use the global classes from Bootstrap and MDL, decouple the CSS with CSS Modules, and use inline style components with JavaScript. In the next chapter, we will build a Twitter streaming app, and we'll get familiar with the basics of the streaming API. Also, we will implement a state management container library, Redux.

4

Real-Time Twitter Streaming

The objectives of this chapter are to learn how we can implement Meteor's built-in real-time capabilities with one of the Twitter developer APIs--the streaming API. On the frontend side, in the earlier chapters, we managed the data flow with the react-meteor-data module, which reactively checked for any data changes and re-rendered our components. Updates on the collections updated the props and that forced the re-rendering of the components with the new data. We managed the state of the components with react's internal state, which is fine in certain cases. When your application grows and the user interactions are becoming more and more complex, managing state between components becomes very difficult and prone to bugs and unexpected behavior. In this chapter, we will introduce a library, called Redux, to manage the applications' state.

Here's what this chapter covers:

- Learning about the Twitter's streaming API
- Learning how Redux works and the benefit of adding it to your stack
- Building a real-time Twitter streaming app that will perform simple sentiment analysis
- Adding a real-time visualization chart for the sentiment analysis

Twitter streaming

As per the writing of this chapter, there are 317 million monthly active users of the Twitter social service. More and more people are relying on social media services to obtain the latest news and opinions of other users. Twitter is a very friendly platform for developers; and with their APIs, you can access its core data via two main categories: REST and Streaming. What you can do with all that data is almost limitless.

You can track and build an opinion analysis of a person, technology product, or a global issue. Politicians and celebrities are the heart of the Twitter platform, and news usually breaks on Twitter first and later on the other social media outlets.

Before you start hacking with the Streaming API, you need to provide Twitter with a few things:

1. You need a Twitter account.
2. You have to create an app and get access tokens.
3. To connect to the service, you need four credentials: Consumer key, Consumer Secret, Access Token, and Access Token Secret.

After you create your Twitter account (if you don't have one or you don't want to use your personal one), you have to go to `https://dev.twitter.com/`, navigate to **My apps**, and **Create New App**:

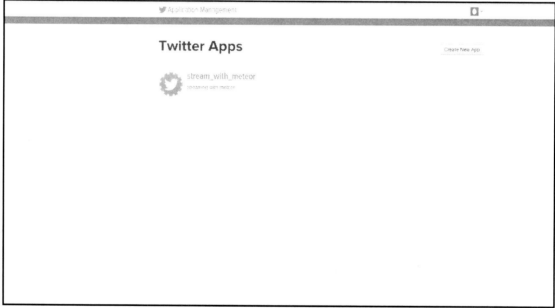

Next, you need to enter all the required fields in the details page. The application should have a unique name and, for the **Website** field, you can have a temporary `http://127.0.0.1:3000` or something like that; you can change it later to the real one; you can leave out the **Callback URL** field.

There are two types of OAuth authentication of Twitter: application-only authentication and application-user authentication. In our app, we'll use application-only authentication because we won't require the users to access the service directly on behalf of our app:

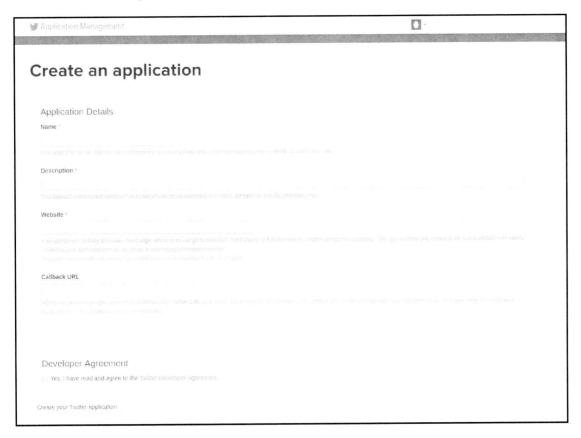

Once you have all the fields verified, you have to create your access tokens. Click on the **Create my access token** button:

That's all you need to create a Twitter application.

The application structure

On the frontend, we will have a Single Page App with three client-routed pages: **Filters**, **Sentiment**, and **Tweets**.

On the **Filters** page, the user will be able to specify filters (phrases, keywords) that will be passed on to the server side where we will parse all incoming tweets containing that keyword. The incoming tweets from the stream will be geolocation-based, which can be specified as latitude and longitude pairs.

The reason for not directly using the filter passed by the user is that each time a new filter is specified, we have to disconnect from the stream and reconnect again with the new parameters. After a certain amount of reconnections, Twitter will rate limit us for all connections that are using the same credentials for. There is no public information on how many times we can reconnect to a stream in a period of time.

Streaming tweets filtered by location also has its limitations. We will only get the location-enabled tweets that are falling into that geo *bounding box* defined by the Lat and Long pairs. On a side note, the feature of adding location to your tweets by default is **off**; this will create a gap in the data for users who tweet without having enabled that feature.

In a real-world application, you can create and combine different strategies of mining your data. You can offer the users predefined filters that you won't disconnect frequently on the backend and only serve analytics based on the collected data for each filter to the user. For example, if you build an election poll app, you can filter the candidates and/or the political parties.

The second page of the app will be the visual sentiment analysis presentation. On the server, if we get a match of the keyword that the user sent, we will run an analysis on the tweet text and get a score based on the content of the text.

The last page of the App will be the **Tweets** page. We will display the tweets in real time as they are pushed from the server:

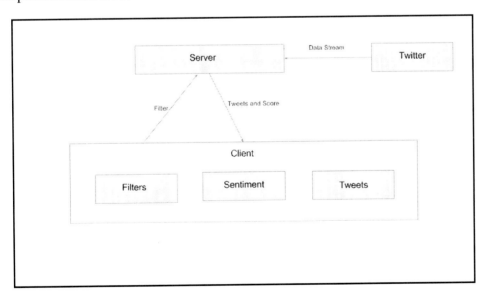

To manage the frontend application state, we will implement a library called Redux. React itself does not enforce any data flow paradigm; and you can add it to any existing framework as the view part. After React was released, Facebook introduced architecture, called Flux, that follows the unidirectional data flow from top to bottom instead of two-way data binding. What we get with Redux is something simpler than Flux and easier to implement.

Meteor with Redux

The functionality of the Filter page is the following:

- The user should be able to create as many filters as he wants (list of filters)
- The user should be able to edit and delete the created filters
- The user should be able to activate one filter at a time
- The user should be able to see incoming tweets in real time by an activated filter
- On the **Sentiment** page, the user should see the statistics only on the currently active filter

For the purpose of learning how we can manage the application's state, we will persist all the user actions on the client using Redux.

Every single JavaScript framework currently on the market has an example of the famous To-do list app demonstrating the core functionalities of the framework, such as a data flow, data bindings, and more.

You can think of the Filters a as To-do list.

Redux and pure functions

In JavaScript, there are five primitive types: undefined, null, boolean, string, and number; everything else is an object. If we pass an object to a function (which itself is an object), then the object is passed by reference and not by value.

If the function modifies that object, it is something that we call an **impure** function; this is also known as a *function with side effects*.

Let's create a very basic sample to grasp the idea:

```
function getNewMessage(old_message){
  old_message.message = 'new message'
```

```
return old_message
}

var old_message = {
  message: 'old message'
}

var newMessage = getNewMessage(old_message)
console.log(newMessage)
console.log(old_message)  // the old_message changed
```

In this sample, we created a function called getNewMessage that modifies the property message of the passed object and returns the same object with the updated property. If you run that code, you will see how that function modified the object that was declared outside. So, it has a side effect, and we lose the initial value of the old_message once the function is executed.

This may not seem a big deal at first because we needed the latest updated new value, but now we can imagine that the new value can be processed on the server with an async call from the client; for example, if that was the case, we really don't know when the old_message will be updated with the new value.

What will be really nice and helpful is that if we have something like a storage where the old_message is always available and accessible from the entire app at any given time, we can get a snapshot of the current state/value of it. It will be even nicer if we also know what the previous value before the update, or even better, all the previous values from the beginning of the page load were. This is what we get with Redux--a fully predictable state container.

Let's change the function from impure to pure to see how we can return the new value without modifying the passed object:

```
function getNewMessage(old_message){

var new_message = {
    message: 'new message'
}

var newObject = Object.assign({},old_message, new_message);
  return newObject
}

var old_message = {
  message: 'old message'
}
```

```
var newMessage = getNewMessage(old_message)
console.log(newMessage)
console.log(old_message)
```

Here, the difference is that we passed the original value and, instead of modifying it, we directly created a brand new object by merging both the objects into a `newObject`; by doing so, we didn't modify the original object. The function is pure, which means that it never modifies the inputs; it only produces new output based on the input.

Now, let's rewrite the preceding example in ES6:

```
const getNewMessage = (old_message) => {
let message = {
    message: 'new_message'
}
 return  { ...old_message, ...message }
}

let old_message = {
 message: 'old message'
}

let newMessage = getNewMessage(old_message)
console.log(newMessage)
console.log(old_message)
```

The main difference here is that we used **object spread syntax** instead of `Object.assign()`, and it does the exact same thing.

The Redux parts

There are a few components of the Redux architecture: actions, a reducer function, and the store. The **reducer** is a pure function that gets a state and an action for an input, and then returns a new single (reduced) state object.

Actions are plain objects that *must* include a property *type* that will be used by the reducer function to perform a type of action to create the next state.

The only way to change a state is through dispatching actions. Redux strictly follows the Flux's unidirectional data flow architecture, and updating the state should happen only from actions to a reducer and then to the store. The following diagram shows the data flow of Redux:

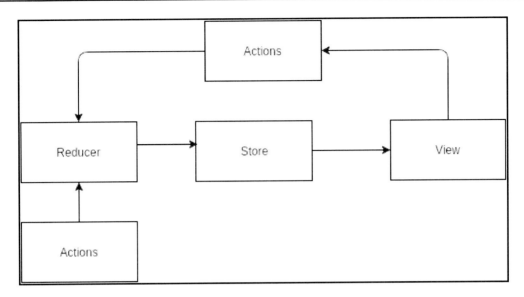

The **Store** is where the state is persisted, and it's only *one* store for the entire application. It has the following methods:

- dispatch:(action)
- getState:getState()
- replaceReducer:replaceReducer(nextReducer)
- subscribe:subscribe(listener)
- Symbol(observable):observable()

For now, we are interested in the first two: dispatch(action) and getState().

Why do we need Redux when we have Minimongo on the client?

Minimongo is great at keeping a snapshot of the current data on the server-side MongoDB. To have a persisted state on the client, our options are to have local collections, session variables/reactive dictionaries, and/or components' internal state, which makes it hard to maintain with all globals and internals passing down from parent to children components.

Another benefit of using Redux is that your client data layer (the store) does not depend on the data source. The client can query data with HTTP, GraphQL, WebSockets, and gRPC (there is not yet support for the browser at the time of this writing, but that will probably change soon) and then pass it down for rendering.

With Redux, we get excellent developer tools. Every update of the state is persisted in the store; you can go back in time and check every single user interaction, which is the ultimate debugging tool. If you are building an application that has tons of components (and you keep adding new ones), you will eventually need access to a global, reliable state accessible from anywhere in the app, and Redux is your best bet.

Building the App

Let's start with creating and installing all the necessary packages.

In the Terminal, perform the following steps:

1. Create the app using the following command:

```
>> meteor create twitter_redux
>> cd twitter_redux
>> npm install
```

2. Install React and React DOM:

```
>> npm install react --save
>> npm install react-dom --save
```

3. Install React Router:

```
>> npm install react-router --save
```

4. Install Redux:

```
>> npm install redux --save
```

5. Install React Redux:

```
>> npm install react-redux --save
```

6. Install React Router Redux:

```
>> npm install react-router-redux --save
```

7. Install Redux logger. It is very useful middleware for logging all actions and states to the browser's console:

```
>> npm install redux-logger --save
```

8. Install Redux Thunk middleware-- middleware to support async actions:

```
>> npm install redux-thunk --save
```

9. Install the sentiment module to perform sentiment analysis on tweets:

```
>> npm install sentiment --save
```

10. Install recharts--a great set of chart components to visualize data:

```
>> npm install recharts --save
```

11. Install bootstrap CSS and font-awesome:

```
>> npm install bootstrap@4.0.0-alpha.5 --save
>> npm install font-awesome --save
```

12. Meteor webpack integration (this is optional; you can use Meteor):

```
>> meteor add webpack:webpack
>> meteor add webpack:react
```

13. Remove the ecamascript package (this is optional; you can use Meteor):

```
>> meteor remove ecmascript
```

Webpack needs to know the entry of the browser and server files.

In the package.json, add the following lines:

```
"main": "server/index.js",
"browser": "client/index.js",
```

Folder structure client

A common code structure of Redux is to place all actions in the `actions` folder, all reducers in the `reducers` folder, and all the action types defined as constants in the `constants` folder:

As I mentioned earlier, Redux has only one store for the entire application. The store will persist the entire state as one big JavaScript object. We can think of the store as one MongoDB collection. When the app grows in functionality, managing the state with one reducer function becomes very difficult.

We can split the functionality of the store by creating many reducers that are exported and combined into one single `reducer` function.

The way we do that is a straightforward task:

```
import {combineReducers} from 'redux'
combineReducers({reducer_one_key: reducer_one, reducer_two_key:
reducer_two});
```

With the `combineReducers` function, we can combine as many reducers as we need as key and value pairs. The key is how the reducer will appear in the store object.

Let's start creating the reducers that we'll need for our app:

We will have two reducer functions that will manage two different parts of the state object.

The filters will take care of all the filters that the user will create, modify, delete, and set to an active state.

The filter state object consists of three fields: `text`, `id`, and `active`:

```
const initialState = [{
text: 'filter default text',
    id: 0,
active: false
}]
```

- `text`: The filter text that the user will send to the server for parsing the tweets.
- `id`: We need an ID of each filter in order to modify, delete, and set to active by ID. Also, it will be used as a render key in the React list component.
- `active`: The user can set each filter from active to inactive.

```
export default function filters(state = initialState, action) {
  switch (action.type) {
    case ADD_FILTER:
      return [
        ...state,
        {
          id: state.reduce((maxId, filter) => Math.max(filter.id, maxId),
```

```
-1) + 1,
        text: action.text,
        active: false
    }
  ]
... other actions
```

Here, we defined a pure function--`filters`--and passed two objects; the first one is the initial state and the other is the action. The initial state is optional; you can just default it to an empty array.

In the switch statement, if the `action.type` was ADD_FILTER, we will return a new state without mutating the original.

The next thing is to write the action that we passed to the `reducer` function.

In the `actions` folder, we can write the `action` function as follows:

```
export const addFilter = text => ({type: types.ADD_FILTER, text})
```

In Redux, these functions are called **Action Creators**; their job is to create an action.

In another file, the type is defined as a constant:

```
export const ADD_FILTER = 'ADD_FILTER'
```

The Action Creator `ADD_FILTER` gets a text as input and returns object type and the text.

For now, we have the Action Creator and the reducer function. The next thing we need is the `store`, where the state will be persisted:

```
import {createStore } from 'redux'
import reducer from './reducer'
const store = createStore(reducer)
```

We create the store by passing the exported `reducer` function to the `createStore()` function imported from Redux.

After the `store` is initialized, we can dispatch action functions that will generate the new state and update the store itself.

The flow is as follows:

- The store dispatches an action => the reducer computes and returns a new state => the new state is persisted in the store:

```
store.dispatch(addFilter('some new filter'))
```

- The next type is the delete filter functionality. In the reducer function, add the following code:

```
case DELETE_FILTER:
return state.filter(filter => filter.id !== action.id)
```

- The important thing to note here is that the array `filter` method returns a new array, and that is what we need in order to stay pure and not modify the current state. The delete Action Creator function is as shown:

```
export const deleteFilter = id => ({type: types.DELETE_FILTER, id})
store.dispatch(deleteFilter(0))
```

- To edit the filter, we loop with the array `map` method, and we create a new copy with the new text if the ID matches the ID passed by the action:

```
case EDIT_FILTER:
return state.map(filter => filter.id === action.id
? {
...filter,
 text: action.text
}
: filter)
```

That's all we need to have all the functionalities of the filters.

The full code of the filter reducer looks like this:

```
import {ADD_FILTER, DELETE_FILTER, EDIT_FILTER, SELECT_FILTER} from '../constants/ActionTypes'

const initialState = [
  {
    text: 'filter default text',
    id: 0,
    active: false
  }
]

export default function filters(state = initialState, action) {
  switch (action.type) {
    case ADD_FILTER:
      return [
        ...state, {
          id: state.reduce((maxId, filter) => Math.max(filter.id, maxId), -1) + 1,
          text: action.text,
          active: false
        }
      ]
    case DELETE_FILTER:
      return state.filter(filter => filter.id !== action.id)
    case EDIT_FILTER:
      return state.map(filter => filter.id === action.id
        ? {
          ...filter,
          text: action.text
        }
        : filter)
    case SELECT_FILTER:
      return state.map(filter => filter.id === action.id
        ? {
          ...filter,
          active: true
        }
        : {
          ...filter,
          active: false
        })
    default:
      return state
  }
}
```

The tweets that will be pushed from the server will also be stored in a Redux state. You can leave them in the Minimongo and just read and render as they hit the browser:

```
import {RECEIVE_TWEET} from '../constants/ActionTypes'
const tweets = (state = [], action) => {
  switch (action.type) {
    case RECEIVE_TWEET:
```

```
      return [
        ...state,
        {
          id: action.id,
          time: action.time,
          sentiment: action.sentiment,
          phrase: action.phrase,
          tweet: action.tweet
        }
      ]
    default:
      return state
  }
}
export default tweets
```

There is only one action here. When we receive a new tweet, we will add it to the store.

Getting the data from the collection

There are a few options on how we can listen when a collection changes. The first option is to use Meteor's Tracker, which is a tracking system that can track anything that supports reactive updates. In our case, we are interested in the DB collections:

```
let Stats = new Mongo.Collection('stats');
Tracker.autorun(() => {
  let data = Stats.find({}).fetch()
  store.dispatch({type: 'RECEIVE_TWEET', tweets: data})
});
```

`Tracker.autorun` will run each time the `Stats` collection changes and, in there, we can dispatch the action with the data to the reducer.

Another way is to attach an observer to the collection:

```
let Stats = new Mongo.Collection('stats');
Stats.find({}).observe({
  added: function (data) {
    store.dispatch({
      type: 'RECEIVE_TWEET',
      id: data._id,
      time: data.time,
      sentiment: data.score.score,
      phrase: data.phrase,
      tweet: data.tweet
    })
```

```
    }
  });
```

Here, the store will dispatch an action when a new item is in sync with Minimongo.

Both the methods will return the entire documents and not only the new documents.

The third method that we can use is `observeChanges`. When a new document is added, it will return the new document only (with `id` and `fields`):

```
let Stats = new Mongo.Collection('stats');
Stats.find({}).observeChanges({
    added: function (id, data) {
        store.dispatch({
            type: 'RECEIVE_TWEET',
            id: id,
            time: data.time,
            sentiment: data.score.score,
            phrase: data.phrase,
            tweet: data.tweet
        })
    }
});
```

React will re-render the changes only, so we are good in all cases.

Now we have both reducers--the tweets and the filters--in the `index.js` of the reducers folder; we can combine them and export them as one reducer function:

```
import {combineReducers} from 'redux'
import filters from './filters'
import tweets from './tweets'
import {routerReducer} from 'react-router-redux'
export default combineReducers({filters: filters, tweets: tweets, routing:
routerReducer});
```

Here, we also added a react router reducer. We need it to keep all the pages in sync with the store when we are paging through the app.

Async actions in Redux

Out-of-the-box, Redux is synchronous. If you try to dispatch an async function, you'll get an error:

```
Actions must be plain objects. Use custom middleware for async actions.
```

```
import thunk from 'redux-thunk'
import createLogger from 'redux-logger'
const middleware = [thunk]
if (process.env.NODE_ENV !== 'production') {
 middleware.push(createLogger())
}
const store = createStore(reducers, applyMiddleware(...middleware))
```

redux-thunk is middleware that will allow us to dispatch a function and wait for the result; then we can dispatch another action(s).

Here's how we can use async actions:

```
export const track = filter => {
    return dispatch => {
        Meteor.call('track_phrase', filter.phrase, err => {
            if (!err) {
                dispatch(selectFilter(filter.id));
            }
            //do something if you have an error. you can dispatch another
action
        })
    }
}
```

In the action, we call a standard Meteor method by passing a filter phrase to the server; then if there was no error on the callback, we dispatched another action--selectFilter(filter.id).

Here are all our actions:

```
import * as types from '../constants/ActionTypes'
export const addFilter = text => ({type: types.ADD_FILTER, text})
export const deleteFilter = id => ({type: types.DELETE_FILTER, id})
export const editFilter = (id, text) => ({type: types.EDIT_FILTER, id, text})
export const selectFilter = (id) => ({type: types.SELECT_FILTER, id})

export const track = filter => {
    return dispatch => {
        Meteor.call('track_phrase', filter.phrase, err => {
            if (!err) {
                dispatch(selectFilter(filter.id));
            }
            //do something if you have an erro. another action
        })
    }
}
```

The next step is to define our routes in the root of the client folder:

```
import {Provider} from 'react-redux'
import {Router, Route, browserHistory, IndexRoute} from 'react-router'
import {syncHistoryWithStore, routerReducer} from 'react-router-redux'
…. Code omitted

const history = syncHistoryWithStore(browserHistory, store)
import App from './containers/App';
import Sentiment from './containers/Sentiment';
import AddFilter from './containers/AddFilter'
import Tweets from './containers/Tweets'
import PageNotFound from './components/PageNotFound';

export const renderRoutes = () => (
 <Provider store={store}>
  <Router history={history}>
     <Route path="/" component={App}>
       <IndexRoute component={AddFilter}/>
       <Route path="tweets" component={Tweets}/>
       <Route path="sentiment" component={Sentiment}/>
       <Route path="filters" component={AddFilter}/>
    </Route>
  <Route path="*" component={PageNotFound}/>
 </Router>
</Provider>
);
```

Here, we have four container components: App, AddFilter, Tweets, Sentiment, and a fallback component (PageNotFound) if the page is not found.

We need to add a few new additions to react-router in order to have Redux store passed down to all components.

We wrap all our container components in the Provider component from Redux; by doing so, the store will be passed down to all its children so that they can read from it. The second thing is the syncHistoryWithStore function.

Here, we pass two arguments: the react-router browser history and the store. With that, the location will be kept in the store as a plane object and, each time the browser location changes, an action will be fired--LOCATION_CHANGE--and the state will be updated; with that we don't have to manage the state ourselves.

Creating the App components

Let's start with the container components:

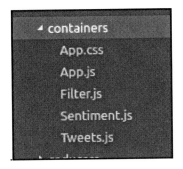

The `App.js` will be nothing more than a wrapper for the whole app. In there, we will render a `NavBar` and a bootstrap class container where we will render all children components passed to the component:

```
import React from 'react'
import NavBar from '../components/NavBar'
const App = ({children}) => (
 <div>
   <NavBar/>
   <div className="container">
     {children}
   </div>
 </div>
)
export default App
```

Connecting the Redux store with the React components

Throughout the book, we have been splitting the components into presentational and container components. There are a few things that we can do with Redux by following that pattern.

The presentational components will not be aware of Redux, and their main job is to present the UI. All markup and CSS classes will be defined in the presentational components. On the other hand, the containers will take care of the data and will barely contain any markup. The main difference is that we will have Redux to generate the containers for us.

Redux is not a React library, and we can get the bindings from the `react-redux` library:

```
import {connect} from 'react-redux'
class Tweets extends React.Component {
  ...
}

const mapStateToProps = (state) => ({tweets: state.tweets, filters:
state.filters})
export default connect(mapStateToProps)(Tweets)
```

Here's how it works:

- We imported the connect method from `react-redux` and mapped the global state values with the props of the component. For this component, we are interested in the tweets and the filters from the state.
- The connect method takes a function and returns another function that takes a component as an argument.

Let's rewrite the component generation to see that it works more clearly:

```
const generateContainer = connect(function(store) {
  return {
    tweets: store.tweets,
    filters: store.filters
  },
})
export default generateContainer(Tweets);
```

In ES6, the following will be the code:

```
const generateContainer = connect(store => {
  return {
    tweets: store.tweets,
    filters: store.filters
  }
})
```

Then, we can even shorten it like this:

```
const generateContainer = connect(store => ({tweets: store.tweets, filters:
store.filters}))
```

The next thing is the actions. The second argument of the connect method is the mapping dispatcher to the props. That gives us the optional functionality of dispatching actions from the components passed as props:

```
const mapDispatchToProps = dispatch => {
    return {
        actions: bindActionCreators(AllActions, dispatch)
    }
}

export default connect(mapStateToProps, mapDispatchToProps)(Filter)
```

Now all the actions will be passed as props and, if you have presentational components, you can pass them as props of type functions:

```
const Filter = ({filters, actions}) => {
    return (
        <div>
            <FilterForm addFilter={actions.addFilter}/>
        </div>
    )
}
```

In the presentational, you dispatch an action like this:

```
export default class FilterForm extends Component {
    this.props.addFilter(text)
}
```

The containers and the components of the App

Here's a diagram of all our components:

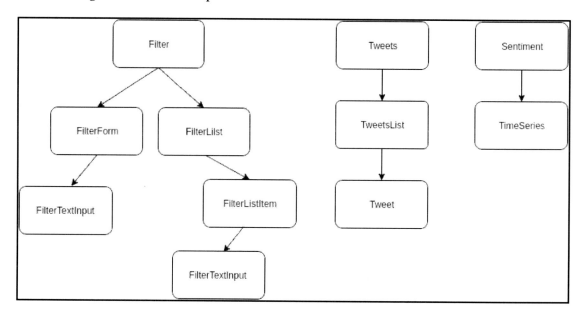

Starting from the **Filter** container, we will build the **Filter** functionality. You can explore more examples of this type of list (To-do List) in the Redux GitHub repository at https://g ithub.com/reactjs/redux/tree/master/examples.

```
const Filter = ({filters, actions}) => {
return (<div>
      <FilterForm addFilter={actions.addFilter}/>
      <FilterList filters={filters} actions={actions}/>
  </div>)
 }
.... Code Ommited
export default connect(mapStateToProps, mapDispatchToProps)(Filter)
```

The Filter components

```
1   import React, {PropTypes, Component} from 'react'
2   import FilterTextInput from './FilterTextInput'
3
4   export default class FilterForm extends Component {
5     static propTypes = {
6       addFilter: PropTypes.func.isRequired
7     }
8
9     handleSave = text => {
10      if (text.length !== 0) {
11        this.props.addFilter(text)
12      }
13    }
14
15    render() {
16      return (
17        <div className="col-md-6">
18          <div className="form-group">
19            <FilterTextInput newFilter onSave={this.handleSave} placeholder="Enter Filter"/>
20          </div>
21        </div>
22      )
23    }
24  }
```

The `FilterForm` renders the `FilterTextInput` component by passing three
props: `handleSave`, a callback that will dispatch and action, `addFilter()`, a
`placeholder`, the placeholder value of the textbox, and a `newFilter`. From the component
diagram, you'll note that we rendered the `FilterTextInput` component from the
`FilterForm` and the `FilterListItem`. From the `FilterForm`, we will create a new filter
and from the `FilterListForm`, we use the same component for editing the existing filters.
If we render it with `newFilter` as a prop, the component can be used for adding; if we
don't pass it, the text input can be used for editing.

Here's how it looks:

```
1   import React, {Component, PropTypes} from 'react'
2
3   export default class FilterTextInput extends Component {
4     static propTypes = {
5       onSave: PropTypes.func.isRequired,
6       text: PropTypes.string,
7       placeholder: PropTypes.string,
8       editing: PropTypes.bool,
9       newFilter: PropTypes.bool
10    }
11
12    state = {
13      text: this.props.text || ''
14    }
15
16    handleSubmit = e => {
17      const text = e.target.value.trim()
18      if (e.which === 13) {
19        this.props.onSave(text)
20        if (this.props.newFilter) {
21          this.setState({text: ''})
22        }
23      }
24    }
25
26    handleChange = e => {
27      this.setState({text: e.target.value})
28    }
29
30    handleBlur = e => {
31      if (!this.props.newFilter) {
32        this.props.onSave(e.target.value)
33      }
34    }
35
36    render() {
37      return (<input
38        className="form-control"
39        type="text"
40        placeholder={this.props.placeholder}
41        autoFocus="true"
42        value={this.state.text}
43        onBlur={this.handleBlur}
44        onChange={this.handleChange}
45        onKeyDown={this.handleSubmit}/>)
46    }
47  }
```

Here, we have three vanilla JavaScript events: `onblur`, `onchange`, and `onkeydown`. The only difference is that they are camel cased in JSX syntax--`onblur` is `onBlur`, `onchange` is `onChange`, and `onkeydown` is `onKeyDown`. When the user presses *Enter* (the `keyCode` is 13), we will fire the `onSave` callback (passed as a prop) and the `FilterForm` parent component will dispatch an action and update the store. If the `newFilter` prop was passed, we will clear the input box by setting the component's state to empty. `onChange` – `handleChange`. Here, we simply set the component state with the input text value for every change in the input box. `onBlur` –`handleBlur`. `onBlur` fires as soon as the input loses its focus. We will save the new text only if we are updating an existing filter, ignore it otherwise. The `FilterList` component is as follows:

```
import React, {Component, PropTypes} from 'react'
import FilterListItem from './FilterListItem'

export default class FilterList extends Component {
  static propTypes = {
    filters: PropTypes.array.isRequired,
    actions: PropTypes.object.isRequired
  }

  render() {
    const {filters, actions} = this.props
    return (
      <div className="col-md-6">
        <ul className="list-group">
          {filters.map(filter => <FilterListItem key={filter.id} filter={filter} {...actions}/>)}
        </ul>
      </div>
    )
  }
}
```

The Unordered list component gets two props, all the filters, and all the actions, and renders a list of child components--FilterListItem--by passing filter as prop and all actions. The FilterListItem::

```
render() {
    const {filter, deleteFilter, track} = this.props

    let element

    if (this.state.editing) {
        element = (<FilterTextInput
            text={filter.text}
            editing={this.state.editing}
            onSave={(text) => this.handleSave(filter.id, text)}/>)

    } else {
        element = (
            <div className="row">
                <div className="col-sm-11">
                    <div onDoubleClick={this.handleDoubleClick}>
                        {filter.text}
                    </div>
                </div>
                <div className="col-sm-1">
                    <span onClick={() => deleteFilter(filter.id)}>
                        <i className="fa fa-times" aria-hidden="true"></i>
                    </span>
                </div>
            </div>
        )
    }

    return (
        <li
            className={classnames("list-group-item", {'list-group-item-success': filter.active})}
            onClick={() => track({id: filter.id, phrase: filter.text})}>
            {element}
        </li>
    )
}
```

Let's see what is happening in the render method. Here, we will conditionally render the FilterTextInput component. If the component state is in editing mode, we will render it by passing the onSave callback prop, the editing true or false, and you will note that we didn't pass the newFilter prop; with this, we are using this component to edit an existing filter. If the state.editing is equal to false, we will render an element with two events: onDoubleClick and onClick.

Here are all the event methods:

```
handleDoubleClick = () => {
  this.setState({editing: true})
}
handleClick = () => {
  this.props.deleteFilter(id)
}
handleSave = (id, text) => {
    if (text.length === 0) {
      this.props.deleteFilter(id)
    } else {
      this.props.editFilter(id, text)
    }
    this.setState({editing: false})
}
```

On double-click, we set the state editing to `true`. On single-click on the delete icon, we will dispatch the `deleteFilter` action. If the input box is empty on `handleSave`, we will delete the filter; we will edit it and set the editing state to `false` otherwise:

```
return (
    <li className={classnames("list-group-item",
        {'list-group-item-success': filter.active})}
          onClick={() => track({id: filter.id, phrase: filter.text})}>
      {element}
</li>)
```

This is the last piece of the component. On a click on the entire component, we will dispatch the `track` async action, where we call the `Meteor` method and pass data to the server. If there is no error, we update the state of the filter to active:

```
export const track = filter => {
  return dispatch => {
    Meteor.call('track_phrase', filter.phrase, err => {
      if (!err) {
        dispatch(selectFilter(filter.id));        }
          //do something if you have an error. another action      })    } }
```

Tweets component

The complete code of the `Tweets` component is as follows:

```
class Tweets extends React.Component {

  render() {
    const {tweets, filters} = this.props
    let filteredTweets = []
    let activeFilter = filters.filter(filter => filter.active === true)
    if (activeFilter[0]) {
      filteredTweets = tweets.filter(tweet => tweet.phrase === activeFilter[0].text);
    }
    return (
      <div>
        <TweetsList tweets={filteredTweets}/>
      </div>
    )
  }
}

Tweets.propTypes = {
  tweets: PropTypes.array.isRequired,
  filters: PropTypes.array.isRequired
}
const mapStateToProps = (state, dispatch) => {
  return {tweets: state.tweets, filters: state.filters}
}
const generateComponent = connect(mapStateToProps)

export default generateComponent(Tweets);
```

We want to render tweets filtered by an active filter and not all incoming tweets so that each user goes to the Tweets page. We will query the store, get the currently active filter, and filter out the tweets in a new array by matching phrase:

```
const TweetsList = ({tweets}) => {
  const text = (
    <div>
        {tweets.map(data => <Tweet key={data.id} tweet={data.tweet}
    score={data.sentiment}/>) }
    </div>);
  return(
    <div>{text}</div>)
  }
```

There's nothing really special in the `TweetsList` component. We loop through all the tweets (filtered and passed as props) and render a child component--`Tweet`--which will take care of the look of each tweet:

```
const Tweet = ({tweet, score}) => {
return (
<div className="card">
   <div className="card-block">
    <h4 className="card-title">Score {score}</h4>
    <p className="card-text">{tweet}</p>
 </div>
</div>) }
```

The Sentiment component

The last page is the Sentiment. We will represent all tweets by time and score. When a new tweet is saved to the database, we save the time it arrived and the sentiment score; later (or in realtime) that information can be used to analyze the data over a period of time:

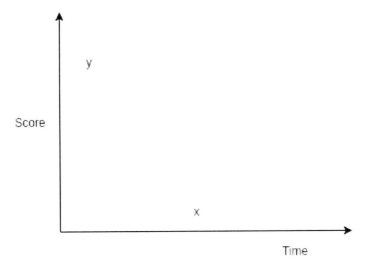

Again, we want the user to visualize tweets by the currently active filter:

```
import React, {PropTypes} from 'react'
import {Link} from 'react-router'
import {connect} from 'react-redux'
import TimeSeries from '../components/TimeSeries'

class Sentiment extends React.Component {

    render() {
        const {tweets, filters} = this.props
        let filteredTweets = []
        let activeFilter = filters.filter(filter => filter.active === true)
        if (activeFilter[0]) {
            filteredTweets = tweets.filter(tweet => tweet.phrase === activeFilter[0].text);
        }
        return (
            <div>
                <TimeSeries data={filteredTweets}/>
            </div>
        )
    }
}

Sentiment.propTypes = {
    tweets: PropTypes.array.isRequired,
    filters: PropTypes.array.isRequired
}
const mapStateToProps = (state) => ({tweets: state.tweets, filters: state.filters})

export default connect(mapStateToProps)(Sentiment)
```

Here, we query and filter the store exactly the same way as we did in the `Tweets` component. The last piece is the chart. For this example, I am using recharts, a very nice charting library with tons of examples; you can refer to it at `http://recharts.org/en-US`.

```jsx
import React, {PropTypes} from 'react'
import {
  ResponsiveContainer,
  LineChart,
  Line,
  XAxis,
  YAxis,
  Tooltip,
  CartesianGrid,
  Legend,
  ErrorBar
} from 'recharts';

const TimeSeries = ({data}) => {

  return (
    <ResponsiveContainer minWidth={1000} minHeight={500}>
      <LineChart
        data={data}
        margin={{
          top: 20,
          right: 50,
          left: 20,
          bottom: 5
        }}>
        <XAxis dataKey="time"/>
        <YAxis/>
        <CartesianGrid strokeDasharray="3 3"/>
        <Tooltip/>
        <Legend/>
        <Line type="monotone" dataKey="sentiment" stroke="#82ca9d"/>
      </LineChart>
    </ResponsiveContainer>
  )

}

export default TimeSeries
```

Here, we have the time for x (axis); and the line will draw the sentiment score. Any time a new tweet arrives, the chart will re-render with the latest update. It should look like this:

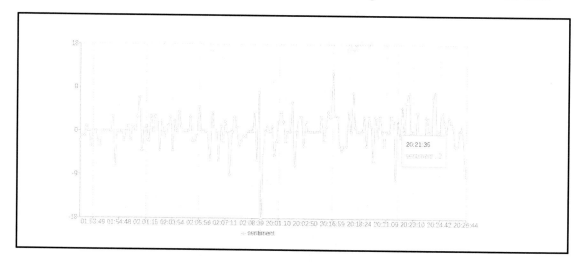

On the Server

On the server, we need just two libraries to have all that working. The sentiment that will score every text (tweet) that we pass in, `https://github.com/thisandagain/sentiment`, from the `GitHub` repository:

```
var sentiment = require('sentiment');
var r1 = sentiment('Cats are stupid.');
console.dir(r1);
// Score: -2, Comparative: -0.666
var r2 = sentiment('Cats are totally amazing!');
console.dir(r2);
// Score: 4, Comparative: 1
```

Twitter is the second one that we will use to hook up to the Twitter's Streaming API.

`https://github.com/desmondmorris/node-twitter`

The first thing we need to do is to initialize a new client with our credentials that we got when we created the Twitter app at the beginning of the chapter:

```
require('../env')
import Twitter from 'twitter'
let client = new Twitter({
```

```
consumer_key: process.env.CONSUMER_KEY,
consumer_secret: process.env.CONSUMER_SECRET,
access_token_key: process.env.ACCESS_TOKEN_KEY,
access_token_secret: process.env.ACCESS_TOKEN_SECRET});
```

I have placed my credentials in a `.env.js` and then loaded it as a module. In there, I can have all my credentials as node globals.

```
process.env['CONSUMER_KEY'] = 'jPd5vh5aHWzPhx2r7tBts3dp3'
```

Here, we are creating the stream filtered by geolocation lat-long pairs. The `'-180,-90,180,90'` pairs will give us the whole Earth. Then, we subscribe an event--`on('data')`, and we get the tweet on the callback:

```
let stream_geo = client.stream('statuses/filter', {'locations':
'-180,-90,180,90'});
 stream_geo.on('data', data => {
        if (data.lang === 'en') {
                parser(data.text)
        }
});
```

 Error: Meteor code must always run within a Fiber. Try wrapping callbacks that you pass to non-Meteor libraries with `Meteor.bindEnvironment`.

This is the error that you will get and, by following the suggested solution from the error log, we can fix it like this:

```
stream_geo.on('data', Meteor.bindEnvironment(data => {
    if (data.lang === 'en') {
        parser(data.text)
    }
}));
```

After we have connected to the stream and tweets are incoming in realtime, we need to get the filter phrase from the user and check it against every tweet.

We send the filter from the frontend with the `Meteor` method that we dispatched from a Redux action; for this non-trivial example, we assign the phrase as one global variable--`filter_phrase`:

```
Meteor.methods({
        track_phrase: function (phrase) {
        filter_phrase = phrase
    }
```

```
});
```

The `parser` functionality is pretty simple. If the phrase is in the tweet, we insert it in the `Stats` collection and that will sync it with the client Minimongo:

```
const filter = (data) => {
        const {tweet, phrase_filter} = data
        return tweet.includes(phrase_filter)
};
const parser = (data) => {
        if (filter({tweet: data, phrase_filter: filter_phrase})) {
            let d = new Date();
            let n = d.toISOString().substr(11, 8);
            Stats.insert({
              time: n,
              score: sentiment(data),
              phrase: filter_phrase,
              tweet: data,
              timestamp: Date.now()
            })
        }
}
```

Test it out and improve it!

You can improve many things in this app by adding new features. For example, you can save the filters for each user in a collection. You can break down what is returned by sentiment module and add more visualizations of the sentiment. There are many technologies that can do better in sentiment analysis than simply counting negative and positive phrases. On the server, you can connect to a more sophisticated **Natural Language Processing (NLP)** service, or you can build a training algorithm with some of the currently available frameworks. Try different lat-long pairs to get the tweets by location, or perhaps let the user select the location. Here is a simple tool that can generate a bounding box for you--`http://boundingbox.klokantech.com`.

You can also improve your development experience on the frontend with Redux development tools. The very basic logger middleware works great in tracking each action in the browser console. Here's a collection of some great tools currently available at `https://github.com/gaearon/redux-devtools`.

Summary

In this chapter, we covered the process of creating a Twitter app in the Twitter developer's console. We got familiar with the state management of the frontend using the *pure* functional programming library, Redux. We also added Filter List (similar to a To-do List) functionality to our app and went through the complete list of items, CRUD using Redux's store state and the React internal component's state.

On the backend, we created a stream of tweets by location; then, with the specified filter by the user, we parsed each tweet and we ingested the tweets into MongoDB based on the findings. We also performed sentiment analysis on each matching tweet and all score results and tweets were pushed in real time to the user with the reactiveness of Meteor.

5
Developing Kanban Project Management Tool

In Chapter 2, *Building a Shopping Cart*, we built a **Create Read Update Delete (CRUD)** application and managed reactivity by creating **Higher-Order Component** (**HOC**); we did this by wrapping our container components with the react-meteor-data package. We used this package to do the fetching and passing of data down to the container components and their children as props.

We generated our container components as follows:

```
export default createContainer(() => {
 return {
products: ProductsCollection.find({department: 'books'}).fetch()
  };
}, Books);
```

In Chapter 4, *Real-Time Twitter Streaming*, we introduced a client-side state container library, called Redux. With Redux, we persisted the application state by connecting our containers to a single store that had a single JavaScript object presentation of the state. Note that we persisted the data on the client side only. The data (tweets) was pushed from the server to the client using Meteor's *Data on the Wire* feature, and every newly inserted document on the server was available in Minimongo—the client's database. On the client side, we subscribed to a collection event that fired on every change (added document) made on the server; we then dispatched actions with our Redux store and updated the state with the new data.

The subscription to the collection event was defined as:

```
Stats.find({})
  .observe({
added: function (data) {
store.dispatch({
        type: 'RECEIVE_TWEET',
        id: data._id,
        time: data.time,
        sentiment: data.score.score,
        phrase: data.phrase,
        tweet: data.tweet
    })
  }
});
```

In this chapter, we will combine what we learned in `Chapter 2`, *Building a Shopping Cart*, and `Chapter 4`, *Real-Time Twitter Streaming*. We will build a simple Kanban application that will manage the client state with Redux, and we will wire all the Meteor Methods and subscriptions through the Redux store, which will guarantee the correct state of our app at any given time. We will also learn how to extend the functionality of a React component by writing Higher-Order Components.

If I were to give a very lean description, the Kanban management method describes the progress of a given process in a visual way. To represent a Kanban app, we will have a single page Board application on the front-end. This is where we will add and remove tasks that could be in either one of the three states: to-do, in-progress, and done. Also, this is where users will be able to change the state of each task by dragging and dropping them into three sub-boards or lists (to do, in-progress, and done). Also, Board will listen for changes on the tasks and update itself in real time. For example, if one user moves a task from **in progress** to **done**, all other users of the application will be able to see the updated Board without the need for refreshing the page or clicking on the refresh button.

Drag and drop in React

We can't have a Kanban Board app without a drag and drop (DnD) UI functionality, which is the core UI of any Kanban software. Thanks to *Dan Abramov* for his DnD React library, we can now easily implement and customize such a functionality in React. The library is built on top of Flux—the original unidirectional data architecture from Facebook (Redux was later developed by *Dan Abramov*, who was influenced by Flux)—and can beautifully fit into our stack without having any fears about breaking the data flow pattern.

The best way to get familiar with the library is by building a React DnD introduction app and exploring the API in a step-by-step manner.

Fire up your terminal and create a Meteor app:

```
>> meteor create dnd-intro
```

Install React and DnD packages:

```
>> npm install react —save
>> npm install react-dom —save
>> npm install react-dnd —save
>> npm install react-dnd-html5-backend —save
```

As shown in the following diagram, the library consists of three main components:

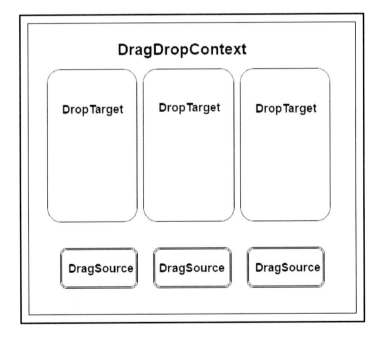

- There is a main root container that is built on top of the drag and drop HTML API, called **DragDropContext**
- Then there is a drag source component (**DragSource**), which can transform any of our standard React components into draggable UIs
- Lastly, there is the drop target (**DropTarget**) component, which accepts draggable components to be dragged and dropped into and out of it

Since we are building a Kanban app, let's name the components close to what they will represent in our app. The Board component will be at the root of our app and will be generated by the `DragDropContext` function. We also need three list components: `Todo`, `In Progress`, and `Done`. They will be our drop targets since the tasks/cards can be dragged and dropped into and out of them. Cards represent a single task on Board, and they will be generated by the `DragSource` function.

We will build it with very minimalistic setup, just basic HTML, CSS, and three React components. When done, it should look something like this:

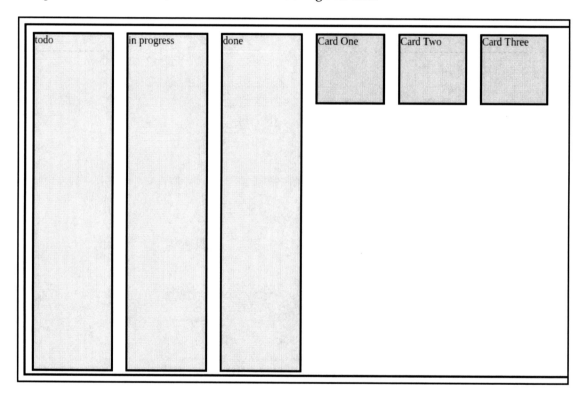

Here we have our board (in light cyan color) that renders three children list (in gray) components and three **Card** components.

Let's start writing these components by creating the files in the root `client` folder:

You can also use this sample app for reference if you already have a parent top-level component and you want to make some of its children draggable and droppable. Follow the ensuing steps to add `DragDropContext` to it. After importing React, we will need to import the `DragDropContext` forms, called `react-dnd` and `HTML5Backend`. That's all we need to convert it:

```
import {DragDropContext} from 'react-dnd';
import HTML5Backend from 'react-dnd-html5-backend';

const Board = () => {
 return (
  <div className="board">
    <div>
      <CardList listName={"todo"}/>
      <CardList listName={"in progress"}/>
      <CardList listName={"done"}/>
    </div>
    <div>
      <Card name='Card One'/>
      <Card name='Card Two'/>
      <Card name='Card Three'/>
    </div>
  </div>
 );
}
```

There is one problem, though. If you try to generate this component, you will get an error:

```
modules.js:4560 Warning: Stateless function components cannot be given refs
(See ref "child" in Board created by DragDropContext(Board)). Attempts to
access this ref will fail.
```

The error is pretty descriptive, and all we need to do is convert it into a class component. For more information on the difference between class and stateless components, refer to Chapter 1, *Foundation of Meteor*, in case you skipped it.

Here we convert it into a class component that extends React's Component class and adds the render() method:

```
class Board extends Component {
render() {
  return (
   <div className="board">
    <div>
      <CardList listName={"todo"}/>
      <CardList listName={"in progress"}/>
      <CardList listName={"done"}/>
    </div>
    <div>
      <Card name='Card One'/>
      <Card name='Card Two'/>
      <Card name='Card Three'/>
    </div>
   </div>
  );
 }
}
```

Our next step is to enhance it with the functionality returned from the DragDropContext function:

```
export default DragDropContext(HTML5Backend)(Board);
```

It takes HTML5Backend as the first parameter, then returns a function that takes our Board component as a parameter.

Moving on to the drop target component, the wrapper DropTarget requires three parameters:

```
DropTarget(types, spec, collect)
```

1. types: This is a plain JavaScript object that describes what the dragged items are.

   In our case, it is the item with the object that has the key CARD:

   ```
   const ItemTypes = {
     CARD: 'card'
   }
   ```

In the `DropTarget` function, we pass it as:

```
DropTarget(ItemTypes.CARD, spec, collect)(CardList)
```

2. `specification`: This is another object that will specify the functionality of the drop container. There are three methods that we can access in it, **drop, hover,** and **canDrop**:

```
DropTarget(ItemTypes.CARD, spec, collect)
```

For now, we are interested in the `drop` method only. It can take three parameters, `props`, `monitor`, and `component`:

```
const spec = {
drop(props, monitor, component) {
  ...
   }
};
DropTarget(ItemTypes.CARD, spec, collect)(CardList)
```

Here, `props` are the properties of the `CardList` component; `component` is our `CardList` component.

The second parameter is `monitor`, and that is the interesting one. It returns information about the dragged component, and it has a lot of methods. To keep it simple, we only need information about what was dropped, and to access this data, we will call `monitor.getItem()`.

What returns this method depends completely on the dragged component:

```
const spec = {
drop(props, monitor, component) {
const item = monitor.getItem();// returned data from the
dragged component
return {moved: true, listName: props.listName};
  }
};
```

In the `drop` method, our `CardList` can have data that was passed from the dragged `Card` component. The return of the `drop` method, on the other hand, will be accessible from the dragged component.

To illustrate the data flow, check out the following diagram:

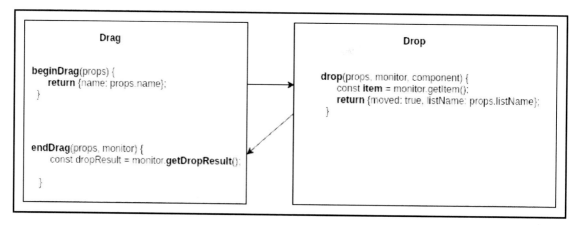

The workflow can be described as follows. As soon as the user starts dragging `Card` (the drag-enabled component), it will fire the `beginDrag` method; this is where we can return any data we need to be accessible on the drop component.

Once the card is successfully dropped, the drop method will fire and return the values we specified.

The next event that will be fired is `endDrag`; it will be fired on the `Card` component, where we can get the return from the `drop()` with `monitor.getDropResult()`.

If we place logs in all the methods in the browser console, we will see the following sequence:

fired `beginDrag`

fired `drop`

fired `endDrag`

3. The third parameter required is the `collection` function where we can return `connect.dropTarget()`:

```
const collect = (connect) => {
  return {
  connectDropTarget: connect.dropTarget()
  }
}
```

The returned function `connectDropTarget` is needed in our `render()` method in order to connect the component to the HTML DnD API. `DropTarget` will take it as an argument and pass it down as a prop to our `CardList` component.

In our `render()` function, we can use it like this:

```
render() {
  const {name, connectDropTarget, listName } = this.props;
    return connectDropTarget(
      <div className="cardList">{listName}</div>
    )
}
```

The complete code of `CardList` is as follows:

```
import React, {PropTypes, Component} from 'react';
import {DropTarget} from 'react-dnd';
const ItemTypes = {
  CARD: 'card'
}
const spec = {
drop(props, monitor) {
  let item = monitor.getItem();
  console.log("fired drop")
  return {moved: true, listName: props.listName};
  }
};
const collect = (connect) => {
  return {
connectDropTarget: connect.dropTarget()
  }
}
class CardList extends Component {
  render() {
    const {name, connectDropTarget, listName} = this.props;
      return connectDropTarget(
          <div className="cardList">{listName}</div>
      )
```

```
    }
  }
  export default DropTarget(ItemTypes.CARD, spec, collect)(CardList);
```

The last component is the `Card`. The function we need to convert our `Card` component into a draggable source is `DragSource`:

```
  export default DragSource(ItemTypes.CARD, spec, collect)(Card);
```

It is the same as that of `DropSource`; `DragSource` takes three parameters: the `type` object, `specification` object, and `collect` function. In order to make `DropSource` aware of this component, both their types should match:

```
  const ItemTypes = {
    CARD: 'card'
  }
  export default DragSource(ItemTypes.CARD, spec, collect)(Card);
```

The `spec` object can have all these methods: `beginDrag` (`props`, `monitor`, and `component`), `endDrag` (`props`, `monitor`, and `component`), `canDrag` (`props`, `monitor`), and `isDragging` (`props` and `monitor`).

For now, we are interested in the first two: `beginDrag` and `endDrag`.

The last parameter, the `collect` function, will return a connection to the HML DnD API, and it will also be injected into our props using the `DragSource` generator:

```
  export default DragSource(ItemTypes.CARD, spec, collect)(Card)
```

The entire code of the `Card` component is as follows:

```
  import React, {Component, PropTypes} from 'react'
  import {DragSource} from 'react-dnd'
  const ItemTypes = {
   CARD: 'card'
  }
  const spec = {
  beginDrag(props) {
     console.log("fired beginDrag")
  return {name: props.name};
   },

  endDrag(props, monitor) {
    console.log("fired endDrag")
    let dropResult = monitor.getDropResult();
    if (!dropResult) {
       return
```

```
      }
        alert("moved " + dropResult.moved + " listName ")
      }
    };
    const collect = (connect) => {
     return {
    connectDragSource: connect.dragSource()
      };
    }
    class Card extends Component {
     render() {
     const {name, connectDragSource} = this.props;
        return (connectDragSource(
          <div className="card">
            {name}
          </div>
        ))
      }
    }
    export default DragSource(ItemTypes.CARD, spec, collect)(Card);
```

Let me explain the code from top to bottom. First, we defined our `ItemType`: `CARD`. In the `spec` object, we had two methods, `beginDrag`, and `endDrag`, where we had all of the data passed to the drop source and received from it. The `collect` function returned a `connectDragSource` function that `DragSource` injected into our component's props.

Here is the CSS of the app:

```css
.card {
  float: left;
  height: 100px;
  width: 100px;
  border-style: solid;
  content: "";
  margin: 10px;
  background-color: lightsteelblue
}
.cardList {
  float: left;
  height: 500px;
  width: 120px;
  border-style: solid;
  content: "";
  margin: 10px;
  background-color: lightgrey;
}
.board {
```

```
    border-style: solid;
    height: 520px;
    background-color: lightcyan;
  }
```

Test it out!

Try passing data between the drag and drop targets and get comfortable with the minimal functionality we have now. If you run the app, you'll see that we are not actually dropping Cards into Lists, and even though the events are fired, the UI location is unchanged. We will do the actual dropping by updating their properties in the next section.

Building the App

Similar to what we have in the previous example, the Kanban app will have a Board and three List containers (To do, In Progress, and Done). For the tasks, we will have a form with a few fields where the user could enter the title and description of the new task.

Let's start by creating a new Meteor app:

```
>> meteor create kanban
```

This time, instead of manually installing all the packages, copy and replace the package.json file with the default one that was generated in your app:

```
{
  "name": "kanban",
  "private": true,
  "scripts": {
  "start": "meteor run"
},
  "dependencies": {
  "babel-runtime": "6.18.0",
  "bootstrap": "^4.0.0-alpha.5",
  "classnames": "^2.2.5",
  "font-awesome": "^4.7.0",
  "marked": "^0.3.6",
  "meteor-node-stubs": "~0.2.0",
  "react": "^15.4.1",
  "react-dnd": "^2.1.4",
  "react-dnd-html5-backend": "^2.1.2",
  "react-dom": "^15.4.2",
  "react-redux": "^5.0.1",
```

```
    "react-router": "^3.0.0",
    "react-router-redux": "^4.0.7",
    "redux": "^3.6.0",
    "redux-logger": "^2.7.4",
    "redux-thunk": "^2.1.0"
  },
  "babel": {
  "plugins": [
  "transform-class-properties"
  ]
  },
  "devDependencies": {
  "babel-plugin-transform-class-properties": "^6.19.0"
  }
}
```

Now just run `npm install` and wait until all the dependencies are installed.

Starting from the client, this is how the `client` folder structure will appear:

The `actions` and `reducers` folders are all part of Redux, and the `components` and `containers` split is our standard way of decoupling React components into two categories.

Go ahead and create all the folders and files using the screenshot.

From where can we start building all of that functionality? What we can do is define the actual *actions* that the user will perform and start building on top of the definitions. Note that each action will be persisted in the store; you will have to decide which action should be persisted in the Redux store and which one should be persisted in the React component's state.

Let's define the types in an `ActionTypes.js` file in the `constants` folder:

- The user should be able to create a new card. We can write this as the action type `export const ADD_CARD = 'ADD_CARD'`.
- The user should be able to change the status of any card by dragging it to different lists. We can write this as the action type `export const UPDATE_STATUS = 'UPDATE_STATUS'`.

- The user should be able to delete a card from the Board. This can be described as `export const DELETE_CARD = 'DELETE_CARD'`.

- The user should be able to see all the preceding actions without reloading the page in real time. If another user adds a new card, for example, we would want to see the card appearing on our Board. The action type, in this case, should be `export const RECEIVE_CARD = 'RECEIVE_CARD'`.

- When the user launches the application, we would want to have all the cards on the Board. For this, we would need to call the server and get all the records on the initial app load. We can name this action type `export const INITIAL_LOAD = 'INITIAL_LOAD'`.

The full code of `ActionTypes.js` file is as follows:

```
export const INITIAL_LOAD = 'INITIAL_LOAD'
export const RECEIVE_CARD = 'RECEIVE_CARD'
export const ADD_CARD = 'ADD_CARD'
export const DELETE_CARD = 'DELETE_CARD'
export const UPDATE_STATUS = 'UPDATE_STATUS'
```

The next thing we need to do is define the action functions; we can refer to them as **Action Creators** (function that creates an action) in Redux.

In the `actions` folder, we'll create an `index.js` file where we'll define all the functions. This is a small app and we can have them in one file, which is as follows:

- Type `INITIAL_LOAD` in the Action Creator `export const initialLoad = data => ({type: types.INITIAL_LOAD, data})`.

  Query the backend and when you get the requested data, dispatch an `initialLoad` action: `dispatch(initialLoad(data))`.

- Type `RECEIVE_CARD` in the Action Creator. We will receive cards without actually requesting them. They will be *pushed* from the server as soon as a new card is added to the database. And the Action Creator can be written as `export const receiveCard = (id, title, task, status) => ({type: types.RECEIVE_CARD, id, title, task, status})`.

    Using `dispatch(receiveCard(id, data.title, data.task, data.status))`, the server will push `id`, `title`, `task`, and `status`.

- Type `ADD_CARD`. Now the user adds a new card to the database. We'll use the action function `export const addCard = (id, title, task, status) => ({type: types.ADD_CARD, id, title, task, status})` `dispatch(addCard(result._id, result.title, result.task, result.status))`. We will dispatch this action when the data is successfully inserted into the database. The ID will be returned from the server.

- Type `DELETE_CARD`. It'll use the `export const deleteCard = id => ({type: types.DELETE_CARD, id})` action.

    This will be dispatched on the success of the deletion action on the server, using `dispatch(deleteCard(id))`.

- Type `UPDATE_STATUS`. Here, the action creator is `export const updateCardStatus = (id, status) => ({type: types.UPDATE_STATUS, id, status})` `dispatch(updateCardStatus(id, status))`.

Before we move on to reducers, we need to have some way to send data to the server whenever a user creates, deletes, or changes the status of a card.

We will use Meteor methods to do this. Start by defining server methods, then, client calls.

In the `main.js` file on the server, type this:

```
Meteor.startup(() => {
  // code to run on server at startup

  Meteor.methods({
    ....
```

We'll keep the same order. The `initial_load` will be as follows:

```
Meteor.methods({

initial_load() {
    return Tasks.find({}).fetch()
},
```

Calling this method from the client will fetch all the records from the `Tasks` collection; if there is no error, we can dispatch our Redux action:

```
export const initial_load = () => {
  return dispatch => {
   Meteor.call('initial_load', (err, data) => {
      if (!err) {
   dispatch(initialLoad(data))
      }
      //you can do something if you have an error. another action
    })
   }
}
```

Next, we have the `add_card` method:

```
add_Card(data) {
    let id = Tasks.insert({title: data.title, task: data.task, status:
data.status})
    return Tasks.findOne({_id: id})
},
```

Calling this method from the client will insert the new record and return the inserted record. The insertion is synchronous, and you can return the data directly to the client.

Note that for all those methods for which you didn't do any validation against a collection schema, you can add the validations later.

Now check out the `client` method call:

```
export const add_Card = (data) => {
  return dispatch => {
  Meteor.call('add_Card', data, (err, result) => {
    if (!err) {
  dispatch(addCard(result._id, result.title, result.task, result.status))
      }
      //you can do something if you have an error. another action
    })
   }
}
```

To delete a card, simply pass an `id` and remove it from the collection:

```
delete_Card(data) {
    Tasks.remove({_id: data.id});
},
```

The action performed on the client to do this is as follows:

```
export const delete_Card = id => {
  return dispatch => {
    Meteor.call('delete_Card', {id}, (err) => {
      if (!err) {
        dispatch(deleteCard(id))
      }
       //you can do something if you have an error. another action
    })
  }
}
```

Next, we have the update card status:

```
update_CardStatus(data) {
    Tasks.update({_id: data.id}, {
      $set: {
      status: data.status
      }
    });
}
```

And on the client, update the card status as mentioned:

```
export const update_CardStatus = (id, status) => {
  return dispatch => {
    Meteor.call('update_CardStatus', {id, status }, (err) => {
        if (!err) {
            dispatch(updateCardStatus(id, status))
        }
        //you can do something if you have an error. another action
      })
  }
}
```

The complete code on the server should look like this:

```
import {Meteor} from 'meteor/meteor';
import {Tasks} from '../shared/tasksCollection'

Meteor.startup(() => {

  Meteor.methods({

    initial_load() {
      return Tasks.find({}).fetch()
    },

    add_Card(data) {
      let id = Tasks.insert({title: data.title, task: data.task, status: data.status})
      return Tasks.findOne({_id: id})
    },

    delete_Card(data) {
      Tasks.remove({_id: data.id});
    },

    update_CardStatus(data) {
      Tasks.update({_id: data.id}, {
        $set: {
          status: data.status
        }
      });
    }

  });
});
```

The complete code for `actions/index.js` is as follows:

```
import * as types from '../constants/ActionTypes'
export const initialLoad = data => ({type: types.INITIAL_LOAD, data})
export const receiveCard = (id, title, task, status) => ({type: types.RECEIVE_CARD, id, title, task, status})
export const addCard = (id, title, task, status) => ({type: types.ADD_CARD, id, title, task, status})
export const deleteCard = id => ({type: types.DELETE_CARD, id})
export const updateCardStatus = (id, status) => ({type: types.UPDATE_STATUS, id, status})

export const initial_load = () => {
    return dispatch => {
        Meteor.call('initial_load', (err, data) => {
            if (!err) {
                dispatch(initialLoad(data))
            }
        })
    }
}
export const add_Card = (data) => {
    return dispatch => {
        Meteor.call('add_Card', data, (err, result) => {
            if (!err) {
                dispatch(addCard(result._id, result.title, result.task, result.status))
            }
        })
    }
}
export const delete_Card = id => {
    return dispatch => {
        Meteor.call('delete_Card', id, (err) => {
            if (!err) {
                dispatch(deleteCard(id))
            }
        })
    }
}
export const update_CardStatus = (id, status) => {
    return dispatch => {
        Meteor.call('update_CardStatus', {
            id,
            status
        }, (err) => {
            if (!err) {
                dispatch(updateCardStatus(id, status))
            }
        })
    }
}
```

Our next step is to create the reducer.

First, we will import all the action types defined as constants in the `constants/ActionTypes.js` file:

```
import {ADD_CARD,
        DELETE_CARD,
        UPDATE_STATUS,
        RECEIVE_CARD,
        INITIAL_LOAD}
  from '../constants/ActionTypes'
```

We name our reducer function `cards`:

```
export default function cards(state = [], action) {
```

In ES6, we could default our parameters in the function definition; here, we can set our state to an empty array, which will be the initial state of our app.

There are a few things you need to be aware of the initial state in Redux: a few ways in which you can have the initial state passed to the store. One way is to preload it and pass it to the `createStore` function as the second parameter:

```
let preloadedState = {
    cards
}
const store = createStore(reducers, preloadedState,
applyMiddleware(...middleware));
```

This is a very common way of preloading the state in universal apps (apps rendered on the server). We can query the database on the server, build our store, and pass it to the client as a global JavaScript variable. In Meteor, we can do this by querying the server with a Meteor method and passing the result to the `createStore` function:

```
Meteor.startup(() => {

    Meteor.call('initial_load', (err, cards) => {
        if (!err) {
            let preloadedState = {
                cards
            }
        const store = createStore(reducers, preloadedState,
applyMiddleware(...middleware));
        render(
          <Provider store={store}>
            <App/>
          </Provider>, document.getElementById('root'));
    }
  })
```

The second way is to create the store with a default empty array for the state and dispatch an action to load the data from the server once the store is initialized. This action looks like this:

```
const store = createStore(reducers, applyMiddleware(...middleware))
store.dispatch(initial_load());
  render(
    <Provider store={store}>
      <App/>
    </Provider>, document.getElementById('root'));
```

This is where we previously defined the action as:

```
export const initialLoad = data => ({type: types.INITIAL_LOAD, data})
export const initial_load = () => {
 return dispatch => {
    Meteor.call('initial_load', (err, data) => {
        if (!err) {
 dispatch(initialLoad(data))
        }
    })
  }
}
```

The third way of loading initial data is more specific to Meteor. We subscribe to the collection, and as soon as the record is added to the client-side Minimongo, we despatch an action:

```
Tasks.find({}).observeChanges({
 added: function (id, data) {
    store.dispatch(receiveCard(id, data.title, data.task, data.status))
    }
});
```

The next logical step is to write our reducer function.

The reducer function

We start with the action type INITIAL_LOAD:

```
export default function cards(state = [], action) {
    switch (action.type) {
    case INITIAL_LOAD:
        return action.data;
```

Here, we return the new data; notice we do not mutate our state. The second one is the `ADD_CARD` action:

```
case ADD_CARD:
if (state.filter(card => card._id === action.id).length > 0) {
    return state;
}
  return [
    ...state, {
    _id: action.id,
    title: action.title,
    task: action.task,
    status: action.status
    }
  ]
```

In our app, when we create a new card, we dispatch the `ADD_CARD` action, and at the same time, we listen for collection changes. Since we are changing the collection (adding a new card), we will dispatch the `RECEIVE_CARD` action. To prevent adding one item twice, we return the original state if the card is already added. We can add a filter condition in both actions; this way, we won't have to worry about race conditions, especially since the data on the client MongoDB will be updated first before it reaches the server side:

```
case ADD_CARD:
  if (state.filter(card => card._id === action.id).length > 0) {
    return state;
  }
case RECEIVE_CARD:
if (state.filter(card => card._id === action.id).length > 0) {
    return state;
}
```

The `DELETE_CARD` action is pretty simple. Again, we do not mutate the state as we return a new filtered array:

```
case DELETE_CARD:
  return state.filter(card => card._id !== action.id)
```

The last one is `UPDATE_STATUS`. We loop through the array, and if the passed `id` matches the item, we return a new state:

```
case UPDATE_STATUS:
    return state.map(card => card._id === action.id
    ? {
    ...card,
    status: action.status
    }: card)
```

The complete code of the reducer function is as follows:

```
import {ADD_CARD, DELETE_CARD, UPDATE_STATUS, RECEIVE_CARD, INITIAL_LOAD} from '../constants/ActionTypes'

export default function cards(state = [], action) {
    switch (action.type) {
        case INITIAL_LOAD:
            return action.data;
        case ADD_CARD:
            if (state.filter(card => card._id === action.id).length > 0) {
                return state;
            }
            return [
                ...state, {
                    _id: action.id,
                    title: action.title,
                    task: action.task,
                    status: action.status
                }
            ]
        case DELETE_CARD:
            return state.filter(card => card._id !== action.id)
        case UPDATE_STATUS:
            return state.map(card => card._id === action.id
                ? {
                    ...card,
                    status: action.status
                }
                : card)
        case RECEIVE_CARD:
            if (state.filter(card => card._id === action.id).length > 0) {
                return state;
            }
            return [
                ...state, {
                    _id: action.id,
                    title: action.title,
                    task: action.task,
                    status: action.status
                }
            ]
        default:
            return state
    }
}
```

At this point, we have created all the action types, all the functions (Action Creators), and our reducer as well; we have also created all the Meteor Methods on the server and the method calls on the client. We then subscribed to observe the changes of the collection and dispatched the proper actions.

Now we need to build our components and containers. We will have only one `App` container and a few components:

From the top, we have the `Board` component, then we have `Card`. We also have a simple form, `CardForm`, where the user can enter the title and the task description. We will render three `CardList` components for the statuses (`todo`, `in-progress`, and `done`).

We want to have some type of Modal for the form, for better user experience. The Modal will show with the form and hide when the form is submitted. We could use the Bootstrap Modal, but for this app, we will build one ourselves with React.

The `NavBar` object, for now, will not have any functionality; later, we will add some links to it.

The user will click on a button and the Modal will show up with the form. The `NewTask` component is that button that will open the Modal with the form.

On the `container` side, we only have the `App.js` component that will connect to the Redux store, map all props to the store's state, and bind all the actions creators. Doing it this way, the rest of the components will not be aware of Redux.

The `App` component is as follows:

```
class App extends React.Component {
 render() {
 const {cards, actions} = this.props
  return (
   <div>
     <NavBar/>
     <Board cards={cards} {...actions}></Board>
   </div>
  )
 }
}

App.propTypes = {
 cards: PropTypes.array.isRequired,
 actions: PropTypes.object.isRequired
}
const mapStateToProps = (state) => {
 return {cards: state.cards}
}
const mapDispatchToProps = dispatch => ({
actions: bindActionCreators(AllActions, dispatch)
})
const generateComponent = connect(mapStateToProps, mapDispatchToProps)
export default generateComponent(App);
```

What we did here is defined our `App` component and rendered `NavBar` and `Board` in the `render` method. We did some type checking with `App.propTypes` and then mapped all the states from the Redux store to the `cards` props. After this, we imported and bound all the actions to the `actions` props using the `bindActionCreators` function. Binding the actions this way will decouple Redux from the rest of the components. We don't have to pass the dispatcher or import the actions in other components; in order to dispatch them, we can simply call the functions by name.

`Board` is our parent component generated by `DragDropContext`, and every child it renders can be defined draggable and droppable:

```
render() {
    const {cards, delete_Card, update_CardStatus, add_Card} = this.props
    return (
        <div className="container">
            <div className="row">
                <div className="col-sm-12"><NewTask add_Card={add_Card}/></div>
            </div>
            <div className="row">
                <div className="col-sm-4">
                    <CardList
                        title={"To-Do"}
                        listName
                        ={"todo"}
                        delete_Card={delete_Card}
                        update_CardStatus={update_CardStatus}
                        cards={cards.filter((card) => card.status === "todo")}/>
                </div>

                <div className="col-sm-4">
                    <CardList
                        title={"In Progress"}
                        listName
                        ={"inprogress"}
                        delete_Card={delete_Card}
                        update_CardStatus={update_CardStatus}
                        cards={cards.filter((card) => card.status === "inprogress")}/>
                </div>

                <div className="col-sm-4">
                    <CardList
                        title={"Done"}
                        listName
                        ={"done"}
                        delete_Card={delete_Card}
                        update_CardStatus={update_CardStatus}
                        cards={cards.filter((card) => card.status === "done")}/>
                </div>
            </div>
        </div>
    )
```

Here everything is happening in the render method. We render the `NewTask` component by passing the `add_Card` action as a prop. Then, we render the three `CardList` components for each status. If we look at each `CardList` filter, you'll see all the cards based on their statuses:

```
cards={cards.filter((card) => card.status === "todo")}
cards={cards.filter((card) => card.status === "inprogress")}
cards={cards.filter((card) => card.status === "done")}
```

We are also in control of which children components get passed, which actions each component needs, and so on.

Finally, we enhance it with `DragDropContext` and export it as a standard React component: `export default DragDropContext(HTML5Backend)(Board)`.

Building the Modal

In our app, we want to open a popup/modal on a user action and then close it either by clicking on the close button inside the modal or anywhere outside of it.

Let's build a sample Modal app and see how it'll work in a step-by-step fashion. Later, we can implement it in the Kanban app. Open the terminal and create a modal app: `meteor create modal`. To save on typing and installing packages one by one, copy and replace this `package.json` file with the one that was generated by Meteor. Then, run `npm install`:

```json
{
  "name": "modal",
  "private": true,
  "scripts": {
  "start": "meteor run"
},
  "dependencies": {
  "babel-runtime": "6.18.0",
  "classnames": "^2.2.5",
  "meteor-node-stubs": "~0.2.0",
  "react": "^15.4.2"
},
  "babel": {
  "plugins": [
  "transform-class-properties"
  ]
},
  "devDependencies": {
```

```
"babel-plugin-transform-class-properties": "^6.19.0"
  }
}
```

To keep it clear and descriptive, we will create the Modal app with just four files. Delete all the default files in the client folder and create the following files:

In index.html, have the bare minimum Meteor React HTML set up:

```
<head>
<meta charset="UTF-8">
  <title>Modal</title>
</head>
  <body>
    <div id='root'></div>
</body>
```

The first thing we need is a test button through which we can click and open the Modal:

```
Meteor.startup(() => {
 class App extends React.Component {
   render() {
      return (
    <div>
       <button type="button">Open Modal</button>
      </div>)
    }
  }
    render(
     <App/>, document.getElementById('root'));
});
```

We created a very basic class component with one rendered button; the next thing is to add the click event to the button using `<button type="button" onClick={() =>` `this.openModal()}>Open Modal</button>`.

The corresponding method is `openModal() {    alert() }`.

Once Meteor refreshes the page, click on the button to make sure you have done everything right; you should get the alert popup.

The Modal will be in two states, `open` and `close`, and this is a perfect case where we can have that state persisted in the component instead of the Redux store or any other storage. This state is purely UI-related, and there is no need for it to be in the store. If the requirements of the Modal change over time and you need it persisted and accessible across the whole app, you can map its state to the props and have it persisted by dispatching an action.

To have the component's state, add the *constructor* class method and set the default state there. By default, it will be hidden.

The next thing we need to do is set the state to `open` when we click on the button. To do this, use the following:

```
openModal() {    this.setState({isModalOpen: true}) }
```

The Modal is a popup UI, and it will be on top of all other elements. There are two ways to close it (hide it): either have a close button in the modal or have the user click on anything inside the background. The parent component `App` needs to track the close event and set its state; for this, pass a function that will fire back from the Modal component:

```
closeModal() {    this.setState({isModalOpen: false})   }
```

The corresponding function `onClose` is passed as a prop:

```
<Modal onClose={() => this.closeModal()}></Modal>
```

The last thing we need is to pass a prop with this state:

```
<Modal isOpen={this.state.isModalOpen} onClose={() =>
this.closeModal()}></Modal>
```

The entire `App` component will appear as follows:

```
import React from 'react'
import {render} from 'react-dom'
import Modal from './Modal'

Meteor.startup(() => {

  class App extends React.Component {
    constructor(props) {
      super(props)
      this.state = {
        isModalOpen: false
      }
    }
    openModal() {
      this.setState({isModalOpen: true})
    }
    closeModal() {
      this.setState({isModalOpen: false})
    }

    render() {
      return (
        <div>
          <button type="button" onClick={() => this.openModal()}>Open Modal</button>
          <Modal isOpen={this.state.isModalOpen} onClose={() => this.closeModal()}></Modal>
        </div>
      )
    }
  }
  render(
    <App/>, document.getElementById('root'));

});
```

To set its visibility, we can use pure CSS classes; all we need is three classes:

```
.modal {
    position: fixed;
    z-index: 2;
    min-width: 500px;
    min-height: 400px;
    overflow: auto;
    top: 50%;
    left: 50%;
    transform: translate(-50%, -50%);
    background-color: #fefefe;
    z-index: 2;
```

```
}
.hidden{
  display: none;
}
.overlay-modal {
  position: fixed;
  width: 100%;
  height: 100%;
  top: 0; left: 0; bottom: 0; right: 0;
  z-index: 1;
  background-color: grey;
}
```

Here we have a `.modal` class, which is a container centered in the middle of the screen. Second, we have the `.hidden` class, which we will add and remove from the element in order to control the visibility of the Modal. Lastly, we have the `overlay-modal` class, which will be stretched in the entire window as a background backdrop. The `z-index` will control which element is on the top or the stack order of the elements. The Modal will be on top of all the other elements and should have the highest `z-index`; just below, it will be the `overlay-modal` class.

To build the Modal, start from the `render` method. In there, we have a close button, which will set the visibility to hidden, and an overlay container (`div`) styled with the `.overlay-modal` class as the background, which can also hide the Modal:

```
render() {
  const modalClass = classnames('modal', {
   hidden: !this.props.isOpen
  });
  const overlayClass = classnames('overlay-modal', {
   hidden: !this.props.isOpen
 });
 return (
     <div>
   <div className={modalClass}>
   <button type="button" onClick={(e) => this.handleClose(e)}>Close
Modal</button>
   </div>
    <div className={overlayClass} onClick={(e) => this.handleClose(e)}></div>
     </div>
   )
 }
```

A few things are happening in the render method. We control the visibility by adding and removing the CSS class .hidden with the help of the classnames module. We can see that the Modal is controlled from outside passed props, and the only way to close it is by re-rendering it with new props. This way, we don't break the unidirectional data flow from the parent to the child. Visually, this data flow can be presented with the following diagram:

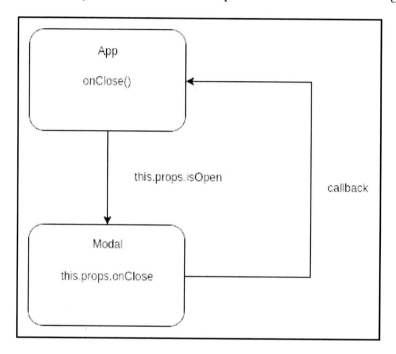

The Modal fires back the onClose function passed as props, and the parent app will update props.isOpen. This will force to re-render the Modal and pass the updated props.

Here is the complete code of the Modal:

```
import React, {Component} from 'react'
import classnames from 'classnames'

class Modal extends Component {
    handleClose(e) {
       e.preventDefault()
  this.props.onClose()
   }
render() {
  const modalClass = classnames('modal', {
    hidden: !this.props.isOpen
});
```

```
  const overlayClass = classnames('overlay-modal', {
    hidden: !this.props.isOpen
  });
  return (
    <div>
      <div className={modalClass}>
        <button type="button" onClick={(e) => this.handleClose(e)}>Close
Modal</button>
    <div>
         {this.props.children}
      </div>
    </div>
        <div className={overlayClass} onClick={(e) =>
this.handleClose(e)}></div>
    </div>
    )
  }
}
export default Modal
```

We added the `handleClose` method that fires back to the parent component when you click on either the overlay or close button.

We also added `this.props.children}` to the render method; this way, we could have the Modal render anything passed from the parent without knowing what will that be in advance. Then test it from the parent app, have the `<p>Test</p>` line wrapped in the `Modal` component:

```
<Modal isOpen={this.state.isModalOpen} onClose={() => this.closeModal()}>
    <p>Test</p>
</Modal>
```

You will notice that `<p>Test</p>` was rendered in the `{this.props.children}` placeholder.

That's all we need for our Modal in the Kanban app. Copy and paste `Modal.js` into `Modal.js` in the Kanban app. To open the Modal, the `NewTask` component will have the exact same functionality as that of our `App.js`:

```
import React, {Component, PropTypes} from 'react'
import Modal from '../Modal'
import CardForm from '../CardForm'

class NewTask extends Component {
    constructor(props) {
        super(props)
        this.state = {
            isModalOpen: false
        }
    }
    openModal() {
        this.setState({isModalOpen: true})
    }
    closeModal() {
        this.setState({isModalOpen: false})
    }
    render() {
        return (
            <div>
                <button
                    type="button"
                    className="btn btn-success btn-lg"
                    onClick={() => this.openModal()}>Create Task</button>
                <Modal isOpen={this.state.isModalOpen} onClose={() => this.closeModal()}>
                    <CardForm add_Card={this.props.add_Card} onClose={() => this.closeModal()}/>
                </Modal>
            </div>

        )
    }
}

export default NewTask
```

Here we wrapped `CardForm` in the Modal the same way we did with our test mMdal app. We also passed the `this.closeModal` function to the form, which we can fire back from the form and re-render with the updated props.

Starting from the `render` method, let's build the `CardForm` component:

```
<form onSubmit={(e) => this.handleSubmit(e)}>
  <div className="form-group">
    <label htmlFor="task_title">Task Title</label>
    <input
    onChange={(e) => this.handleChangeTitle(e)}
      type="text"
      id="task_title"
      className="form-control"
      placeholder="Enter Title"
  value={this.state.title}/>
  </div>
  <div className="form-group">
    <label htmlFor="task_descritopn">Description</label>
    <textarea
  onChange={(e) => this.handleChangeTask(e)}
      type="text"
      id="task_descritopn"
      className="form-control"
      placeholder="Enter Description"
 value={this.state.task}/>
  </div>
    <button type="submit" className="btn btn-primary">Submit</button>
  </form>
```

Here we have a form with two fields: one for the task title as the `<input>` HTML element and the other as `<textarea>` for the task description. We also added two `onChange` events for both the fields. This will keep the values of the input in the component's state.

Here we have both the methods:

```
handleChangeTitle(event) {
   this.setState({title: event.target.value});
 }

handleChangeTask(event) {
   this.setState({task: event.target.value});
 }
```

As always, we set the initial state in the `constructor` method:

```
constructor(props) {
super(props);
this.state = {
  title: '',
  task: ''
  };
}
```

The next functionality we need is to save the form data to the database. By clicking on the **submit** button, we fire an `onSubmit` form event where we can dispatch some action with the data.

The `handleSubmit` method will do three things:

1. Dispatch an action and update the store.
2. Set the state with the initial values: `this.state = {title: '', task: '' };`.
3. Close (hide) the Modal by firing back the `onClose()` function.

```
handleSubmit(event) {
  event.preventDefault();
this.props.add_Card({title: this.state.title, task:
this.state.task, status: 'todo'})
this.setState({title: ''});
  this.setState({task: ''});
this.props.onClose()
  }
```

The next component we need to build is the `CardList` component where all the cards will be rendered; it is also our droppable component.

We can start with the `render` method:

```
render() {
 const {listName, cards, delete_Card,update_CardStatus, connectDropTarget,
title } = this.props;
 return connectDropTarget(
  <div className="list-card">
     <div className="card-block">
        <h3 className="card-title">{title}</h3>
     </div>
{cards.map(card =>
     <Card key={card._id} {...card}
      update_CardStatus={update_CardStatus}
```

```
            delete_Card={delete_Card}/>) }
      </div>
  )
    }
```

Starting from the props declaration, we pass a `listName` (todo, inprogress, and Done) to the Board: parent, then the list of `Cards` components (mapped to the Redux store) and two actions `delete_Card` and `update_CardStatus`. Since `connectDropTarget` was injected by the `DropTarget` generator. The last one is the title (text),

```
import React, {PropTypes, Component} from 'react';
import {DropTarget} from 'react-dnd';
import Card from '../Card'

const ItemTypes = {
    CARD: 'card'
}

const spec = {
    drop(props, monitor, component) {
        return {listName: props.listName};
    }
};

function collect(connect, monitor) {
    return {
        connectDropTarget: connect.dropTarget()
    };
}

class CardList extends Component {
    static propTypes = {
        connectDropTarget: PropTypes.func.isRequired
    };

    render() {
        const {listName, cards,delete_Card,connectDropTarget, update_CardStatus, title } = this.props;
        return connectDropTarget(
            <div className="list-card">
                <div className="card-block">
                    <h3 className="card-title">{title}</h3>
                </div>

                {cards.map(card =>
                    <Card key={card._id} {...card}
                    update_CardStatus={update_CardStatus}
                    delete_Card={delete_Card}/>)}
            </div>
        )
    }
}
export default DropTarget(ItemTypes.CARD, spec, collect)(CardList);
```

We already know about all the drop target functionalities of the DnD sample application we did at the beginning of the chapter. In our specification object, we had the drop method that listName to the dragged Card.

The next component is the draggable Card.

In the render method, we have the following:

```
render() {
  const {task, title, _id, update_CardStatus,delete_Card, connectDragSource}
= this.props;
    return connectDragSource(
      <div className="card" style={{...style}}>
        <div className="card-block">
         <h4 className="card-title">{title}</h4>
          <p className="card-text">{task}</p>
            <div className="btn btn-danger" onClick={() =>
delete_Card(_id)}>DELETE</div>
        </div>
      </div>
  )
  }
```

In the CardList, component, we passed down the following props: task (task description), title (a title of the task), update_CardStatus (an action that will update the status), delete_Card (each card can be deleted by dispatching this action), and connectDragSource, which was injected by the Higher-Order Component DragSource:

```
import React, {Component, PropTypes} from 'react'
import {DragSource} from 'react-dnd'

const ItemTypes = { CARD: 'card' };
const style = {margin: '8px' };

const source = {
    beginDrag(props) {
        return {title: props.title, _id: props._id};
    },
    endDrag(props, monitor) {
        const item = monitor.getItem();
        const dropResult = monitor.getDropResult();
        if (dropResult) {
            props.update_CardStatus(item._id, dropResult.listName);
        }
    }
};
const collect = (connect, monitor) =>{
    return {
        connectDragSource: connect.dragSource()
    };
}
class Card extends Component {
    render() {
        const {task, title, _id, update_CardStatus,delete_Card, connectDragSource} = this.props;
        return connectDragSource(
            <div className="card" style={{...style}}>
                <div className="card-block">
                    <h4 className="card-title">{title}</h4>
                    <p className="card-text">{task}</p>
                    <div className="btn btn-danger" onClick={() => delete_Card(_id)}>DELETE</div>
                </div>
            </div>
        )
    }
}
export default DragSource(ItemTypes.CARD, source, collect)(Card);
```

The interesting thing here is happening in the endDrag method. When the Card is
successfully dropped into the list, we get the listName that is returned from the droppable
component CardList from the monitor. Then we dispatch update_CardStatus with the
ID and the listName (todo, inprogress, or done).

Test it out!

Open multiple browser tabs and launch the app. Then, try adding, deleting, and moving cards from one list to another. All the app instances should be updated in real time, and this is what we are looking for from a real-time Kanban application.

We got the reactivity we wanted by subscribing to the collection events; one thing we didn't have was a mechanism of unsubscribing (stopping) from the subscriptions. For example, if we add another page and the user leaves the Board and navigates there, he will still receive updates from the subscriptions. This is not a big deal in small apps; however, you could imagine in big multipage apps, this can become a pure waste of CPU cycles. React's API provides all the life cycle methods we need to stop a subscription. We can stop our subscriptions when the component is unmounting `componentWillUnmount()` and when the component is mounting `componentDidMount()`.

Another consideration is the way we subscribed to the collection. We have that in our `observe.js` file:

```
Tasks.find({})
  .observeChanges({
    added: function (id, data) {
store.dispatch(AllActions.receiveCard(id, data.title, data.task,
data.status))
    }
});
```

Here we have `Tasks.find({})`, which will give us all the records (unfiltered); however, what if the product owner decides that for the next sprint, he or she wants to have a board that can update the to-do list in real time only and nothing else. We can create another subscriber file and just have the exact thing with a new query:

```
Tasks.find({status: 'todo'})
  .observeChanges({
    added: function (id, data) {
store.dispatch(AllActions.receiveCard(id, data.title, data.task,
data.status))
    }
});
```

This approach is not reusable at all. Another option is to create an observer module that could get the `for` parameter a collection query. We still have to unsubscribe and subscribe directly to the App container component's life cycle methods. We can extend the functionality of a React component by creating a Higher-Order Component.

Higher-Order Components

Initially, Facebook used mixins to extend the component's functionality. Mixins are basically a way in which we can merge or mix objects. `Object.assign` is a perfect example of how to do this:

```
let newObject = Object.assign({}, object_1, object_2);
```

We've been using this in our Redux reducer function for generating a new state without modifying the original object. One problem of using this as an extension of objects in big apps is the control of the functionality of all those base (mixins) objects. Consider the following example:

```
let obj_1 = {};
obj_1.sayHi = () =>{
  console.log('hi from object one')
}

let obj_2 = {};
obj_2.sayBye = () =>{
    console.log("bye from object two")
  }

let newObj = Object.assign({}, obj_1, obj_2)
newObj.sayHi()
newObj.sayBye()
```

Here, we created two objects: `obj_1` and `obj_2`. Each object has its own method, `sayHi()` and `sayBye()`, respectively. Later, instead of writing these two methods again, we can just merge (mix) them into our newly created `newObj`. This is a pretty powerful way of sharing functionality, but as the app gets bigger, we won't really know where all the mixins will get used and which other objects will depend on them. Let's imagine that a different developer just adds one extra method to `obj_2`:

```
let obj_2 = {};
obj_2.sayBye = () =>{
  console.log("bye from object two")
}
obj_2.sayHi = () =>{
  console.log('hi from object two')
}

let newObj = Object.assign({}, obj_1, obj_2)
newObj.sayHi()
newObj.sayBye()
```

This will print the following:

```
hi from object two  bye from object two
```

This is a result of the dynamic nature of JavaScript, very powerful and yet difficult to maintain for large-scale applications.

If we just replace the order of the objects in the `Object.assign()` method, we will have this:

`let newObj = Object.assign({}, `**`obj_1, obj_2`**`)` with `let newObj = Object.assign({}, `**`obj_2, obj_1`**`)`

We get the expected result. To solve this, we should not touch mixins that have been used in many components and have many levels of dependencies. Adding can create a problem. Imagine what will happen if we remove or rename some of the methods in a large application.

How can we reuse code then? The first thing we should consider is what functionality we need to reuse. Small functions that do one thing can be exported and imported as modules into your React components. Facebook favors composition over inheritance, and Higher-Order Components are just components wrapping our components and adding functionality to them without modifying them. This is the same pattern as that of our container components that dealt with the data and rendered presentational children components that were responsible for the look of the data.

Back to our Kanban app, we can create a Higher-Order Component that will take care of subscribing to and unsubscribing from a collection that is passed to it:

```
let query = Tasks.find({});
const higherOrderComponent = HOC(query)(App);
```

This is the most common signature of HOC: it is a function that returns another function.

To understand what is going on underneath, we can write a simple example like this:

```
const firstFunction = (arg_1) => (arg_2) => {
  const secondFunction = () => {
    console.log(arg_1 + arg_2)
  }
  return secondFunction;
}
```

This syntax is also known as Currying in JavaScript. Instead of listing all the function arguments in a certain order, such as `firstFunction(param_1, param_2)`, we can pass each argument one by one:

```
let first = firstFunction(1)
let second = first(2)
second()
```

Alternatively, in short, we pass them as this:

```
let newFunction(1)(2)
newFunction()
```

Let's create the HOC for our Kanban app. It will take a collection query and our component as arguments and will return a new component `const HOC = (Collection) => (Component) => {}`. The code is as follows:

```
const HOC = (Collection) => (Component) => {
  return class Observe extends Component {
      constructor(props) {
      super(props)
      }
    }
}
```

The next thing we will have is an event handler variable for each event in the `constructor` method:

```
return class Observe extends Component {
      constructor(props) {
      super(props)
      this.addedHandle = {};
      this.changedHandle = {};
      this.removedHandle = {};
      }
  }
```

When the component is mounted, we will assign them to the collection observers:

```
componentDidMount() {
   let self = this;
    this.addedHandle = Collection.observeChanges({
        added: function (id, data) {
         self.props.action({type: 'ADDED', result: data, id: id})
      }
    });
  this.changedHandle = Collection.observeChanges({
        changed: function (id, data) {
```

```
              self.props.action({type: 'CHANGED', result: data, id: id})
          }
      });
      this.removedHandle = Collection.observeChanges({
        removed: function (id) {
          self.props.action({type: 'REMOVED', result: [], id: id})
        }
      });
  }
```

When the component is unmounted, we stop the subscriptions:

```
componentWillUnmount() {
    this.addedHandle.stop()
    this.changedHandle.stop()
    this.removedHandle.stop()
}
```

Finally, we will render the second argument (the component) by passing through all the props:

```
render() {
    return (<Component{...this.props}/>)
}
```

Now we can use this component to generate multiple containers. We can generate our App container like this:

```
const generateComponent = connect(mapStateToProps, mapDispatchToProps)
let query = Tasks.find({});
const higherOrderComponent = HOC(query)(App);

export default generateComponent(higherOrderComponent);
```

First, we connect to the Redux store by mapping the state to the props and all the actions—nothing changed there. Next, we generated a new HOC component by passing a collection query and our App component. Last, we passed our generated component as the second parameter of the Redux generator.

To test this, we can create another container called TodoBoard, which is the exact same thing as App; however, now we know we can filter observer events:

```
const generateComponent = connect(mapStateToProps, mapDispatchToProps)
let query = Tasks.find({status: 'todo'})
const higherOrderComponent = HOC(query)(TodoBoard)
export default generateComponent(higherOrderComponent)
```

Test it out!

Add links to different pages on `NavBar` and see how the component unsubscribes as soon as it is unmounted. You can also assign static methods of the HOC component and have it call them to the generated one:

```
Observe.dataChanged = Component.dataChanged;

  Observe.dataChanged({
    props: self.props,
     data: {
       type: 'REMOVED',
       result: [],
       id: id
     }
  })
```

In the `App` component, we declared it as:

```
static dataChanged(params) {
   //dispatch actions
 }
```

Summary

In this chapter, we started with the React DnD library by creating a sample app and exploring the minimum API needed to create a drag and drop interface for our Kanban app. Then we moved on to what we learned from it in the Kanban app. We also explored data handling by subscribing to a database collection and overviewed a few ways of loading the initial data from the server to the Redux store. During the development of the components, we also did a quick Modal app that we later imported into our project. Our final step was an overview of React's paradigm on code reusability, which we did by creating a Higher-Order Component. In the next chapter, we will add a full-text search feature in a Meteor application with MongoDB.

6
Building a Real-Time Search Application

In this chapter, we will explore the full-text search functionality of MongoDB by developing a simple search application with the main stack that we've been using for the past few chapters: Meteor, React, and Redux, adding a few new libraries along the way. We'll start by importing sample data to the MongoDB collection, then we will create an index on some of the fields and perform search queries directly from the sample data which can be found in the official MongoDB documentation at `https://docs.mongodb.com/getting-started/shell/import-data/`.

The direct link to the data is `https://raw.githubusercontent.com/mongodb/docs-assets/primer-dataset/primer-dataset.json`. The dataset contains over 25,000 documents of restaurants in the New York City area, which is a perfect dataset for what we will build. If you click on the preceding link, you would probably notice that the data contains the coord field (latitude and longitude). We will use this field to visually locate the returned results from the search. The functionality of the application does not need much explanation. We will keep it very simple and intuitive to the user by building it in a way that is similar to any search and locate applications, such as Google Maps, Bing Maps, Foursquare, and so on.

The app will contain three main components: a search bar where the user can type search requests, a list on which we will display the returned results, and a map where the user can visually locate the results.

Importing the data

They are many ways of importing existing data into MongoDB. It depends on many factors, but the two most important ones are the source and data model. Our data sample is in JSON format, which is the format of the documents stored in MongoDB collections. The way MongoDB works is that behind the scenes, it encodes the JSON documents in a binary format—BSON (Binary JSON)—with some additional metadata, and when we query the collections, we get plain JSON objects. JSON is what we, JavaScript developers, naturally think of data that makes MongoDB extremely easy to work with; this is also the main reason why it is one of the most popular NoSQL databases.

How we model our collections is completely different from how we'd model our tables in a relational database. Data modeling in MongoDB is a big topic and it's out of the scope of this book; however, we actually did a bit of data modeling in our Redux stores in the previous chapters. We started modeling our stores with the question, "what state our application needs to persist?" and the way we think in MongoDB is, "what data does our application UI need?" In both cases, we start data modeling from the UI, which is the opposite of how we would usually do data modeling in relational databases.

For this app, we can do a direct import of the sample JSON dataset into one collection and build our frontend on the defined model, which is fine for the purpose of learning the full-text search topic.

First, let's create the app and launch the mongo shell from the app directory:

```
>> meteor create search
```

We need to keep our app running in order to launch the shell. Open another terminal and change the directory to the root of the app, then execute the following command:

```
>> meteor mongo
```

If the app is running, it will return the MongoDB version and the connection to the database instance:

```
MongoDB shell version: 3.2.6
connecting to: 127.0.0.1:3001/meteor
```

The next step of importing the data is to save it as a JSON file on the disk. We can use the same name as that of the data from the `primer-dataset.json` link. Copy and paste the data from the link: `https://raw.githubusercontent.com/mongodb/docs-assets/primer -dataset/primer-dataset.json` into the file. Importing data with the MongoDB import tool is a straightforward task. Note that you need to execute it outside the Meteor mongo shell. Launch another terminal and execute the command:

```
mongoimport -h localhost:3001 -db meteor -collection restaurants -type json
-file  ~/chapter_six/search/primer-dataset.json
```

The first argument (`-h`) is the hostname of the database where we need to connect (`localhost:3001`). The database's name is meteor (the default name when we created the app). We then specify where we want to import the data (the restaurants collection); the data type is JSON and the last argument is the path of the file. If you have never had MongoDB installed outside a Meteor project, you may get an error if you run the tool. To fix this, you need to install the `mongo-clients` package:

```
>>sudo apt install mongo-clients
```

Let's summarize all the steps we did so far:

1. Create the app using `meteor create search`.
2. Change the directory to the app and install `cd search npm install`.
3. Run `npm start`.
4. Press *Ctrl* + *Alt* + *T* to open another terminal and install the `mongo-clients` package; use `sudo apt install mongo-clients`.
5. Import the data:

```
mongoimport -h localhost:3001 -db meteor -collection restaurants -type json
-file  ~/chapter_six/search/primer-dataset.json
```

Index a text field

In order to do a full-text search on a collection, we need to index a text field(s). Any field in our collection of the type string can be indexed; it can be just one field or all of them.

Let's start exploring the imported data by querying it in the shell.

Without stopping the application, open another terminal in the app directory and start the mongo shell:

```
>> meteor mongo
```

To see all the databases in our application, we can use the following command:

```
meteor:PRIMARY> show dbs
local 0.009GB
meteor 0.005GB
```

To switch to the `meteor` database, use:

```
meteor:PRIMARY> use meteor
switched to db meteor
```

To show all the collections in the database, use:

```
meteor:PRIMARY> show collections
restaurants
```

To count the number of documents in the restaurant collection, use:

```
meteor:PRIMARY> db.restaurants.count()
25359
```

We have imported 25,359 documents in our collection. To get the first document of the collection, we can perform the following query:

```
meteor:PRIMARY> db.restaurants.findOne()
{
  "_id" : ObjectId("588d6860448c71e9482cf244"),
  "address" : {
    "building" : "1007",
    "coord" : [
    -73.856077,
      40.848447
  ],
    "street" : "Morris Park Ave",
    "zipcode" : "10462"
  },
  "borough" : "Bronx",
  "cuisine" : "Bakery",
  "grades" : [
    {
      "date" : ISODate("2014-03-03T00:00:00Z"),
      "grade" : "A",
      "score" : 2
    },{
      "date" : ISODate("2013-09-11T00:00:00Z"),
      "grade" : "A",
      "score" : 6
    },{
```

```
            "date"  :  ISODate("2013-01-24T00:00:00Z"),
            "grade" : "A",
            "score" : 10
        },{
            "date"  :  ISODate("2011-11-23T00:00:00Z"),
            "grade" : "A",
            "score" : 9
        },{
            "date"  :  ISODate("2011-03-10T00:00:00Z"),
            "grade" : "B",
            "score" : 14
    }
],
    "name" : "Morris Park Bake Shop",
    "restaurant_id" : "30075445"
}
```

Another way to get the first record is using the `limit()` method:

```
db.restaurants.find().pretty().limit(1)
```

In the returned result, we can see that we have an address object with nested object coordinates (coord), street, building, and a zip code. We also have a field borough, cuisine type, a list of ratings, the name of the restaurant, and ID of each restaurant.

Let's say we want to find a restaurant name that contains the word, `Morris`. In SQL, this can be done with the `LIKE` operator; in MongoDB, the equivalent query is a regular expression using the `$regex` operator.

For SQL, the code is as follows:

```
SELECT * FROM restaurants
WHERE name LIKE '%Morris%'
```

Here's MongoDB using the `$regex` operator:

```
db.restaurants.find({"name" : {$regex: /Morris/}})
```

We can also use pattern matching without the `$regex` operator:

```
db.restaurants.find({"name" : /Morris/})
```

If you add the `count()` method to the query, you'll see that there are five restaurants that contain the word Morris in their name. Regular expressions are nothing more than pattern matching strings in a query. What the query did was it scanned the entire collection and performed a pattern string search on the value of the key name. The `$regex` operator also comes with options that we can add to additionally refine it.

We can use $options: "i" for lowercase matching:

```
db.restaurants.find( { name: { $regex: /morriS/, $options: "i" } } )
```

We can use $options: "x" to ignore white spaces:

```
db.restaurants.find( { name: { $regex: /Morri s/, $options: "x" } } )
```

Mix both options using $options: "xi":

```
db.restaurants.find( { name: { $regex: /morri s/, $options: "xi" } } )
```

Regular expressions work great in many cases, for example, if we want to find all the restaurants that contain the word Morris in their name in the borough of Bronx. With options of white spaces and lowercase matching, we can query it like this:

```
db.restaurants.find({ name: { $regex: /morri s/, $options: 'xi' },
borough:"Bronx" })
```

If you count the records, you will see that we narrowed the records from five to three.

Is searching the same as querying? There is a big difference between query and search. With queries, the result will be 100 percent correct—if the query is written correctly to describe the question, in other words, the query will give us exactly what we are looking for. This is not exactly true with the search. We don't know for sure what we'll get and the result can be completely off from what we are expecting, which of course depends on the search engine. Good search engines are way more complex systems than straight questions to the database. They can perform queries and rankings; they can implement complex algorithms and learn from previously asked questions. We are not going to get a Google search with the MongoDB full-text search, and this is completely fine for many applications that we could use it for.

Let's say we are building a photo gallery app where users can browse photos and make a purchase. If you have a search bar in the application, naturally the users will search for anything related to the context of the app. Imagine now they type landscape in the search box looking for landscape photos and the query returns local landscape contractors. This is not exactly what we are expecting from an inventory search. In this case, we have predefined audience and what data will be included in the search.

On the other hand, if the application grows and we want to add search functionality to a type of social media, such as comments, user profiles, groups, and product ratings, we will need a more powerful search solution than MongoDB's full-text search. There are two very popular open source options, Solr and Elasticsearch, built on top of Apache Lucene. They can go beyond the MongoDB search functionality. That said, running a search store in parallel with your database has its challenges, such as keeping both data stores in sync.

Let's create a simple test collection and index some of the fields and see how MongoDB's search works:

```
meteor:PRIMARY> db.createCollection('test')
{ "ok" : 1 }
```

Insert the following records:

```
db.test.insert({name:'Harry Potter', 'age':10, movie:'Harry Potter and the
Order of the Phoenix'})
db.test.insert({name:'John J. Rambo', age:30, movie:'First Blood'})
db.test.insert({name:'John McClane', age:35, movie:'Die Hard'})
db.test.insert({name:'Dejah Thoris', age:28, movie:'John Carter of Mars'})
```

To create an index on a text field, use the `createIndex` method:

```
meteor:PRIMARY> db.test.createIndex({name:"text"})
{
  "createdCollectionAutomatically" : true,
  "numIndexesBefore" : 1,
  "numIndexesAfter" : 2,
  "ok" : 1
}
```

Here we can see that, by default, there is already an indexed field. To find all the indexes, use the following command:

```
meteor:PRIMARY> db.test.getIndexes()
[
  {
    "v" : 1,
    "key" : {
    "_id" : 1
   },
    "name" : "_id_",
    "ns" : "meteor.test"
  },
  {
    "v" : 1,
    "key" : {
    "_fts" : "text",
    "_ftsx" : 1
  },
    "name" : "name_text",
    "ns" : "meteor.test",
    "weights" : {
      "name" : 1
  },
```

```
      "default_language" : "english",
      "language_override" : "language",
      "textIndexVersion" : 3
  }
]
```

By default, MongoDB names the text index with the `name_text` value. What is actually happening here is that the text index can be only one per collection, which can have many fields. Let's drop the index and add another one to see how it works:

```
meteor:PRIMARY> db.test.dropIndexes()
{
  "nIndexesWas" : 2,
  "msg" : "non-_id indexes dropped for collection",
  "ok" : 1
}
```

Now let's add another field to the `text` index:

```
meteor:PRIMARY> db.test.createIndex({name:"text",movie:"text"})
{
    "createdCollectionAutomatically" : false,
    "numIndexesBefore" : 1,
    "numIndexesAfter" : 2,
    "ok" : 1
}
```

As you can see, there are two indexes still. Execute the `getIndexes` method to check how MongoDB indexes them:

```
{
    "v" : 1,
    "key" : {
    "_fts" : "text",
    "_ftsx" : 1
},
    "name" : "name_text_movie_text",
    "ns" : "meteor.test",
    "weights" : {
      "movie" : 1,
      "name" : 1
},
    "default_language" : "english",
    "language_override" : "language",
    "textIndexVersion" : 3
}
```

By default, the index fields are chained with underscore and text: `name_text_movie_text`.

The next important thing is the weights key. According to the official MongoDB documentation, here's how weights are used:

For a text index, the weight of an indexed field denotes the significance of the field relative to the other indexed fields in terms of the text search score. For each indexed field in the document, MongoDB multiplies the number of matches by the weight and sums the results.

If the `weights` option is not provided, both the `movie` and the `name` fields will be set to `1`. Let's change that. First, drop all indexes in the `db.test.dropIndexes()` collection and create a new one:

```
>> db.test.createIndex({name: "text", movie: "text"},{ weights: { name: 2,
movie: 5 }})
{
    "createdCollectionAutomatically" : false,
    "numIndexesBefore" : 1,
    "numIndexesAfter" : 2,
    "ok" : 1
}
```

Now if you run the `db.test.getIndexes()` method, you will see that the weights are changed. You can also override the default name of the index by passing the `name` option:

```
db.test.createIndex({name: "text", movie: "text"},{ weights: { name: 2,
movie: 5 },name:"myIndexName"})
```

We need two things to perform a search on a collection: the `$text` query operator and the `$search` operator. A simple search query looks like this:

```
meteor:PRIMARY> db.test.find({$text:{$search:"McClane"}}).pretty()
{
    "_id" : ObjectId("58916ba53f4876962bb3687b"),
    "name" : "John McClane",
    "age" : 35,
    "movie" : "Die Hard"
}
```

An example of a search for the word `John` in our collection is as follows:

```
meteor:PRIMARY> db.test.find({$text:{$search:"John"}}).pretty()
{
    "_id" : ObjectId("5896445e1570d9a933699269"),
    "name" : "John J. Rambo",
    "age" : 30,
    "movie" : "First Blood"
}
{
    "_id" : ObjectId("5896445e1570d9a93369926a"),
    "name" : "John McClane",
    "age" : 35,
    "movie" : "Die Hard"
}
{
    "_id" : ObjectId("5896445f1570d9a93369926b"),
    "name" : "Dejah Thoris",
    "age" : 28,
    "movie" : "John Carter of Mars"
}
```

The search returned three documents: two containing the word `John` in the field name and one in the `movie` field. The only reason the search included the third record `"movie"`: `"John Carter of Mars"` was because we included the `movie` field in the index.

To test this, drop the index, then recreate it with only one field:

```
db.test.dropIndexes()
db.test.createIndex({movie:"text"})

db.test.find({$text:{$search:"John"}}).pretty()
```

Now the search will scan only the `movie` field for the text `John`. The result is as follows:

```
{
    "_id" : ObjectId("5896445f1570d9a93369926b"),
    "name" : "Dejah Thoris",
    "age" : 28,
    "movie" : "John Carter of Mars"
}
```

We move on to language-specific stop words. The search will ignore language-specific stop words, such as `and`, `or`, `of`, and so on.

Let's test this:

```
db.test.find({$text:{$search:"of"}}).pretty()
```

No records were returned even if the text `of` was in the field `"movie": "John Carter of Mars"`.

Single characters that are not stop words will be included in the search. If you have both the movie and name text indexed, the following query will return a result:

```
meteor:PRIMARY> db.test.find({$text:{$search:"J"}}).pretty()
{
  "_id" : ObjectId("5896445e1570d9a933699269"),
  "name" : "John J. Rambo",
  "age" : 30,
  "movie" : "First Blood"
}
```

What will happen if we change the document from `John J. Rambo` to `John A. Rambo`. The character `A` is an English stop word. Let's test it:

```
db.test.update({_id: ObjectId("5896445e1570d9a933699269")},{
$set:{name:"John A. Rambo"}})
```

The following search query will not return a result as expected:

```
db.test.find({$text:{$search:"A"}}).pretty()
```

If we want the search to include stop words, we need to specify the language option to `none` when we create the index or add it as an option to the search:

```
db.test.createIndex({name: "text", movie: "text"}, { default_language:
"none" })
db.test.find( { $text: { $search: "A", $language: "none" } } ).pretty()
```

Now, the search query will return the result that we are looking for:

```
{
    "_id" : ObjectId("5896445e1570d9a933699269"),
    "name" : "John A. Rambo",
    "age" : 30,
    "movie" : "First Blood"
}
```

There are some more options that we can use to refine/tune our search:

- `$caseSensitive`: Case sensitivity, by default, is `false`. To include it, simply add it to the query, `{ $caseSensitive: true}`.
- `$language`: By default, language is set to English `en`; the search supports over 20 languages.
- `$diacriticSensitive`: This is false by default. To include diacritical marks (such as ā, ä, or ă), we can use `{$diacriticSensitive: true}`.
- `"\ " some phrase \ ""`: We can use double escaped quotes for phrase matching.

Note that adding the options `$caseSensitive` and `$diacriticSensitive` (and setting them to `true`) can impact the performance.

Try it out!

Out-of-the-box, we get pretty powerful search functionalities with MongoDB, and you can explore the search further by trying out options from the preceding examples in the test collection; you can also insert new documents and find out how to build your search queries for different scenarios. For example, if you insert the following document, which is in French, would the search ignore the À character assuming that the default language is English? Also, what do we need to do in order to ignore this character? Check this out using the following:

```
db.test.insert({name:'André Marcon', age:50, movie:'À vendre'})
```

Another great feature we get with MongoDB full-text search is that there is no need for manual reindexing of our data in order to make it searchable. In the previous examples, we inserted documents and searched on the content right away, without any extra steps. The content was available immediately, which makes the search real time. Other more powerful solutions, such as Solr, offer a near real-time search, which means the documents will be available almost immediately for the search. Usually, the more powerful a solution is, the more complex the live indexing of data. If you really need an enterprise search that handles everything from data synchronization to zero downtime and data center replications, there are commercial solutions available, such as Datastax Enterprise with Solr and Amazon Elasticsearch Service.

Now that we have a good understanding of how the search works, let's build our search application.

Building the app

The UI of the app should look something like this:

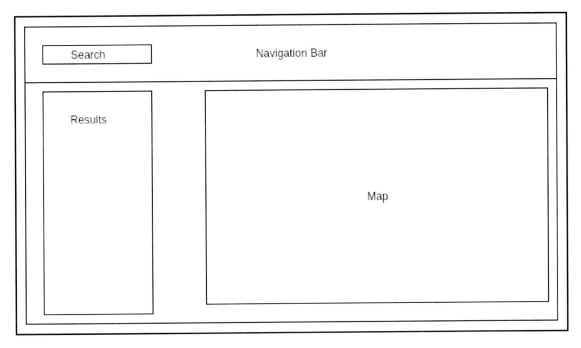

It will have a search bar, a result list, and a map where we can visually locate the search results. We have already created the app and imported the data; now open it with the editor of your choice and start creating the required folders and files:

As you may have noticed, we are keeping the same folder structure as we did in the previous chapters. Since we will be using Redux to store some of the application's state, our first step is to define the user actions and what state we want to persist. Let's list them:

- A text query: We can persist the user input in our store
- Returned results: We will persist the result from the query and pass it down to the children components for rendering
- Going to a location: The user should be able to click on an item in the result list and the map should be updated to that location based on the latitude and longitude of the record

Let's start creating all the actions creators and action types in one file; after that, we can split them into more logical files/directories.

For the query, we can have an action type and the corresponding action creator function:

```
export const QUERY = 'QUERY'
export const query = (query_string) => ({type: types.QUERY, query_string})
```

When we receive the results from the server, we need an action to pass them down to the reducer:

```
export const RECEIVE_RESULT = 'RECEIVE_RESULT'
export const receiveResult = (result) => ({type: types.RECEIVE_RESULT,
result})
```

For this example, we can just persist the entire JSON object into the store without any parsing and filtering of the records.

The third action is when the user clicks on an item in the list and goes to the location (locate the restaurant on the map):

```
export const GO_TO = 'GO_TO'
export const goTo = (lat, lng, restaurant_name, cuisine) => ({type:
types.GO_TO, lat, lng, restaurant_name, cuisine})
```

With this action, we are persisting the latitudes-longitudes, the restaurant name, and the cuisine type; they will be passed down as props in our Map component for rendering and navigating to the location.

We have all the actions and types; now let's create an `index.js` file in the `actions` folder and move all the action creators there. We can copy and paste the action types in an `ActionTypes.js` file in the `constants` folder.

The complete code for action creators in the `actions/index.js` file is as follows:

```
import * as types from '../constants/ActionTypes'
export const query = (query_string) => ({type: types.QUERY, query_string})
export const receiveResult = (result) => ({type: types.RECEIVE_RESULT,
result})
export const goTo = (lat, lng, restaurant_name, cuisine) => ({type:
types.GO_TO, lat, lng, restaurant_name, cuisine})
```

The action types in the `constants/ActionTypes.js` file is as follows:

```
export const QUERY = 'QUERY'
export const RECEIVE_RESULT = 'RECEIVE_RESULT'
export const GO_TO = 'GO_TO'
```

Our next logical step is to create the reducer function. In the `reducers` folder, create a file called `serach.js`:

Using the ES6 default parameter feature, we can define our initial state directly in the function declaration like this:

```
export default function search(state = {
    isFetching: false,
    result: [],
    lat: 40.748817,
    lng: -73.985428,
    restaurant_name: '',
    cuisine: ''
}, action) {
```

We default most of the fields to empty or false, except lat-long. Our dataset contains restaurants in the New York City area, and we can default the location of the map to Manhattan (40.748817 - 73.985428 are the coordinates of the Empire State Building). We have one field `isFetching` set to `false`; we will use it later when we start pulling the data from the server.

In the same order, we created the actions; we can start the reducer function with the first type, namely QUERY:

```
case QUERY:
  return {
    ...state,
    query_string: action.query_string,
    isFetching: true
  }
```

Without mutating the state, we return a new one using the ES6 object spread operator.

We do a similar thing with the RECEIVE_RESULT type:

```
case RECEIVE_RESULT:
  return {
    ...state,
    result: action.result,
    isFetching: false
  }
```

The last one is the GO_TO type:

```
case GO_TO:
  return {
    ...state,
    lat: action.lat,
    lng: action.lng,
    restaurant_name: action.restaurant_name,
    cuisine: action.cuisine
  }
```

Here's the full code of the reducer:

```
import {QUERY, RECEIVE_RESULT, GO_TO} from '../constants/ActionTypes'

export default function search(state = {
    isFetching: false,
    result: [],
    lat: 40.7484,
    lng: -73.9857,
    restaurant_name: '',
    cuisine: ''
}, action) {
    switch (action.type) {
        case QUERY:
            return {
                ...state,
                query_string: action.query_string,
                isFetching: true
            }
        case RECEIVE_RESULT:
            return {
                ...state,
                result: action.result,
                isFetching: false
            }
        case GO_TO:
            return {
                ...state,
                lat: action.lat,
                lng: action.lng,
                restaurant_name: action.restaurant_name,
                cuisine: action.cuisine
            }
        default:
            return state
    }
}
```

With these three steps, we are now done with most of the Redux part; the next thing we will build are the React components.

We can start from the container component, which will be connected to the store and act as the application's main data container.

In the `containers` folder, create the `App.js` file, and in there, define the component as a class component:

```
class App extends React.Component {
  render() {
    const {search, actions} = this.props
      return (
      <div>
        <NavBar {...actions}/>
        <Main search={search} actions={actions}/>
      </div>)
    }
  }
}
```

We rendered two presentational components, namely `NavBar` and `Main`, where we will pass the actions and the state as props.

For a shorter syntax, you can use the ES6 object spread operator for passing down the props: `<NavBar {...actions}/>` and `<Main {...this.props}/>`.

To bind the actions and map the state to the props, use the Redux connect Higher-Order Component:

```
import {connect} from 'react-redux'

const mapStateToProps = (state) => {
 return {search: state.search}
}
const mapDispatchToProps = dispatch => ({
 actions: bindActionCreators(AllActions, dispatch)
})
const generateComponent = connect(mapStateToProps, mapDispatchToProps)
export default generateComponent(App);
```

Let's build the first rendered component: `NavBar`. This will render the search bar:

```
class NavBar extends React.Component {
  render() {
    return (
      <nav className="navbar navbar-light bg-faded">
        <SearchForm {...this.props}/>
      </nav>)
    }
}
export default NavBar;
```

We defined it as a pure presentational component (styled with Bootstrap), which only passes the incoming props to the child component `SearchForm`.

When the user types a query, they can press *Enter* on the keyboard or click on a search button to submit the query to the server. This can be easily done with a standard HTML form using the `onsubmit` (in JSX, `onSubmit`) event. Create a `SearchForm.js` file in the `SearchForm` folder.

Start from the `render()` method:

```
render() {
return (
    <form className="form-inline" onSubmit={this.handleSubmit}>
     <input
        className="form-control mr-sm-2"
        type="text"
        placeholder="Search"
        autoFocus="true"
        value={this.state.query_string}
        onChange={this.handleChange}/>
      <button className="btn btn-outline-success my-2 my-
sm-0">Search</button>
    </form>
    )
  }
```

To the text input field, we are adding the `onChange` event; when it fires, we will persist its value locally to the React's state. Now we need to create and bind two methods to the class context. As always, the best place to set the initial state and bind all the methods is the `constructor` method:

```
constructor(props) {
 super(props);
  this.state = {
   query_string: ''
 };
 this.handleChange = this.handleChange.bind(this);
 this.handleSubmit = this.handleSubmit.bind(this);
 }
```

When `onChange` is fired, we keep resetting our state:

```
handleChange(event) {
   this.setState({query_string: event.target.value});
 }
```

The last piece we need to hook up is the on submit event on the form. Since we passed all the actions bound to the dispatcher, all of them can be called as any regular JavaScript function, which makes this component unaware of Redux:

```
handleSubmit(event) {
   event.preventDefault()
   this.props.search(this.state.query_string)
 }
```

The default behavior of the HTML form on submit event is to submit the form data to the server. We want to do this ourselves with an action and preserve the form data (from the input field) in the store. To prevent the default `submit` method (which will also refresh the page), we use the `preventDefault()` method.

The full code of the `SearchForm` component is as follows:

```
import React, {Component, PropTypes} from 'react'

class SearchForm extends Component {
    constructor(props) {
        super(props);
        this.state = {
            query_string: ''
        };
        this.handleChange = this.handleChange.bind(this);
        this.handleSubmit = this.handleSubmit.bind(this);
    }

    handleChange(event) {
        this.setState({query_string: event.target.value});
    }

    handleSubmit(event) {
        event.preventDefault()
        this.props.search(this.state.query_string)
    }
    render() {
        return (
            <form className="form-inline" onSubmit={this.handleSubmit}>
                <input
                    className="form-control mr-sm-2"
                    type="text"
                    placeholder="Search"
                    autoFocus="true"
                    value={this.state.query_string}
                    onChange={this.handleChange}/>
                <button className="btn btn-outline-success my-2 my-sm-0">Search</button>
            </form>
        )
    }
}
export default SearchForm
```

There is one action search that we need to add to our actions; when dispatched, it will call a Meteor Method and pass the query string to the server. Before we move on and build the rest of the components, let's set up our collection for the search and have the functionality of sending queries to the server from the client.

Keeping the app running, open another terminal, change the directory to the root of the app, then launch the mongo shell:

```
meteor mongo
use meteor
```

Let's clear all the previously created indexes and start from scratch:

```
meteor:PRIMARY> db.restaurants.dropIndexes()
{
  "nIndexesWas" : 2,
  "msg" : "non-_id indexes dropped for collection",
  "ok" : 1
}
```

There are a lot of records in our collection, over 25,000 documents. We want to somehow limit the number of returned results. The first thing we can do after creating a text index on a field (name) is use the limit aggregation to return a certain number of records.

Create a text index on name:

```
meteor:PRIMARY> db.restaurants.createIndex({name:"text"})
{
  "createdCollectionAutomatically" : false,
  "numIndexesBefore" : 1,
  "numIndexesAfter" : 2,
  "ok" : 1
}
```

Without limiting the records, if we search for the word new, the search will return 648 records, which will be a pretty bad user experience if we try to load all of them in the app:

```
meteor:PRIMARY>
db.restaurants.find({$text:{$search:"new"}}).pretty().count()
648
```

With the limit() method, we can return any reasonable number of records, such as 20, for example:

```
meteor:PRIMARY>
db.restaurants.find({$text:{$search:"new"}}).pretty().limit(20)
{
    "_id" : ObjectId("5892ca96caf6e23d867f91ac"),
    "address" : {
    "building" : "700",
     "coord" : [
       -74.01322760000001,
        40.6423101
     ],
     "street" : "Fifth Ave. At 55 St.",
     "zipcode" : "10019"
},
. . . . . .
```

The question is which 20 documents from the 648 will the search return? The answer is there is no particular order in which documents will be included in the result. Since we are performing a search and not just a query, we want to have the best matches in the 20 records. We can use the `sort()` method to sort the records by the highest score with the `$meta` query operator and then limit the number of returned results.

To visualize the score, we can include it in the result:

```
db.restaurants.find({$text: {$search: "new"}}, {score: {$meta:
"textScore"}}).sort({score:{$meta:"textScore"}}).limit(10)
    ......
 "name" : "New Wai Ling Chinese Restaurant/New Fresco Tortillas Ii Taco",
 "restaurant_id" : "50004367",
 "score" : 0.8999999999999999


. . . . . . . .

 "name" : "New Corner",
 "restaurant_id" : "40365355",
 "score" : 0.75


. . . . . .

 "name" : "The New School",
 "restaurant_id" : "40934234",
 "score" : 0.75
```

The first record returned scored `0.8999` out of `1.0`; the string `New` appeared twice in the indexed search field name. The remaining nine records were scored at `0.75`.

Before we move this query to the server-side application, we have to consider a few things that use the MongoDB full-text search with Meteor. Methods such as `limit()` and `sort()` are not natively present in the Meteor collections API. Full-text search is not available in the front-end database Minimongo. One option to have the search functionality in Meteor is using the native Node.js MongoDB driver, which supports everything we did in the mongo shell.

Let's move through our search query step by step. First, we need to install the driver:

```
>> npm install mongodb —save
```

In the `server/main.js` file, import the module:

```
const MongoClient = require('mongodb').MongoClient
```

The next step is to establish a connection with a running MongoDB server:

```
const url = 'mongodb://127.0.0.1:3001/meteor'
MongoClient.connect(url, (err, db) => {....})
```

The callback returns two parameters, an error, and an initialized database object. Before we write the method, let's visualize how the client request, database connection, and **Meteor Method** fit together:

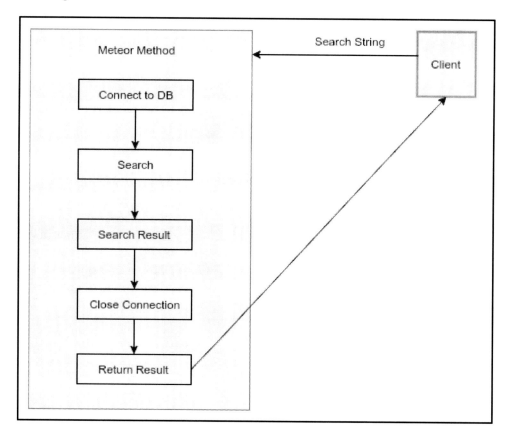

The **Client** calls a **Meteor Method** by passing a search string. In this method, we will establish a connection to the running MongoDB instance and perform a search. After we get the result, we will close the connection and return the result to the client.

All I/O over the network are asynchronous, and the **Search** and **Search Results** steps from the preceding diagram are exactly that. Usually, the way we handle async actions in JavaScript is by writing callback functions. You may notice that all our **Meteor Methods** are written without callbacks. Meteor abstracts all the async actions for us in a way that we wouldn't have to deal with callbacks. In many cases, like this one, we need to call external services and wait for the result. After a certain amount of time, when we receive it, we can pass it to the method's caller. There are a few ways in which we can write callback-free async format functions, Fibers and Promises are some of the good choices. To see how they work, let's write an async function with a callback and convert it into a callback-less function using Fibers and Promises:

```
const asyncFunction = (callback => {
  console.log('called asyncFunction')
  setTimeout(() => {
      callback('hi')
  }, 5000);
})

asyncFunction(result => {
    console.log(result)
})
asyncFunction(result => {
    console.log(result)
})
....
```

Callbacks allow us to write non-blocking code, which is the heart of the Node.js architecture. If you call this function multiple times, one after the other, you will see that the function executes the log message called `asyncFunction` many times first, then after 5 seconds of each function call, it will return the result `hi`. This is a pretty simple example with only one function, but in reality, we can have one callback function depending on another callback function's result. This could end up looking something like this:

```
asyncFunctionOne(result_one => {
    asyncFunctionTwo(result_one, result_two => {
        asyncFunctionThree(result_two, result_three => {
            console.log(result_three)
        })
    })
})
```

Here, `asyncFunctionTwo` takes the result from the callback of `asyncFunctionOne` and `asyncFunctionThree` takes the result from `asyncFunctionTwo`. This type of nesting callback functions is known as **callback hell**. What we want to have is the ability to write asynchronous functions with synchronous signatures. The goal is to have a syntax that is similar to this:

```
let result_one = asyncFunctionOne()
let result_two = asyncFunctionTwo(result_one)
let result_three = asyncFunctionThree(result_two)
console.log(result_three)
```

Let's convert the function using Fibers. The Meteor API is built on top of Node.js using `fibers` to handle callback-less syntax, and there is no need to install the fibers module; it is already included in Meteor:

```
import Future from 'fibers/future'
const asyncFunction = () => {
    let future = new Future();
     Meteor.setTimeout(()=> {
       future.return('hi');
    }, 5000);
    return future.wait();
 }
```

The recommended way of using `fibers` is with the **Future** API (from the official GitHub page `https://github.com/laverdet/node-fibers`). Two important things happened in the preceding function. We created a new instance of the Future function and then immediately returned the `future.wait()` method, and after 5 seconds, the `future.return` was called. They are two ways of calling this function in sync style without using callbacks:

```
import Fiber from 'fibers'
 Fiber(() => {
   let result = asyncFunction(); //sync style
   console.log(result)
 }).run();
```

The first way is to wrap and call it in a Fiber instance. The second way is using the Future API to create a function that would automatically run in its own fiber. Note that we are actually getting the result when then fiber returns `future.return()`, which will resolve the `call_fiber()` function with the result in a callback:

```
let call_fiber = function () {
    let result = asyncFunction(); //sync style call
    return result
}.future();

call_fiber().resolve((err, result) => {
    console.log(result)
});
```

If we still get the result with a callback, what is the benefit of using Fibers then? Let's remove the nested callbacks using ES6 arrow functions and see how much cleaner the code will be then:

```
asyncFunctionOne()
  .resolve(result_one => asyncFunctionTwo(result_one))
  .resolve(result_two => asyncFunctionThree(result_two))
  .resolve(result_three => console.log(result_three))
```

The same thing can be accomplished with Promises:

```
const asyncFunction = () => {
    console.log('called asyncFunction')
    return new Promise((resolve, reject) => {
        Meteor.setTimeout(() => {
            resolve('hi')
        }, 5000);
    })
}
```

As you can see, the `Promise` API is very similar to the Future API. How we call them is also very similar:

```
asyncFunction().then(result => {
    console.log(result)
})
```

Using ES6 arrow functions, we can chain promisified functions similarly to the Future API:

```
asyncFunctionOne()
  .then(result_one => asyncFunctionTwo(result_one))
  .then(result_two => asyncFunctionThree(result_two))
  .then(result_three => console.log(result_three))
```

Now we have a good understanding of how promises and fibers work and the benefits we get out from them. Let's create two search methods and test them:

```
Meteor.methods({
  search_with_fibers(query_string) {
   let future = new Future();
   ... async code
   return future.wait()
  },
  search_with_promises(query_string) {
   return new Promise(function (resolve, reject) {
    .... async code
  });
}
```

The next thing we need is to connect to the database:

```
Meteor.methods({
  search_with_fibers(query_string) {
    let future = new Future();
    MongoClient.connect(url, (err, db) => {
    ... connected to the database
    });
    return future.wait()
  },
  search_with_promises(query_string) {
    return new Promise(function (resolve, reject) {
    MongoClient.connect(url, (err, db) => {
    ... connected to the database
    });
  });
}
```

After we connect to the database, we can access the collection through the db object:

```
Meteor.methods({
  search_with_fibers(query_string) {
    let future = new Future();
    MongoClient.connect(url, (err, db) => {
      let col = db.collection('restaurants')
      ... perform queries
    });
    return future.wait()
  },
  search_with_promises(query_string) {
    return new Promise(function (resolve, reject) {
      MongoClient.connect(url, (err, db) => {
        let col = db.collection('restaurants')
        ... perform queries
      });
    });
  });
}
```

Now, we can have access to all the native MongoDB methods that we used in the mongo shell. Let's write the search query and test it in the shell first. Open a new terminal and navigate to the project directory. In the shell, declare pure JavaScript variables:

```
meteor:PRIMARY> var search_query = "new"
```

Declare the query as well:

```
meteor:PRIMARY> db.restaurants.find({$text: {$search:
query_string}},{score: {$meta: "textScore"}}).sort({score: {$meta:
"textScore" }}).limit(10).pretty()
{
  "_id" : ObjectId("5892ca96caf6e23d867f95c3"),
  "address" : {
  "building" : "349",
  "coord" : [
  -73.9721409,
  40.677148
],
  "street" : "Flatbush Avenue",
  "zipcode" : "11238"
},
  "borough" : "Brooklyn",
  "cuisine" : "Asian",
  "grades" : [
{
  "date" : ISODate("2014-08-26T00:00:00Z"),
  "grade" : "B",
```

```
    "score" : 19
  },
  {
    "date" : ISODate("2014-01-24T00:00:00Z"),
    "grade" : "A",
    "score" : 12
  }
  ],
  "name" : "New Wai Ling Chinese Restaurant/New Fresco Tortillas Ii Taco",
  "restaurant_id" : "50004367",
  "score" : 0.8999999999999999
}
{
...
```

Now we can just copy it to our `Meteor` **Methods:**

```
Meteor.methods({
  search_with_fibers(query_string) {
    let future = new Future();
    MongoClient.connect(url, (err, db) => {
      let col = db.collection('restaurants')
      col.find({$text: {$search: query_string}},{score: {$meta:
"textScore"}}).sort({score: {$meta: "textScore" }}).limit(10)
    });
    return future.wait()
  },
  search_with_promises(query_string) {
    return new Promise(function (resolve, reject) {
    MongoClient.connect(url, (err, db) => {
    let col = db.collection('restaurants')
      col.find({$text: {$search: query_string}},{score: {$meta:
"textScore"}}).sort({score: {$meta: "textScore" }}).limit(10)
    });
  });
}
```

The last step is to return the result from the queries. We fetch the results in the native driver by converting them into an array with the `toArray()` function. We can add `toArray()` after the `limit()` method, and when we fetch them, they will be available in the callback. Then, we close the `db` connection and resolve (in `Promise`) or return (in `Fiber`) them to the client.

In the `search_with_fibers` method:

```
col.find({$text: {$search: query_string}},{score: {$meta:
"textScore"}}).sort({score: {$meta: "textScore" }})
.limit(10)
.toArray((err, result) => {
    db.close()
    future.return(result);
});
```

In the `search_with_promises` method:

```
col.find({$text: {$search: query_string}},{score: {$meta:
"textScore"}}).sort({score: {$meta:          "textScore" }})
.limit(10)
.toArray((err, result) => {
    db.close()
    resolve(result);
});
```

With these steps, we have completed the backend of our app. Now we need to be able to call these methods from the client using Redux's actions. In the `actions/index.js` file, add the following action:

```
export const search = (query_string) => {
  return dispatch => {
    dispatch(query(query_string))
      Meteor.call('search_with_fibers', query_string, (err, result) => {
        if (!err) {
          dispatch(receiveResult(result))
        }
      })
    }
  }
}
```

The search action is dispatched from `SearchForm`, passing `query_string`. This is a Redux async action, and in order to get this to work, we need to have an async middleware-like redux-thunk (we will wire it up in our next step). The second action query it will persist in the store is `query_string`. The next thing in the workflow is the call to the Meteor method `search_with_fibers` by passing `query_string`. Once we get the result, we dispatch the `receiveResult` action to persist all the results in the store.

In the following diagram, we can visualize the workflow:

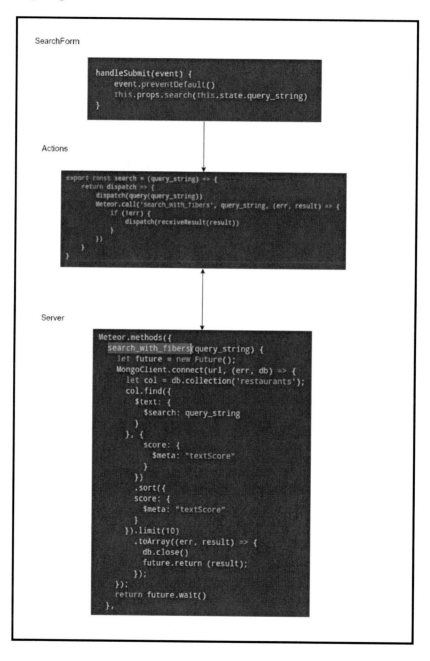

Now we have all the Redux actions defined. We also have the `App.js` data container and `SearchForm`. We also have the backend ready for queries. To run what we have by now, let's render the data container.

In the `index.js` client, import `App.js` and all the required modules:

```
import React from 'react'
import {render} from 'react-dom'
import App from './containers/App'
import reducers from './reducers'
import createLogger from 'redux-logger'
import thunk from 'redux-thunk'
import {Provider} from 'react-redux'
import {createStore, applyMiddleware} from 'redux'
```

Besides the core React modules, here we have imported reducers (one, in our case, search), the thunk middleware required for async action calls, the Provider Redux, a component required to pass down to all the rendered children, and the store; the rest are a few utilities (`createStore`, `applyMiddleware`, `createLogger`, and so on):

```
const middleware = [thunk]
  if (process.env.NODE_ENV !== 'production') {
     middleware.push(createLogger())
}
Meteor.startup(() => {
    const store = createStore(reducers, applyMiddleware(...middleware))
    render(
      <Provider store={store}>
         <App/>
      </Provider>, document.getElementById('root'));
});
```

When `Meteor.startup` is executed, we create the store and pass it as a prop to Provider and render the container component App. At this point, we can search and receive the results. The next logical step is to load them into the result list.

Create the following folders and files:

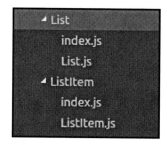

One thing is different in this app when compared to other apps from previous chapters: we don't have the client database Minimongo synced with the server MongoDB. We used methods for data loading, just as we would use a standard Ajax call to the server. Since they are asynchronous, the data may come at any time, and we don't really have control of it. For better user experience, we need to show to the user that the request is submitted and data fetching is in progress. The standard way of providing this type of indication is by showing and hiding the loading indicator. We can define that there will be two states describing the action: data is being fetched (isFetching = true) and data is received (isFetching =false). We already have this object in our store now; we can use it in our component. By default, isFetching is set to false. When the user sends a query to the server, we set it to true; when we receive data, we set it back to false.

In our List component, we can add this visual feature. Starting from the render() method, let's see how this is going to work:

```
render() {
  let spinner = null
    if(this.props.search.isFetching) {
      spinner = <div className="centered"><Spinner/></div>
  }
const list = (
  <div>{this.props.search.result.map(data =><ListItem
key={data.restaurant_id} onClickItem ={this.onClickItem}
{...data}/>)}
    </div>
);
return (
    <div>
       {spinner}
       {list}
    </div>
  )
}
```

First, we create a variable spinner set to null. From the props (mapped to the store), we access the `isFetching` object state. If it is equal to `true`, we assign the `spinner` variable to the `Spinner` component (we will build this next); if `isFetching` is set to `false`, it will not render. Here's the complete code of the list:

```
import React, {PropTypes} from 'react'
import ListItem from '../ListItem'
import Spinner from '../Spinner'

class List extends React.Component {
    constructor(props) {
        super(props)
        this.onClickItem = this.onClickItem.bind(this)
    }

    onClickItem(item) {
        this.props.actions.goTo(item.coord[1], item.coord[0], item.restaurant_name, item.cuisine)
    }
    render() {
        let spinner = null
        const {result} = this.props;
        if (this.props.search.isFetching) {
            spinner = <div className="centered"><Spinner/></div>
        }
        const list = (
            <div>
                {result.map(data => <ListItem key={data.restaurant_id} onClickItem ={this.onClickItem} {...data}/>)}
            </div>
        );
        return (
            <div>
                {spinner}
                {list}
            </div>
        )
    }
}

export default List
```

In the preceding screenshot, you can see that we have a method `onClickItem` that we bound in the constructor and passed down to the `ListItem` component. In this method, we dispatch the action `goTo` by passing the coordinates, the restaurant name, and cuisine type.

The `Spinner` component has nothing to do with data handling or have any internal state; we can define it as a pure presentational component. It is a simple arrow function that will render one animated `<svg>` element.

In the `Spinner` folder, create the `Spinner.js` file and add the following function:

```
const Spinner = () => {
  return (
  <svg
    version="1.1"
    id="loader-1"
    x="0px"
    y="0px"
    width="40px"
    height="40px"
    viewBox="0 0 40 40"
    enableBackground="new 0 0 40 40">
   <path
    opacity="0.2"
    fill="#000"
d="M20.201,5.169c-8.254,0-14.946,6.692-14.946,14.946c0,8.255,6.692,14.946,1
4.946,14.946s14.946-6.691,14.946-14.946C35.146,11.861,28.455,5.169,20.201,5
.169z
M20.201,31.749c-6.425,0-11.634-5.208-11.634-11.634c0-6.425,5.209-11.634,11.
634-11.634c6.425,0,11.633,5.209,11.633,11.634C31.834,26.541,26.626,31.749,2
0.201,31.749z"/>
   <path
    fill="#000"
d="M26.013,10.047l1.654-2.866c-2.198-1.272-4.743-2.012-7.466-2.012h0v3.312h
0C22.32,8.481,24.301,9.057,26.013,10.047z">
   <animateTransform
    attributeType="xml"
    attributeName="transform"
    type="rotate"
    from="0 20 20"
    to="360 20 20"
    dur="0.5s"
    repeatCount="indefinite"/>
   </path>
  </svg>
  )
}
export default Spinner
```

You can replace the content of the render method with anything you like; it doesn't have to be even an cv `<svg>` element. A simple div, such as `<div>Loading...</div>`, will also work. It may not be pretty, but it will indicate the state.

Next, comes the `ListItem` component. We have built many lists through the book so far, and this list item will have nothing new for us:

```
import React, {PropTypes} from 'react'

class ListItem extends React.Component {
    constructor(props) {
        super(props)
        this.handleClick = this.handleClick.bind(this)
    }
    handleClick() {
        this.props.onClickItem({coord: this.props.address.coord, restaurant_name: this.props.name, cuisine: this.props.cuisine})
    }
    render() {
        return (
            <div className="card" onClick={this.handleClick}>
                <div className="card-block">
                    <h4 className="card-title">{this.props.name}</h4>
                    <p className="card-text">Cuisine: {this.props.cuisine}</p>
                </div>
            </div>
        )
    }
}

export default ListItem
```

It is a presentational component that fires back the `onClickItem` function upon a click; it is passed from the parent `List` component as a prop.

The next component we need to build is the Map. There are quite a few map APIs that we can use. The Google Maps API is probably one of the most popular APIs; it is de facto a mainstream **geographic information systems (GIS)** field. Other popular options are Leaflet.js, OpenLayers, and ArcGIS API for JavaScript. For our needs to display a location visually, the Leaflet.js library is a great option. It's a very light API with many versatile plugins, and the best part is that open source React components are available for Leaflet maps. We can quickly plug a map with just a few steps. To install the needed packages, run the commands in the app directory:

```
npm install leaflet —save
npm install react-leaflet —save
```

Leaflet.js requires leaflet CSS in order to work, and you can add it to the `index.html` file in the `<head>` tag:

```
<link rel="stylesheet"
href="https://unpkg.com/leaflet@1.0.3/dist/leaflet.css" />
```

In the Folder `Map`, create a `Map.js` component and import the required components:

```
import React from 'react'
import {render} from 'react-dom'
import {Map, Marker, Popup, TileLayer} from 'react-leaflet'
```

The component will have the Map, a Marker (or a pin), and a Popup. When the user clicks on the Marker, a popup will display the restaurant name and the cuisine type. The last imported component is the map layer. The way most of the map APIs work is that the data on the map is added as a layer(s) that usually is on top of the base map:

```
class MapComponent extends React.Component {
  constructor(props) {
    super(props)
    this.state = {
      zoom: 16
    }
  }

  componentDidMount() {
    let map = this.map.leafletElement;
    map.on('zoomend', () => {
      this.handleZoom(map.getZoom());
    });
  }
  handleZoom(level) {
    this.setState({zoom: level});
  }
  render() {
    const position = [this.props.search.lat, this.props.search.lng];
    return (
      <Map
        center={position}
        zoom={this.state.zoom}
        ref={map => {this.map = map}}>
      <TileLayer
        attribution='&copy; <a
href="http://osm.org/copyright">OpenStreetMap</a> contributors'
        url='http://{s}.tile.osm.org/{z}/{x}/{y}.png'>
      </TileLayer>
        <Marker position={position}>
          <Popup>
            <span>{this.props.search.restaurant_name}
            <br/>{this.props.search.cuisine}</span>
          </Popup>
      </Marker>
    </Map>
    )
  }
}
export default MapComponent;
```

The `Map` component takes two props: the center (with lat-long), which we default in our store to the coordinates of Manhattan, and the zoom level, which we persist in the component's internal state. In some cases, when we work with third-party APIs, we need to have access to the DOM element. To get the element, we can use React's `ref` attribute. When a component is mounted, React will call `ref`, and in the callback, we can get the element node:

```
ref={map => { this.map = map}
```

Here we get the `map` element and store a reference in `this.map` local variable; like this, we can have access to all the DOM APIs. In this case, we are interested in the map event zoom end. When this event is fired, we get the current zoom level with the `map.getZoom()` method and persist it in the component's state.

We render the `Map` and the `List` in the `Main` component, which is a presentational component responsible for the main layout of the app. In the `Main` folder, create the `Main.js` file and add the following code:

```
import React from 'react'
import Map from '../Map'
import List from '../List'

class Main extends React.Component {
  render() {
    return (
      <div className="container-fluid">
        <div className="row">
          <div className="col-4" style={{height: '1000px,
overflowY:'scroll'}}>
              <List {...this.props}/>
          </div>
          <div className="col-8">
              <Map {...this.props}/>
          </div>
        </div>
      </div>
    )
  }
}
export default Main;
```

The final look of our search should look something like this:

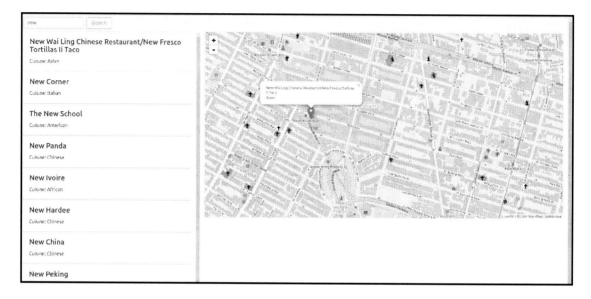

Test it Out!

Explore the imported data as you try different search queries. Add another text index to a different field and set different weight properties on the fields and see how the search scores the results. What result will the current search return if we enter the `li` string? Try options such as `caseSensitive` and ignore language stop words. You can import different data sources and build your app around the JSON model.

At `https://catalog.data.gov/dataset`, you can find plenty of useful data that you can use to build all kinds of apps just by doing what you learned in this chapter.

Summary

In this chapter, you learned how MongoDB full-text search works by importing sample data and building a search and locate app. We went over text indexing and implemented some of the available options in the search API by performing search queries in the mongo shell. Also, when you moved the query from the shell to the app's backend, you learned how you can call async functions in Meteor Methods using Fibers and Promises. To use methods such as `sort()` and `limit()`, we used the official MongoDB for the Node.js driver, which helped us smoothly move from the mongo shell to Meteor. Finally, we built and assembled all our frontend components with the addition of a third-party mapping library called Leaflet.js.

In `Chapter 7`, *Real-Time Maps*, we will build a mapping application by exploring further topics, such as the built-in user account functionality in Meteor and user authentication flow in the redux-react-router module. As always, we'll take advantage of Meteor's full-stack reactivity by adding real-time user interactions to our app.

7
Real-Time Maps

In all of our previous applications, we referred to the application's users as persons who can interact with the software and not necessarily users with a unique user identity persisted in our database. In real-life applications, these types of users are often called visitors since they can just visit the application without leaving behind any personal information. There are many scenarios where we can have users using the app without registration. Typically, we would use some type of software analytics to track the number of visitors, but at some point, we may need to have them registered. Let's discuss some example cases where we need to maintain user accounts' functionality in our applications.

First, let's look at monetization. Users will be provided with the option to pay for services provided by the app, and we need to register them securely with their payment information. Then we have advertisers paying for putting advertisements in our application, and they may need better statistics, such as what our users are interested in, not just the monthly traffic. If a tech company is a public-traded company, such as Twitter, for example, the number of monthly active users is one of the key performance indicators of how popular the product is. And this can affect the stock price.

Second, we have enterprise security. If our app is deployed within an enterprise organization, user accounts can be used as general security access. Usually, such users are managed by the internal IT team and are often part of user groups, which is beyond the scope of this chapter.

One of the most important aspects is the user experience: registered users should be able to create their own customized personal space in our app.

Building the entire sign-up/login workflow from scratch is a quite a hard task. Even if we use well-tested libraries for this, we would still need to have a pretty good understanding of how security works; we also need to design the database model to maintain this sensitive information. If we need to quickly prototype an app and don't want to spend all our time on creating user accounts workflows, the good news is that we can add that functionality to our Meteor app by just adding a few packages that will do the heavy lifting for us.

In this chapter, we will build a mapping application where we will require the users to register before using the application. After they are registered and successfully logged in, we will use their identity to give them the ability to create and read posts from other registered users. You can think of it as a Facebook user who can post on someone's timeline or read posts from other users. Since the main UI of the application will be a map, we will track all the user's locations and activities in real time, using Meteor's real-time APIs.

Before we jump right into building the app, let's see what we are getting for free out of the box with Meteor by creating a small test app.

Open the terminal and create a Meteor app with the following packages:

```
>> meteor create accounts
>> cd accounts
>> npm install
>> npm install react —save
>> npm install react-dom —save
```

In order to just drop user accounts in our app, we need at least these two packages:

```
meteor add accounts-ui accounts-password
```

According to the Meteor official documentation, the way we can quickly prototype an app with user accounts is by using Blaze (the original template engine of Meteor), rendered in our React component (if we are using React as our view layer). In many cases, this is probably sufficient enough to get us started. One way this could be implemented with React is that we have Blaze render a UI login template, and React will render this UI template. Let's add this template to the sample application.

Open the project in your editor and delete the content of the `main.js` and `main.html` files. For a small test app like this one, we can keep the whole code in the `main.js` file.

First, define the app HTML:

```
<head>
    <title>accounts</title>
</head>
<body>
<div id="root"></div>
</body>
```

Import all packages in the `main.js` file:

```
import React, {Component} from 'react'
import ReactDOM from 'react-dom'
import {Template} from 'meteor/templating'
import {Blaze} from 'meteor/blaze'
```

If you don't remove the two packages `meteor/templating` and `meteor/blaze`, they will be installed by default when we create the app. Next, create the React component that will render the `Blaze` template:

```
class AccountsUI extends Component {
  componentDidMount() {
      this.view = Blaze.render(Template.loginButtons,
ReactDOM.findDOMNode(this.refs.container));
  }
  componentWillUnmount() {
  Blaze.remove(this.view);
  }
  render() {
      return <span ref="container"/>;
  }
}
Meteor.startup(() => {
  ReactDOM.render(
    <AccountsUI/>, document.getElementById('root'))
});
```

By just adding three lines of code to our React component, we have a complete user accounts workflow. `Blaze.render` works in a way that is similar to `ReactDOM.render`, and since Blaze would render the template when the component is unmounted, we will use the `Blaze.remove()` method to remove it. Here is a screenshot showing how the default user accounts form will look:

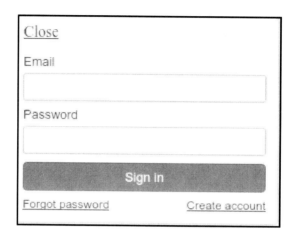

This gives us access to the following functionality: **Create account**, **Forgot password**, **Change password**, **Sign in**, and **Sign out**. Now let's see where all of this information will be saved in the database.

Keep the app running and open another terminal. Change the directory to the root of the app and launch the mongo shell:

```
>> meteor mongo
meteor:PRIMARY> use meteor
meteor:PRIMARY> show collections
meteor_accounts_loginServiceConfiguration
users
```

As soon as we add the two packages `accounts-ui` and `accounts-password`, Meteor will create two collections in the database: `users` and `meteor_accounts_loginServiceConfiguration`. To see how the `users` collection is structured, create a test account and log in to the application. Querying the `users` collection will return a result that will be similar to the following:

```
meteor:PRIMARY> db.users.find({}).pretty()
{
  "_id" : "GSfoKX5Q29qY2ZPch",
  "createdAt" : ISODate("2017-02-24T05:19:41.152Z"),
  "services" : {
```

```
    "password" : {
 "bcrypt" : "$2a$10$9HOqkg1BlUzpCgArijmwMe6tvTDfPatH6gR27UWRa/yAXLQXr4L.u"
 },
  "resume" : {
   "loginTokens" : [
    {
       "when" : ISODate("2017-02-24T05:19:41.173Z"),
       "hashedToken" : "usvTvmaYEZHHOgbq37T0XRsWtjU5AyTa2QDutY/x2f4="
    }
   ]
  }
 },
 "emails" : [
  {
    "address" : "user_one@gmail.com",
     "verified" : false
  }
 ]
}
```

We have _id, which is the default ID of the document created by MongoDB. This ID will also be our unique identifier for the user (later, we will see how to access it in our application). We also have the password encrypted, using the Node.js module bcrypt. If you are interested in exploring how all this works magically, refer to the GitHub repository of the Meteor account's modules at https://github.com/meteor/accounts/tree/master/packages.

There is an easy way in which we can change the default fields in the login form. One way is to configure it using the Accounts UI configuration module. In the same file, let's try a different configuration. Import accounts from meteor/accounts-base, and just before our AccountsUI component's initialization, place the following configuration:

```
import {Accounts} from 'meteor/accounts-base';
Accounts.ui.config({passwordSignupFields: 'USERNAME_ONLY'});
```

When the browser is refreshed, you'll notice that the e-mail field is changed to **Username** and the **Forgot password** functionality is removed (since this functionality is tied to an e-mail account).

Here is the complete list of all the possible account field configurations:

```
USERNAME_AND_EMAIL
USERNAME_AND_OPTIONAL_EMAIL
USERNAME_ONLY
EMAIL_ONLY
```

What we typically want from a user accounts workflow in our application is that after the user logs in, we want to redirect him (give him access) to the actual application. If he logs out, we want to redirect him or her back to the login page. Since we are building **single page applications (SPA)**, we want to handle the flow on the client using client-side routing. Now we have done the actual user login, we can build our application using on the frontend React, React-router, and Redux.

Building the App

Let's visualize what we will build before we start writing the code:

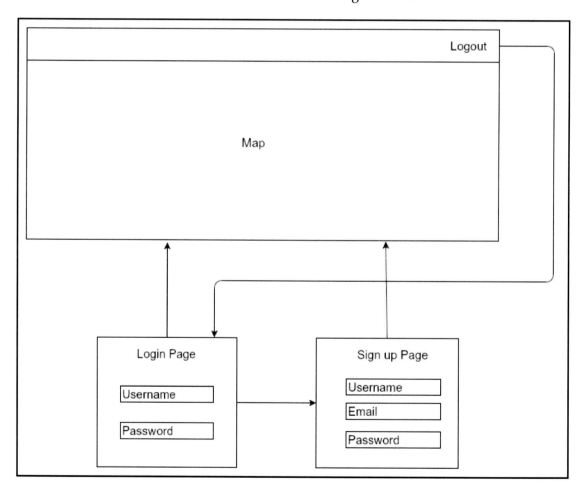

We have three pages in our single page app.

In **Login Page**, the user needs to enter their **Username** and **Password**, and if they are successfully authenticated, we will redirect them to the application; if not, we will display the error message returned from the server.

In Signup Page, the user will save their user credentials in the database; if there are no errors, we will redirect the user to the application (the **Map**).

In the Map page, we have a **Logout** link, which will log out the user and bring them back to **Login Page**.

Out of the box, the user accounts UI comes already styled. What we want from our application is not only to take advantage of the accounts packages functionality but also have full control over the look of the app. We'll build all our pages step by step from scratch and explore how all this fits together.

To have a consistent look and responsiveness across pages, we will style them using the Material Design Lite CSS library.

Let's start by creating the app with the Meteor CLI and installing all the packages. Open the terminal and create the app:

```
>> meteor create map
```

Instead of manually installing all the packages, replace the default packages.json file with the following script:

```
{
    "name": "map",
    "private": true,
    "scripts": {
    "start": "meteor run"
},
    "dependencies": {
    "babel-runtime": "6.18.0",
    "bcrypt": "^1.0.2",
    "classnames": "^2.2.5",
    "leaflet": "^1.0.3",
    "marked": "^0.3.6",
    "material-design-lite": "^1.3.0",
    "meteor-node-stubs": "~0.2.0",
    "react": "^15.4.2",
    "react-addons-pure-render-mixin": "^15.4.2",
    "react-dom": "^15.4.2",
    "react-leaflet": "^1.1.0",
```

```
    "react-redux": "^5.0.1",
    "react-router": "^3.0.2",
    "react-router-redux": "^4.0.7",
    "redux": "^3.6.0",
    "redux-logger": "^2.7.4",
    "redux-thunk": "^2.1.0",
    "turf": "^3.0.14",
    "turf-random": "^3.0.12"
  },
    "babel": {
    "plugins": [
      "transform-class-properties"
    ]
  },
  "devDependencies": {
    "babel-plugin-transform-class-properties": "^6.19.0"
  }
}
```

Since we will build our own account UIs, we only need the `accounts-password` package.

Add it to the stack:

```
meteor add accounts-password
```

Our next step is to create all the folders in the client directory. Remove all the defaults once created by Meteor and create all the folders and files, as shown in the following screenshot:

Now we need to figure out from where we need to start building the app. In this application, we could follow the login workflow from the diagram. Unregistered users need to register before using the app. Let's build the Login page first, then the rest of the pages.

Login, Signup, and the main app components are all entry pages of our app, and they will have to connect to the backend for data. Since they will all be dealing with data, we can create them as React containers instead of presentational components. We can use the same folder structure pattern as our previous applications. All the files and folders in the `containers` folder are listed as follows:

Starting from the render method, let's create and style the `Login` component. We have already created many forms, so this shouldn't be something new for us:

```
<form className="#">
    <div className="mdl-textfield mdl-js-textfield">
        <input
        id="login-username"
        className="mdl-textfield__input"
        type="text"
  onChange={this.handleChangeEmail}
        value={this.state.email}/>
        <label className="mdl-textfield__label" htmlFor="login-
username">Username</label>
    </div>
    <div className="mdl-textfield mdl-js-textfield">
        <input
        id="login-userpass"
        className="mdl-textfield__input"
        type="password"
  value={this.state.password}
```

```
onChange={this.handleChangePassword}/>
        <label className="mdl-textfield__label" htmlFor="login-
userpass">Password</label>
      </div>
    </form>
```

Here we have two input fields with their corresponding labels: one for the username and one for the password. As you noticed, we will use the React component's state to persist the data temporarily between the methods and JSX. This component will essentially be a single page, and for now, it makes sense to style it by wrapping it in the layout classes from MDL. Later, if you add more functionality, you can break it down into children components:

```
<div className="mdl-layout mdl-layout-login">
  <main className="mdl-layout__content-login">
      <div className="mdl-card mdl-shadow--6dp">
        <div className="mdl-card__title mdl-color--primary mdl-color-
text--white">
      <h2 className="mdl-card__title-text">Map</h2>
    </div>
        <div className="mdl-card__supporting-text">
 The form goes here
    </div>
    <div className="mdl-card__actions mdl-card--border">
        <p className="text-center">Don't have an account? Register
            <Link to="/signup">{' '}here</Link>
        </p>
        {error}
    </div>
    <div className="mdl-card__actions mdl-card--border">
      <button
        className="mdl-button mdl-button--colored mdl-js-button mdl-js-
ripple-effect"
  onClick={this.handleSubmit}>Log in</button>
      </div>
    </div>
  </main>
</div>
```

In the `App.css` file, place the following CSS classes:

```
.mdl-layout-login {
  align-items: center;
  justify-content: center;
}
.mdl-layout__content-login {
  padding: 24px;
  margin-top: 100px;
}
```

Once styled and rendered, the page should look like this:

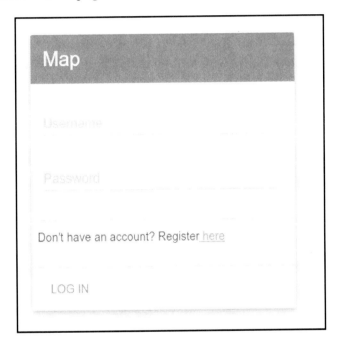

Next thing we need to do is add the login functionality.

Starting from the component definition, we are setting the default state and binding the methods in the constructor method:

```
class Login extends Component {
  constructor(props) {
    super(props);
    this.state = {
      error: '',
      email: '',
      password: ''
    };
    this.handleSubmit = this.handleSubmit.bind(this);
    this.handleChangePassword = this.handleChangePassword.bind(this)
    this.handleChangeEmail = this.handleChangeEmail.bind(this)
  }
```

The `handleSubmit` method is where we will send a request to the server to log in to the user; the rest are standard methods to handle the internal state. Here is the method:

```
handleSubmit(event) {
  event.preventDefault();
  let self = this;
  Meteor.loginWithPassword(this.state.email, this.state.password, (err, result) => {
    if(err) {
    self.setState({error: err.reason})
      } else {
    self.props.router.push({pathname: '/'})
      }
  });
}
```

When the user clicks on the login button, `handleSubmit` will be called. We will then get the values from the local state and pass them as parameters to the `Meteor.loginWithPassword` method. All encryption-decryption and validation of the password will be handled for us; this is great because we don't have to write the code for this. If for some reason, the user cannot log in, an error will be returned from the method. **User not found** is returned if the user does not exist in the database; if the password doesn't match, it will return the **Incorrect password** message. In this app, we won't cover the forgot password case. This will usually require sending an e-mail with a link to a page to create a new password; however, lately, a common workflow is by sending a text message with a verification code or even making a phone call with the code.

If there is no error, we will redirect the user to our main page using, in our case, the `react-router-redux` binding library for `react-router`. When we create the router with all other components, this should work seamlessly.

The next component is the Signup page. It is pretty much the same as Login page. We collect just one extra field: the username. Another bonus we get with the Meteor accounts package is that the user can be authenticated with both their e-mail or username:

```
<form className="#">
  <div className="mdl-textfield mdl-js-textfield">
    <input
      id="signup-username"
      className="mdl-textfield__input"
      type="text"
      onChange={this.handleChangeUserName}
      value={this.state.username}/>
    <label className="mdl-textfield__label" htmlFor="signup-
username">Username</label>
  </div>
  <div className="mdl-textfield mdl-js-textfield">
    <input
      id="signup-mail"
      className="mdl-textfield__input"
      type="text"
      onChange={this.handleChangeEmail}
      value={this.state.email}/>
    <label className="mdl-textfield__label" htmlFor="signup-
mail">Email</label>
  </div>
  <div className="mdl-textfield mdl-js-textfield">
    <input
      id="signup-user-pass"
      className="mdl-textfield__input"
      type="password"
      value={this.state.password}
      onChange={this.handleChangePassword}/>
    <label className="mdl-textfield__label" htmlFor="signup-user-
pass">Password</label>
  </div>
</form>
```

Just by looking at this form, you can figure out all the methods and the state that needs to be defined. Let's see how we can create a user, which is the interesting part in this component.

First, we need to import the `accounts-base` module:

```
import {Accounts} from 'meteor/accounts-base'
```

In the `handleSubmit` method, create the user by calling the `Accounts.createUser` method:

```
handleSubmit(event) {
  event.preventDefault();
    Accounts.createUser({
      email: this.state.email,
      username: this.state.username,
      password: this.state.password
    }, (err) => {
if (err) {
  this.setState({error: err.reason});
      } else {
    this.props.actions.create_new_user({user_id: Meteor.userId, username:
this.state.username})
      this.props.router.push({pathname: '/'})
    }
  });
}
```

This will insert the user into the `users` collection. If there is an error, we will set the error in the local state and display it; otherwise, we will redirect the user directly to the application. We do one extra call before the redirection, which is related to how we want to handle users' information in our collection(s). In a denormalized MongoDB way, we store additional information in the same `users` collection. For example, we may need to add another field, such as the current user location. Personally, I would like to keep secure information, such as user passwords, completely separate from any other data that the app needs. In this app, the users will create posts, and we will also have their location (coordinates). It's very easy to leak passwords to the client if you query the user location directly from the `users` collection, where the same passwords are stored as well. Instead, we can normalize the collection and use `userId` as a user identifier across the application.

In our next step, we will create the routes of the app. In the `routes.js` file, add the following function:

```
export const renderRoutes = () => (
  <Provider store={store}>
   <Router history={history}>
<Route path="login" component={Login}/>
     <Route path="signup" component={Signup}/>
  <Route path="/" component={App} onEnter={requireCredentials}>
       <IndexRoute component={Main}/>
```

```
      </Route>
      <Route path="*" component={PageNotFound}/>
    </Router>
  </Provider>
);
```

One thing we should be aware of is that there is no guarantee that the user would not type the URL of the app and bypass the login page. For example, the login page URL in this router will be `http://localhost:3000/login`, and the user can just remove the `login` string from the URL and browse to `http://localhost:3000/`. Nothing will prevent them from going directly to the main app that we just secured. The way we can enforce security in any of our routes is by using a middleware function(s). Before the page is rendered, we check whether the user exists; if not, we redirect them to the login page. Middleware functions are nothing more than a function with a callback that is called in the middle of two states, as in our example. Before we enter `Route` with the app component, `onEnter` will be fired and the entrance will be blocked until the callback from the middleware function is called. The signature of `onEnter` looks like `onEnter(nextState, replace, callback)`. Here is the middleware function:

```
const requireCredentials = (nextState, replace, next) => {
  if (Meteor.userId()) {
    store.dispatch(AllActions.get_loggedin_user());
    next()
  } else {
    replace('/login')
  next()
  }
}
```

`Meteor.userId()` is a very convenient way to access the user ID for our entire app. In fact, this user ID is built into the core of the Meteor framework. This ID is available in all the methods and publications, even if we do not add user accounts to our application.

Let's take a look at the rest of the code in the `routes.js` file:

```
import React from 'react';
import {Router, Route, browserHistory, IndexRoute} from 'react-router'
import {createStore, applyMiddleware} from 'redux'
import {syncHistoryWithStore} from 'react-router-redux'
import {Provider} from 'react-redux'
import reducers from './reducers'

import Main from './components/Main'
import PageNotFound from './components/PageNotFound'
import Login from './containers/Login'
import App from './containers/App'
```

```
import Signup from './containers/Signup'

import thunk from 'redux-thunk'
import createLogger from 'redux-logger'

import * as AllActions from './actions'
import observe from './observe'

const middleware = [thunk]
if (process.env.NODE_ENV !== 'production') {
  middleware.push(createLogger())
}
const store = createStore(reducers, applyMiddleware(...middleware))
const history = syncHistoryWithStore(browserHistory, store)

store.dispatch(AllActions.load_users_posts());
observe.init(store)
```

From top to bottom, we imported all the necessary modules and components that our router needs to render. We then set up logger middleware to help us debug the Redux store. We also created the store and synced it with the browser history. At the end, we fetched all the users using a Redux action and initialized an observable function for our collections; we'll define both of these later on.

Because we are concentrating more on users, security, and real-time functionality in this app, we can keep the Redux part with a fewer actions and reducer functions.

Create the files, as shown in the following screenshot, in the `actions`, `constants`, and `reducers` folders:

We can handle the entire app functionality with just two actions: user and load (fetching the posts). When a user is successfully logged in, we want to save their username and ID in our store. Having it in the Redux store will give us access to it in every component through the props mapped to the store.

The user function in reducers is as follows:

```
import {CURREN_USER} from '../constants/ActionTypes'
export default function user(state = {}, action) {
    switch (action.type) {
        case CURREN_USER:
        let result = {
            ...state,
            loggedin_user: action.current_user.username,
            user_id: action.current_user.user_id
        }
return result;
    default:
      return state;
      }
  }
}
```

We default the state of this reducer to an empty object { }. If the action type of CURRENT_USER is fired, we will set the username and ID in the state object.

In the next reducer, posts, we will persist all the posts from all the users in our store:

```
import {LOAD_POSTS} from '../constants/ActionTypes'
export default function posts(state = [], action) {
  switch (action.type) {
      case LOAD_POSTS:
         return action.posts
        default:
        return state
      }
  }
```

Each time a user of the app creates a new post, we will load all the posts from the database as one giant object. This is definitely not the best way of updating the store; you can improve this by granulating the updates by separating the object into subtrees.

Now we have the two reducers. Let's combine them with `routerReducer` in the `index.js` file:

```
import {combineReducers} from 'redux'
import posts from './posts'
import user from './user'
import {routerReducer} from 'react-router-redux'
export default combineReducers({posts: posts, user: user, routing:
routerReducer});
```

Next, we focus on actions. We need the following functionalities in our actions:

1. The user creates a new account. After we call `Accounts.createUser`, we call a Meteor method to add the user to the `Posts` collection with the default values.
2. We dispatch an action to persist the current logged in user when the user logs in.
3. The user can create posts. We call a Meteor Method to pass the data to the server and update the `Posts` collection. Notice, we are updating the `Posts` collection and not inserting a new record. Later, we will see how we can update lists (arrays) in a MongoDB collection.
4. We need to fetch all the posts in real time when a new post is created.
5. The application tracks whether a user has changed their location. If they do, we insert their new coordinates into the `Posts` collection.

Here are all the actions:

```
import * as types from '../constants/ActionTypes'
export const user = current_user => ({type: types.CURREN_USER,
current_user})
export const load_posts = posts => ({type: types.LOAD_POSTS, posts})

export const get_loggedin_user = () => {
    return dispatch => {
        Meteor.call('get_loggedin_user', (err, result) => {
            if (!err) {
              dispatch(user(result));
            }
        })
    }
}
export const create_new_user = (params) => {
    return dispatch => {
        Meteor.call('create_new_user', params, (err, data) => {
            if (!err) {
              dispatch(load_posts(data))
            }
```

```
        })
    }
}
export const load_users_posts = () => {
    return dispatch => {
        Meteor.call('get_all_users', (err, data) => {
            if (!err) {
                dispatch(load_posts(data))
            }
        })
    }
}
export const post = (params) => {
    return dispatch => {
        Meteor.call('post', params, (err, data) => {
            if (!err) {
                //do something if you have an error. another action?
            }
        })
    }
}
export const update_location = (params) => {
    return dispatch => {
        Meteor.call('update_location', params, (err, data) => {
            if (!err) {
                //do something if you have an error. another action
            }
        })
    }
}
```

In the `constants` folder in the `ActionTypes.js` file, export these two constants:

```
export const LOAD_POSTS = 'LOAD_POSTS'
export const CURREN_USER = 'CURREN_USER'
```

With this step, our Redux part is completed. We can now start gluing the components.

Under the `components` folder, create all the files listed in the following screenshot:

Before we start building presentational components, we need to have a container that will render and pass down the data. In the `containers` folder, create an `App.js` file and declare the following component:

```
import React, {PropTypes} from 'react'
import {connect} from 'react-redux'
import {bindActionCreators} from 'redux'

import * as AllActions from '../../actions'
import Main from '../../components/Main'
import Map from '../../components/Map'

class App extends React.Component {
    render() {
    const {posts, actions, user} = this.props
```

```
    return (
    <Main user={user}>
        <Map posts={posts} actions={actions} user={user}/>
      </Main>
        )
  }
}
const mapStateToProps = state => {
    return {posts: state.posts, user: state.user}
}
const mapDispatchToProps = dispatch => ({
actions: bindActionCreators(AllActions, dispatch)
})
export default connect(mapStateToProps, mapDispatchToProps)(App)
```

From the bottom up in the preceding code, we pass down the current state by mapping it to the component's props. We also wrap all our action creators around our dispatch function so it can be called directly from any child component.

In the `render` method, we render the `Main` layout component and the `Map` component. Let's build these two next.

In the `Main.js` file, start from the `render` method:

```
render() {
return (
  <div className="mdl-layout mdl-js-layout">
     <header className="mdl-layout__header">
        <div className="mdl-layout-icon"></div>
        <div className="mdl-layout__header-row">
          <span className="mdl-layout__title">Wellcome
{this.state.username} </span>
       <div className="mdl-layout-spacer"></div>
         <nav className="mdl-navigation">
            <a className="mdl-navigation__link" onClick={this.logout}
href="#">Logout</a>
         </nav>
       </div>
       </header>
<main className="mdl-layout__content">
 {this.props.children}
   </main>
   </div>
);
```

This component will do the following: The user will be able to click on a link and log out from the app; the logout will also redirect them to Login Page, where they can log in again.

Meteor offers a convenient method called `logout()`. Simply calling it will log the user out of the application. In the constructor, we bind the method as usual:

```
this.logout = this.logout.bind(this)
```

Here's the method:

```
logout(e) {
 e.preventDefault();
  Meteor.logout();
 browserHistory.push('/login');
 }
```

We click on the `<a>` hyperlink tag and use `e.preventDefault()` to prevent its default HTML behavior, which is redirecting the page to the link provided in the `href` attribute. Doing this, the hyperlink becomes just another placeholder, such as a `<div>` tag.

`Meteor.logout()` will also clear the login session, which will force the user to go to Login Page. Right after that, we push the current location to a new one using the `browserHistory.push()` method:

```
<main className="mdl-layout__content">
{this.props.children}
</main>
```

In the `main` tag, we can render any children components that are wrapped in our Main component; it could be a map or any other UI.

The next component on the line is the Map. To visualize the users on the Map, we want to have something, such as a pin or marker. What would be nice is if we could have the user profile pictures on the map and not just a marker that we need to click to see which user is at that location.

We don't have a functionality for the user to upload their own profile picture(s), and for this demo app, we can just grab some random profile pictures from social media apps, such as Facebook.

If you browse and add any random number, you will probably get a public profile picture: `http://graph.facebook.com/v2.5/ numbergoeshere/picture?height=200&height=200`.

Let's see how this is going to work in our app. In the render method add the following code:

```
return (
<Map  center={this.state.position}  zoom={this.state.zoom} ref={map => {
this.map = map}}>
 <TileLayer attribution='&copy;
            <a href="http://osm.org/copyright">OpenStreetMap</a>contributors'
 v      url='http://{s}.tile.osm.org/{z}/{x}/{y}.png'>
 </TileLayer>
    <LayerGroup>
 {list}
    </LayerGroup>
</Map>
  );
 }
```

In *Chapter 6*, *Building a Real-Time Search Application*, we had a very similar functionality of our main UI, which was also a map. Each time we select an item from the list of results, we render a Marker component pinned on that location. This will almost be the same, but instead, we will display all the users on the map.

We will customize the default Marker, which looks like, to display the users' profile pictures by looping through all the posts and creating a list of custom Markers. Here is how the code looks:

```
render() {
 const {posts, actions} = this.props;
 let list = [];
 for (let i = 0; i < posts.length; i++) {
 let profile_picture = '<img class="img-circle"
src="http://graph.facebook.com/v2.5/' +      posts[i].profile_number +
'/picture?height=200&height=200"></img>'
    let divIcon = L.divIcon({className: 'custom-div-icon', iconSize: null,
html: profile_picture});
  list.push(
    <Marker position={posts[i].location} icon={divIcon} key={posts[i]._id}>
     <Popup>
        <PostForm actions={actions} user_posts={posts[i]}/>
     </Popup>
    </Marker>
  )
 }
```

Let's see what we did from top to bottom in the preceding code.

As always, the props are passed from the parent component, then we loop through all the posts and push them in an array of `Marker` components. In the Marker, we pass two props, position, and the custom icon. Above all of this, we pull a profile picture based on the profile number that we randomly generated during the signup of the user (we will see how this is done when we get to the server part).

Next thing we need is the user location. There is a very nice geolocation API included in `Leaflet.js`. The best place to get the location is when the component is mounted. The method looks like this:

```
componentDidMount() {
let self = this;
const map = this.map.leafletElement;
map.locate({setView: true, watch: true})
.on('locationfound', function (e) {
  self.setState({
      position: [e.latitude, e.longitude]
    })
    self.props.actions.update_location({lat: e.latitude, long:
e.longitude})
  })
  .on('locationerror', function (e) {
    console.log(e);
  });
}
```

We subscribed to two events: location found and location error. From the first event on the callback, we get the latitude and longitude. We then set these values in our state, which will pin our Marker component to that location on the map. The map will also be automatically panned to that location; also, it will keep *watching* for any location changes.

Here is the entire Map component code:

```
class MapComponent extends React.Component {
    constructor(props) {
        super(props)
        this.state = {zoom: 10, position: [40.7484, -73.9857]}
    }
    componentDidMount() {
        let self = this;
        const map = this.map.leafletElement;
        map.locate({setView: true, watch: true})
            .on('locationfound', function (e) {
                self.setState({
                    position: [e.latitude, e.longitude]
                })
                self.props.actions
                    .update_location({lat: e.latitude, long: e.longitude})
            })
            .on('locationerror', function (e) {
                console.log(e);
            });
    }
    render() {
        const {posts, actions} = this.props;
        let list = [];
        for (let i = 0; i < posts.length; i++) {
            let profile_picture = '<img class="img-circle" src="http://graph.facebook.com/v2.5/' + posts[i].profile_number + '/picture?height=200&height=200"></img>'
            let divIcon = L.divIcon({className: 'custom-div-icon', iconSize: null, html: profile_picture});
            list.push(<Marker position={posts[i].location} icon={divIcon} key={posts[i]._id}>
                        <Popup>
                            <PostForm actions={actions} user_posts={posts[i]}/>
                        </Popup>
                    </Marker>
            )
        }
        return (<Map
                center={this.state.position}
                zoom={this.state.zoom}
                ref={map => {
                    this.map = map;
                }}>
                    <TileLayer
                        attribution='&copy; <a href="http://osm.org/copyright">OpenStreetMap</a> contributors'
                        url='http://{s}.tile.osm.org/{z}/{x}/{y}.png'></TileLayer>
                    <LayerGroup>
                        {list}
                    </LayerGroup>
                </Map>
        );
    }
}
export default MapComponent;
```

The user has the option to create (share) posts on their profile or in other user profiles. All users will be pinned on the map and the user can visualize them by a profile picture. What we can do with this is have the popup of the marker render a `PostForm` component where it can open it by simply clicking on the Marker.

Visually, we'll look like this:

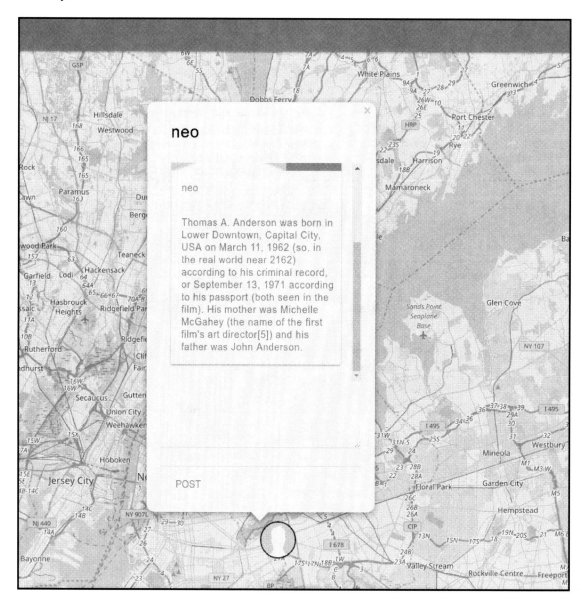

The username is on the top of the popup (username **neo**), and in the popup, we have the list of all the posts listed on this user's wall, just below the list we have the post form.

Let's build what we see in the preceding screenshot. First, we can create the form where the user will insert their posts. In `PostForm`, define our `render` method:

```
render() {
const {user_posts} = this.props
return (
   <div className="mdl-card mdl-card-poup mdl-shadow—1dp">
      <div className="mdl-card__title mdl-card—expand">
         <h6 className="mdl-card__title-text">{user_posts.username}</h6>
      </div>
<PostList user_posts={user_posts}/>
      <form onSubmit={this.handleSubmit}>
         <div className="mdl-textfield mdl-js-textfield">
      <textarea id="user_post"
         className="mdl-textfield__input"
         type="text"
         rows="3"
         onChange={this.handlePostChange}
         value={this.state.post}/>
      <label className="mdl-textfield__label" htmlFor="user_post"></label>
   </div>
   <div className="mdl-card__actions mdl-card—border">
   <button
      className="mdl-button mdl-button—colored mdl-js-button mdl-js-
ripple-effect"
      type="submit">Post</button>
   </div>
  </form>
 </div>
);
}
}
```

Here we wrapped the entire component in a Material Design card component, which has some very useful CSS classes that can help us prototype this interface without too much work. Just above the HTML form, we render the `PostList` component that will take care of the presentational part of the posts.

On the form, we hook up a standard `onSubmit` event; the button is in the `<form>` tag this time and we don't need to have an `onClick` event.

Because the user can write long multiline text, we use `<textarea>` instead of one line, `<input>`. As always, we handle any changes in the form field with the local state.

Here are the two methods in the component:

```
handleSubmit(event) {
  event.preventDefault()
  this.props.actions.post({user_id: this.props.user_posts.user_id, post:
this.state.post})
    this.setState({post: ''});
  }
handlePostChange(event) {
  this.setState({post: event.target.value});
}
```

In `handleSubmit`, we fire a Redux action (post) and save the data on the server. From the props passed from the parent component, we know which user this form belongs to.

The last two components are pretty straightforward to build. One function that is beneficial to have in our list component is the ability to see the latest post on the screen. We can do this by automatically scrolling to the bottom of the list when the component (re)renders.

We can define our `PostList` component as follows:

```
import React from 'react'
import {render} from 'react-dom'
import PostListItem from '../PostListItem'

class PostList extends React.Component {
  scrollToBottom() {
    const scrollHeight = this.postList.scrollHeight;
    const height = this.postList.clientHeight;
    const maxScrollTop = scrollHeight - height;
    this.postList.scrollTop = maxScrollTop > 0 ? maxScrollTop: 0;
  }
  componentDidUpdate() {
  this.scrollToBottom();
  }
 componentDidMount() {
    this.scrollToBottom();
  }
render() {
 const list = (this.props.user_posts.posts.map((post, index) =>
<PostListItem key={index.toString()} post={post}/>))
    return (
     <ul className="mdl-list mdl-message-list"
 ref={(ul) => {
      this.postList = ul;
    }}>
 {list}
  </ul>
```

```
      )
    }
  }
export default PostList
```

In the `render` method, we map the user's posts by creating a list of `PostListItem` components, where we set the keys to the index of the list and also pass down each post as a prop.

To always see the latest posts, we need to scroll to the bottom of the list. We can do this automatically without manually scrolling to the bottom with a few steps. For this, we need to create a variable to hold a reference to the element (`this.postList`). The element is returned from the callback of the `ref` attribute. Notice, that we are modifying the element without the use of props, which is considered antipattern in React. However, this is fine in cases such as this one, where the parent component doesn't really know the height of the list (child component) in pixels. In the `scrollToBottom()` method, we need to scroll to a number of pixels:

```
this.postList.scrollTop = #number of pixels
```

Two things we need to know here: `clientHeight` is the number of pixels of the visible area, including padding, and `scrollHeight` is the height of the element where everything is included in pixels (nonvisible areas, borders, margins, and so on).

When a component mounts or new posts are received, we set the `scrollTop` property to the number of pixels (`scrollHeight clientHeight`). We also want to read the latest post as soon as we open the pop-up form; for this, we call the method in the `componentDidMount()` method.

The last piece is the `PostListItem` component, which is a pure presentational component.

Here is the entire component:

```
import React from 'react'
import {render} from 'react-dom'

class PostListItem extends React.Component {
  createMarkup() {
    return {
        __html: '<img style="height:157px; width:173px;"
src="http://graph.facebook.com/v2.5/' +    this.props.post.profile_number +
'/picture?height=200&height=200"></img>'
    };
  };
  render() {
```

```
      return (
        <li className="mdl-list__item">
          <div className="mdl-card mdl-shadow-2dp">
           <div className="mdl-card__media">
              <div dangerouslySetInnerHTML={this.createMarkup()}/>
          </div>
          <div className="mdl-card__supporting-text">
        {this.props.post.from}
          </div>
           <div className="mdl-card__supporting-text">
      {this.props.post.post}
          </div>
          </div>
        </li>
         )
       }
     }
     export default PostListItem
```

The new thing here is how we set the user profile's `<img>` tag. We pass the profile number from the props and then assign it to the `innerHTML` property of the element. JSX is a JavaScript, and we are setting this HTML from the client code, which is considered a security risk since the client can inject scripts into the components. To prevent this, we need to provide a key, namely __html, and a value of the HTML we need to insert. To make this insertion really obvious that it is a security risk, React has a prop called `dangerouslySetInnerHTML`.

The server side

Let's create the `Posts` collection, which will be shared between the server and the client. In the *shared* folder, create an `index.js` file. We have only one collection and we can define it in the `index.js` file:

```
import {Mongo} from 'meteor/mongo';
export const Posts = new Mongo.Collection('posts');
```

All our data will be passed from the client with Meteor Methods. The first method we can define is `create_new_user()`. We will call this Method when the user signs up for the first time. In `Meteor.startup(() => {}`, let's define the methods:

```
  Meteor.methods({
  create_new_user(data) {
        let profile_number = Math.floor(Math.random() * (10000));
  Posts.insert({user_id: this.userId,
```

```
posts: [],
                        username: data.username,
                        location: random_coordinates(),
                        profile_number: profile_number})
    Meteor.users.update(this.userId, {
        $set: {
profile_number: profile_number
            }
        });
    return Posts.find({}).fetch()
  },
```

A few things are happening here. When the user is created on the client with the `Accounts.createUser({...})` method on the callback (if there is no error), we call this method to complete their account. For the purpose of developing and testing real-time functionality, we will mock up random coordinates with which we can simulate the changing location of the user.

First, we will generate a random profile number that we will use to set the user profile picture. In the `Posts` collection, we insert `user_id`, and since this is a Meteor Method, `userId` will return the currently logged in user. Here is the place where we can default all kinds of data that we may need in our app. We set `posts` to an empty array since it's a brand new account and the rest are the username and some random coordinates.

Next, we modify the users account collection by adding extra information as the profile number. We can query user information from both the collections by `user_id`. You can also have posts in the `users` collection, which is completely up to you—how you want to structure the collections. The only thing you need to be aware of is that the `users` account contains all of the sensitive information. After we insert a new document in the Posts collection and update the `users` collection, we return all the posts to the client, which is completely up to the frontend design.

Let's see how we can generate random coordinates and simulate the location change of the users. For our demo, we want to have users moving around in a certain location like in a real-life scenario. For example, we are in New York City and we see all our friends' locations in real-time around the city. We want to simulate this functionality to test our app.

The first thing we need is to draw a box of coordinates like a fence where we can have random continuously changing points.

We have already installed a helper library named `turf.js` that we can use to generate the points. Here is the method:

```
const random_coordinates = () => {
    let points = turf.random('points', 1, {
    bbox: [-74.103470, 40.652513, -73.809586, 40.949825]
    });
    return [points.features[0].geometry.coordinates[1],
    points.features[0].geometry.coordinates[0]];
}
```

We use the `turf.random` method to generate a point in a box (bounding box). If you put the coordinates on the map—74.103470, 40.652513, -73.809586, 40.949825—it will draw a box around New York City.

To actually move them on the map from the server, we need to update the location in the `Posts` collection and this will re-render the Marker component with the new location of the client. We can create a function to do just that:

```
const move = () => {
  let users = Posts.find({}).fetch()
  _.each(users, function (user) {
    Posts.update({
      _id: user._id
    }, {
      $set: {
        location: random_coordinates()
      }
    });
  });
}
```

We get all the users from the collection and loop through all of them and update their location with random coordinates of the New Your City area. This should be enough to test our user experience and even the performance of our app.

We can call this in `setInterval` and have the location changed over a period of time:

```
Meteor.setInterval(() =>{
    move()
}, 10000);// move every 10 seconds
```

The next method we call from the client is `get_loggedin_user`:

```
get_loggedin_user() {
  let user = Meteor.user();
  return {username: user.username, user_id: user._id};
},
```

Notice we can access user data with the `Meteor.user()` method. A simple method to return all the users' posts is as follows:

```
get_all_users() {
  return Posts.find({}).fetch();
}
```

The last two Methods are `post` (a user-created post) and `update_location()` when the location is updated by the client:

```
post(params) {
  let user = Meteor.user();
  Posts.update({
    user_id: user._id
      }, {
    $push: {
      posts: {
          from: user.username,
          post: params.post,
          profile_number: user.profile_number
        }
      }
  });
},
```

We defaulted each user with a fields posts as an empty array; now we can update the collection as we push a new post to the array. We can denormalize it and push any objects that our app needs:

```
update_location(params) {
  let user = Meteor.user();
  Posts.update({
    user_id: user._id
      }, {
    $set: {
      location: [params.lat, params.long]
      }
  });
}
```

The Leaflet API keeps tracking the user location, and if it changes, we call the `update_location` method with the new coordinates. Keep in mind that the users should allow location sharing in their browser.

Here is a screenshot of all the Methods that we just did:

```
Meteor.methods({
    create_new_user(data) {
        let profile_number = Math.floor(Math.random() * (10000));
        Posts.insert({user_id: this.userId, posts: [], username: data.username, location: random_coordinates(), profile_number: profile_number}
        Meteor.users.update(this.userId, {
            $set: {
                profile_number: profile_number
            }
        });
        return Posts.find({}).fetch()
    },
    get_loggedin_user() {
        let user = Meteor.user();
        return {username: user.username, user_id: user._id};
    },
    get_all_users() {
        return Posts.find({}).fetch();
    },
    post(params) {
        let user = Meteor.user();
        Posts.update({
            user_id: user._id
        }, {
            $push: {
                posts: {
                    from: user.username,
                    post: params.post,
                    profile_number: user.profile_number
                }
            }
        });
    },
    update_location(params) {
        let user = Meteor.user();
        Posts.update({
            user_id: user._id
        }, {
            $set: {
                location: [params.lat, params.long]
            }
        });
    }
});
```

On the client side, we need to listen for any changes in our collections. When a new user is created or the location of any user is changed, we will need to update our UI in real time.

In the `observer.js` file, we can subscribe to the `Posts` collection, and on any changes, we can pull the users' posts from the server:

```
Posts
  .find({})
  .observeChanges({
     changed: function (id, data) {
     store.dispatch(AllActions.load_users_posts())
  }
});
```

Since we are securing our app with user accounts and we want to have actual security in place, doing this will expose all the posts to the client. We really have no control of what the client can do with the collection, which makes our application insecure.

For example, if we dig into the browser console a bit, we can find document id(_id) in the Redux store. As soon as we have this ID, we can go over the code and search for the collection on the client, which is Posts. We can then easily hack into the collection and do all kinds of damage. To delete all the posts from a user, for example, we can just type this into the console query:

```
Posts.remove({ _id: '52rrZ9qgQ4nwRncPn'});
```

To fix this all we have to do is remove the `autopublish` and `insecure` packages:

```
>> meteor remove insecure
>> meteor remove autopublish
```

With this step, we have now completely secured our app and we are in full control of what kind of data we want to send to the client, and the client can update the database only through Methods.

Observing a collection change will not work because we have removed the `autopublish` package. It means that the data on the client will not be automatically pushed from the server.

The way we can keep receiving updates is by implementing Meteor's dependency-tracking system:

```
Tracker.autorun(() => {
    Meteor.subscribe('posts');
    store.dispatch(AllActions.load_users_posts())
});
```

Here we subscribed to the `posts` publisher on the server, and on any changes, we fire our Redux action, which will pull all the users' posts.

And the publisher on the server side looks like this:

```
Meteor.publish('posts', function () {
   if (!this.userId) {
      return this.ready();
   }
   return Posts.find({})
});
```

Test it out!

You can add almost unlimited functionality to this app. You can have some really simple features, such as to track when the users are online and set some visual indication; you can do this simply by saving the status in the database and querying it on changes.

Summary

In this chapter, we started by exploring ways of adding user accounts to our app. We did this by building a simple test application using the pre-made accounts UI and functions available in Meteor. We then moved on to developing own accounts workflow with our stack React, Redux, and the react-router. On the component side, we saw how we can completely customize the look of the map by adding forms in the created custom markers.

In the next chapter, we will build a Chatbot app using the Facebook Messenger platform, using the Wit.ai API.

8
Build a Chatbot with Facebook's Messenger Platform

In this chapter, we will build a chatbot application with Facebook's Messenger platform using a completely different stack from what we were using so far in this book. For our view layer, we will swap **React** with **Angular 2**. To query data from the server, we will use a query language **GraphQL**, and in addition to **MongoDB**, we will add the Cassandra database. We won't be able to cover all of the preceding technologies in a great depth in one chapter, but certainly exploring other technologies can only benefit us as full-stack developers.

First, we can start from the frontend by creating a simple *Meteor* app with implementing Angular 2 as our view layer with all the necessary tooling that we need. We will use TypeScript instead of ES6, which is the recommended (by the Angular team) way of writing Angular 2 apps. TypeScript is a superset of JavaScript that at the end transpiles into a plain JavaScript. That said, it is completely fine to use ES6 or even ES5 with Angular 2.

Angular 2 comes with a very handy CLI tool with which we can explore npm dependencies and the app structure before moving it to the Meteor app. Let's install it and see what is included:

```
sudo npm install -g @angular/cli
```

To create a new app, simply type the following command:

```
ng new angular2-dependencies
```

Here, the app name is *angular2-dependencies*. After all the packages are installed, we can go to the app directory and start the app using the following command:

```
ng serve
```

This will build and bundle all the scripts for us and default the app port to 4200. If you browse the app (http://localhost:4200/), you will see **Loading..** on your screen for a short period and **app works!** after a few seconds, which means we successfully created the app. Open the project in your editor, and let's investigate what is in there.

First, we can start from dependencies in package.json file:

```
"dependencies": {
  "@angular/common": "^2.4.0",
  "@angular/compiler": "^2.4.0",
  "@angular/core": "^2.4.0",
  "@angular/forms": "^2.4.0",
  "@angular/http": "^2.4.0",
  "@angular/platform-browser": "^2.4.0",
  "@angular/platform-browser-dynamic": "^2.4.0",
  "@angular/router": "^3.4.0",
  "core-js": "^2.4.1",
  "rxjs": "^5.1.0",
  "zone.js": "^0.7.6"
},
"devDependencies": {
  "@angular/cli": "1.0.0-rc.1",
  "@angular/compiler-cli": "^2.4.0",
  "@types/jasmine": "2.5.38",
  "@types/node": "~6.0.60",
  "codelyzer": "~2.0.0",
  "jasmine-core": "~2.5.2",
  "jasmine-spec-reporter": "~3.2.0",
  "karma": "~1.4.1",
  "karma-chrome-launcher": "~2.0.0",
  "karma-cli": "~1.0.1",
  "karma-jasmine": "~1.1.0",
  "karma-jasmine-html-reporter": "^0.2.2",
  "karma-coverage-istanbul-reporter": "^0.2.0",
  "protractor": "~5.1.0",
  "ts-node": "~2.0.0",
  "tslint": "~4.4.2",
  "typescript": "~2.0.0"
}
```

The plan is to move some of those packages and the app source to our Meteor app. Let's create our Meteor app and install what we need from the preceding file:

```
>> meteor create chatbot_fb
```

The next step is to copy the Angular app from the `src` folder into the `client/imports` directory and change the extension from `main.js` to `main.ts`. The files and directories should look as in this screenshot:

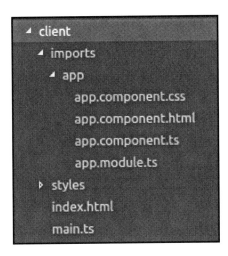

Note that we have the views portion in Angular defined as HTML files. That is different from React, where all the views are written in JavaScript. To have them as HTML files and import them as ES6 modules, we need to install a package `angular2-compilers` and remove `blaze-html-templates`:

```
>> meteor remove blaze-html-templates
>> meteor add angular2-compilers
```

We need a few more packages to make Angular 2 work with Meteor. Here is a complete list of the packages from our Angular app with the addition of Angular-Meteor dependencies, that is, the bare minimum that we need to make it work:

```
npm install --save @angular/common
npm install --save @angular/compiler
npm install --save @angular/core
npm install --save @angular/forms
npm install --save @angular/platform-browser
npm install --save @angular/platform-browser-dynamic
npm install --save @angular/router
npm install --save angular2-meteor
```

```
npm install --save angular2-meteor-polyfills
npm install --save angular2-meteor-tests-polyfills
npm install --save meteor-rxjs
npm install --save babel-runtime
npm install --save reflect-metadata
npm install --save rxjs
npm install --save zone.js
```

Also, we need all development packages:

```
mpm install --save-dev meteor-typings
npm install --save-dev @types/meteor
npm install --save-dev @types/mocha
npm install --save-dev @types/node
npm install --save-dev @types/underscore
npm install --save-dev ts-node
npm install --save-dev tslint
npm install --save-dev typescript
```

The next thing we need is to add two configuration files to configure TypeScript to work with Meteor. From the Angular app, copy, and paste `tsconfig.json` and `typings.d.ts` into the root of our Meteor app.

In `typings.d.ts` file, delete the content and add the following declarations:

```
declare module "*.html" {
  const template : string;
  export default template;
}
declare module "*.css" {
  const style : string;
  export default style;
}
```

The preceding code will tell the TypeScript compiler that all files with extension `.html` can be imported as name template of type string and all files with extension `.css` can be imported as name style of type string. In our code, we can import them as standard ES6 modules:

```
import template from './app.component.html'
import style from './app.component.css'
```

In `tsconfig.json` file, we will need to make a few changes:

```
{
  "compileOnSave": false,
  "compilerOptions": {
  "outDir": "./dist/out-tsc", //delete
  "sourceMap": true,
  "declaration": false,
  "moduleResolution": "node",
  "emitDecoratorMetadata": true,
  "experimentalDecorators": true,
  "target": "es5",
  "lib": [
    "es2016",
    "dom"
  ],
  "types": ["meteor-typings"]
  }
}
```

We don't need to specify `outDir` (we can delete it). Meteor will compile and build our app in `.meteor/local/build folder`, and the only configuration we will add here is `meteor-typings`.

With this last step, we added Angular 2 as a view in our Meteor app. You can also use this setup as your base minimal startup-kit template for Meteor apps with Angular 2 as a view.

To properly render the app, we need to make a few changes on the source of the app itself. Let's start from the main entry of the app `main.ts` file:

```
import "angular2-meteor-polyfills";
import {platformBrowserDynamic} from "@angular/platform-
  browser-dynamic";
import {AppModule} from "./imports/app/app.module";

Meteor.startup(() => {
  platformBrowserDynamic().bootstrapModule(AppModule);
});
```

The first thing we will add is `angular2-meteor-polyfills`, which is basically a package of `polyfills` that will make our Angular 2 app compatible with Meteor.

You can also import them directly, as follows:

```
import 'reflect-metadata';
import 'zone.js/dist/zone-node.js';
import 'zone.js/dist/long-stack-trace-zone';
```

The last thing we need is to boot the app, as we did this many times with React. We bootstrap AppModule on the callback of the Meteor.startup method.

Angular 2 is quite different from other frontend libraries or frameworks, in fact, it is not a just a frontend framework but rather a development platform with which we can develop pure web apps, Mobile Web Apps (hybrids), native mobile apps, and desktop apps. By importing platformBrowserDynamic, we are setting up our app to run on the browser environment as a web application.

Before we move further, let's have a quick high-level overview of Angular 2.

Visually, Angular 2 looks like this:

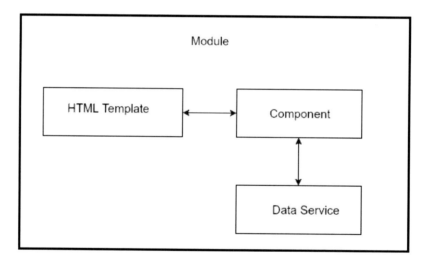

Each app consists of at least one module, one component, and one template. The module acts as a manager of all dependencies needed in order to run our application. Let's take a look at our `app.module.ts` file:

```
import {NgModule} from "@angular/core";
import {BrowserModule} from "@angular/platform-browser";
import {AppComponent} from "./app.component";

@NgModule({
declarations: [AppComponent],
providers: [],
imports: [BrowserModule],
bootstrap: [AppComponent]})

export class AppModule {}
```

If we are following the Angular 2 naming convention, each app should have one root module and one root component named `AppModule` and `AppComponent`; the name of the files are `app.module` and `app.component` respectively. That makes it easy to figure out how the app works by simply finding the app folder and the root module. As for the single entry file of the app, `main.ts` is the file where we bootstrap the root module.

The single root module for the entire application is the `AppModule`. To have that class declared as a module, we import a decorator function `@NgModule`. In that function, we specify metadata (as an object) that tells Angular how to build and run it. In the metadata, we also list all our components in `declarations` array. The providers are the core of Angular architecture. In there, we expose injectable classes to all imported modules; these classes are also called services, singletons, which means we have one instance of an object(s) that we can reuse by injecting it into our components.

Next is the imports key, in that array. We can list modules that should be imported into this root module (a module can import other modules). In this example, we need a `BrowserModule` to render the app, which will let the browser know how to render; it is also the place to list everything our app depends on.

In `bootstrap` array, we specify the starting point of the app; this will bootstrap every component that is listed there. Usually, we specify only one app root component for the entire app. Since this is the root module, we don't need to declare any code in the class, and at the end, we export it as an empty class.

The `AppComponent` class is shown in the following code:

```
import {Component} from '@angular/core';
import template from './app.component.html'
@Component({selector: 'app-root', template})
  export class AppComponent {
title = 'app works!';
  }
```

With the components, we also get a class decorator function, `@Component`, provided by Angular. The metadata, in this case, will associate the code of this component with the view template (imported HTML file as ES6 module). In the class, we can declare methods, set properties, bind events, inject other classes, and import life cycle hooks of the component (very identical to React ones). The selector property is where this component will be rendered. We will declare this selector as a custom HTML tag, which will be invalid and ignored by the browser if we didn't provide BrowserModule before. Let's add that selector into our HTML to see how this looks like:

```
<head>
</head>
<body>
  <app-root>Loading...</app-root>
</body>
```

Meteor injects everything we need in our main HTML page, and in the same way as React, we strip down everything from the HTML page and just leave the bare minimum HTML that Meteor needs. When we bootstrap the component, Angular will start loading all dependencies and components, then the browser will start parsing and rendering all the views. As soon as `AppComponent` is initialized, the selector `<app-root>` will be replaced with the content of our component view. In `app.component.html`, we have that content as shown in the following code:

```
<h1>{{title}}</h1>
```

The value of the title property in our class is bound to this title wrapped using double curly brackets `{{title}}`. There are a few ways we can render data to the view in Angular. The first one is the way we just did it, that is, by binding a property of a class to a template and enclosing that property in `{{}}` notation. That is the simplest way of rendering data in views, the official naming of that method is **Interpolation.**

The second way is by binding a model to the view. The data will flow in one way, from the component to the view. In `AppComponent`, we can create our data model class and bind the HTML element to it:

```
class OneWayBinding {
  text : String;
}
@Component({selector: 'app-root', template})
export class AppComponent {

  one_way : OneWayBinding = {
    text: 'one way binding'
  };


}
```

Just preceding the decorator function, create a `OneWayBinding` class that will be our test model, a class with one property `text` of `String` type. In the component, we can create a property of `OneWayBinding` type, where we assign a value to the property text. This is how we can bind that object to the HTML element:

```
<h1 [innerText]="one_way.text"></h1>
```

Using square brackets `[]` syntax, we can bind our model to the properties or attributes of the HTML elements.

Here is another example of binding a CSS class attribute to the same element:

```
<h1 [class.classExample] = true [innerText]="two_way.text"></h1>
```

Note that we set that binding to `true` in order to render that value. In reality, we can have this style conditionally set, which is a great feature. On the component side, we can also define CSS classes directly in the component's metadata like this:

```
@Component({selector: 'app-root', template,
    styles: [`
    .classExample{
      background-color:LightGray;
    }
`]})
```

In all of the preceding examples, we sent the data from component to the view; if we have input from the UI and change that data, that change will not be sent back to the component automatically. To have that, we need to bind the model in two ways; here is a simple way to do that:

```
class TwoWayBinding {
  text : String;
}
@Component({...
export class AppComponent {
 two_way : TwoWayBinding = {
   text: 'two way binding'
  };
}
```

In the preceding code, we created another sample model, and the syntax in the HTML of binding looks like this:

```
<input [(ngModel)]="two_way.text"/>
<p>{{two_way.text}}</p>
```

Those special keywords reserved for Angular (ngModel) are called directives. We will have a few more examples of other useful directives going forward.

Another way to pass data from the view to our component is by firing events. Let's create a simple button and test it:

```
<button (click)="onHandleClick(two_way.text)">Send to back</button>
```

Note that here we use parentheses () notation to specify the event type.

Back in our component, we define the onHandleClick method:

```
export class AppComponent {
 onHandleClick(data) {
   alert(data);
  }
}
```

One of the most important features of Angular is the reusability of classes in our components. The pattern is known as **Dependency Injection (DI)** , which is the core of the entire platform. We can reuse any class by importing it to another class and injecting it in the constructor.

To test and see how this works, let's create another component and add a simple test service that we can inject in the component(s). In `imports` folder, create the following files:

It will be a simple class that will return an array of items, which our list component will render.

The `ListService` class is shown in the following code:

```
import {Injectable} from '@angular/core';

@Injectable()
export class ListService {
getListItems() : Promise <any> {
 return new Promise(resolve => {
     setTimeout(() => resolve(['item_one', 'item_two',
     'item_three']), 3000);
   });
  }
}
```

Here, the decorator function `@Injectable` is optional. A good practice is to mark this class as injectible, so we know to register it in `providers` array.

With TypeScript in every method or function, we can specify a return type.
The `getListItem()` method has a return type of `Promise`; if you try to return anything else, it will throw an error, which is what we are expecting from TypeScript. To simulate a network request, we resolve `Promise` with a simple array of items in the method after 3 seconds. Let's take a look at how we can import and use this class in our component. The first thing we need to do is to register it in `providers` array; we can also register it in the component that will use it:

```
import {ListService} from "../list/list.service"

@NgModule({
 declarations: [
 AppComponent, ListComponent
 ],
 providers: [ListService],
 imports: [
 BrowserModule, FormsModule, HttpModule
 ],
 bootstrap: [AppComponent]
})
```

Also, register it in `ListComponent` class as shown in the following code:

```
import {Component, OnInit} from '@angular/core';
import {ListService} from './list.service'
import template from './list.component.html'

@Component({selector: 'list', template, providers: [ListService]}) //we can
register it here
export class ListComponent implements OnInit {
  constructor(private listService : ListService) {}
  list : Array <String>;
  getItems() : void {
this.listService.getListItems()
    .then(list => this.list = list)
  }
 ngOnInit() {
    this.getItems()
  }
}
```

A few things are happening here. We import the service as a regular module, then we inject it in `constructor` method where we create a local (private) `listService` variable of type `ListService`, which gives us an access to `ListService` class method(s). Then, we implement an interface (class) `OnInit` using TypeScript which implements keyword. The implementing interface will force us to define its members, in this case, `ngOnInit()` method; if we don't implement it, TypeScript will throw an error as expected.

The `ngOnInit()` life cycle hook will be called right after Angular checks all property bindings of the view, which makes it the best place to start fetching our data. When data is back from the service, we will assign it to the bound property list, which will render or re-render the data in the view. Let's see how we can list that data in our HTML:

```
<ul>
  <li *ngFor="let item of list">
 {{ item }}
  </li>
</ul>
```

The way we manipulate the DOM is one of the fundamental differences between Angular and React. In React, we bring the HTML to the JavaScript by creating virtual DOM; in Angular, we do exactly the opposite, we bring JavaScript to the HTML.

`*ngFor` is another directive that lets us loop through a list.

Test it out!

There is a handy cheat sheet published in the official Angular 2 documentation page, `https://angular.io/docs/ts/latest/guide/cheatsheet.html`; here, you can read about all the core features. Try adding the rest of the life cycle hooks to the components (you can list them with a comma, as follows: implements `OnInit`, `OnChanges`, and so on) and see when they are firing. If you are using Visual Studio Code as your editor, you can find a lot of information about the core classes and properties by holding the *Ctrl* key and hovering over the symbol with your mouse. You can also click on the symbol (while holding the *Ctrl* key), and the editor will take you to the definition of it.

Building the app

We will build an application that will demonstrate a few new technologies that can work well with Meteor. Initially, Meteor was a pretty opinionated framework, which is a good thing for many cases where we can speed up the development by removing the need of gluing or reinventing our own stack from scratch. As for the frontend views, we have a good option of using Angular 1-2, React, and Blaze; for a database, that is not the case. Considering that the whole reactiveness comes from the data on the wire, MongoDB paired with Minimongo is the only option that comes with Meteor. There is an experimental package that can integrate Meteor with SQL databases (PostgreSQL in particular), which doesn't seem to get a lot of traction in the community.

Instead of writing a whole bunch of libraries to support all kinds of databases, a better approach will be to have a unified query language that is completely unaware of the data source(s) and only describes the data that the frontend needs. In 2015, Facebook open sourced their internal query language GraphQL, which does exactly that. There is also a library called `Falcor` developed and open sourced by Netflix which is very similar to GraphQL.

How is this different from having the UI to describe what data needs and just call a REST Service or query a MongoDB collection with DDP?

The problem with these methods is that with REST, for example, we will expose one endpoint where we can request and fetch data from the database and return it to the client. When the app grows and we start having more and more components demanding for different sets of data, the number of REST endpoints will start growing too. We can say that we have them as nicely decoupled services, and each does one thing and it's working quite well. The problem is that with many trips to the server, the app performance will slow down especially if it runs on an unstable Internet connection--a mobile device, for example. With GraphQL, we can pack all the data into a single object and send it to the client in one round-trip.

Another benefit of using GraphQL over REST or DDP is that the data can be easily combined from many different sources. We can fetch many third-party web services or query multiple databases and have one object at the end.

Availability is another thing that we may want to consider. One way to minimize a data loss is by adding a distributed database that can hold critical for the application data replicated across different servers, data centers, and so on.

The following is a diagram of the app that we will build, which will demonstrate the preceding concepts:

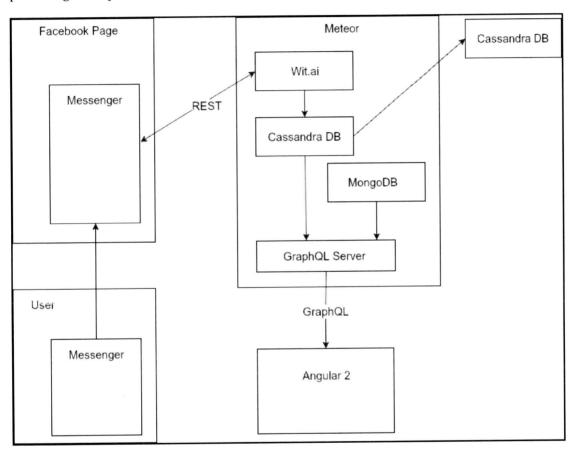

We have a user who will message with their Messenger app on our Facebook page. From there, our Meteor app will receive the messages and will maintain a conversation with our chatbot using `Wit.ai` framework. All the messages will be stored in the Cassandra database, which can be distributed across many servers. To demonstrate the concept of getting data from multiple data sources, some user information will be stored in MongoDB. Our web application will query the entire conversation from Cassandra and will also query the user's data from MongoDB. The important concept is that the client will get the returned results from both databases in one call to the server; the following diagram shows that data flow:

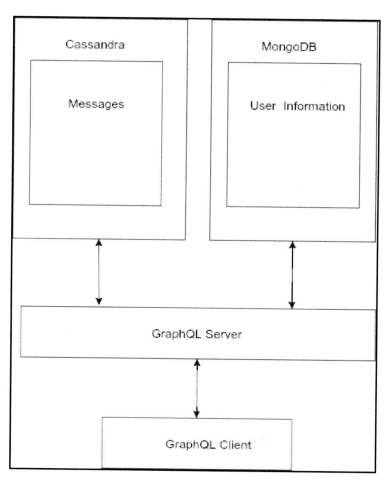

We can start with setting up the Facebook Messenger part first and then add pieces to the backend as we go. After we successfully connect to Messenger, we can start implementing the chatbot to take over the messages. The first thing we need is a Facebook page. If you don't have a Facebook page, go to `https://www.facebook.com/pages/create` and create one:

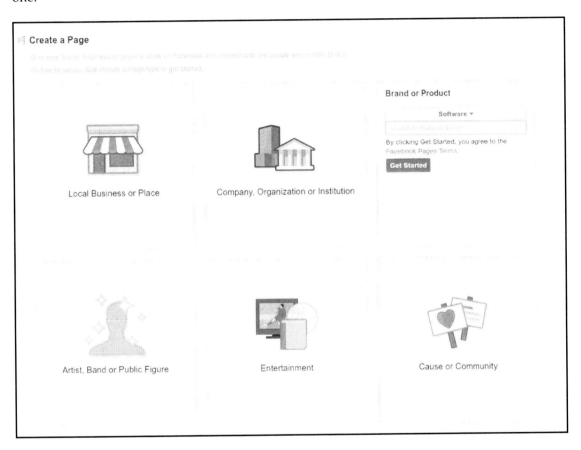

Our app will simulate a business that sells flowers, the users will be able to order flowers directly from the Messenger without installing any third-party apps. We can select **Brand or Product** option, then for the category, you can choose anything you like. A software category is fine since we are testing what we can do with the platform. For a product name, I named mine meteor-chat-bot; you can name yours anything you like. The next thing we need is to create a Facebook application. You can do this by going to `https://developers.facebook.com/quickstarts/?platform=web` as shown in the following figure:

After we enter the name of the app, we need to specify the app category; select **Apps for Messenger**:

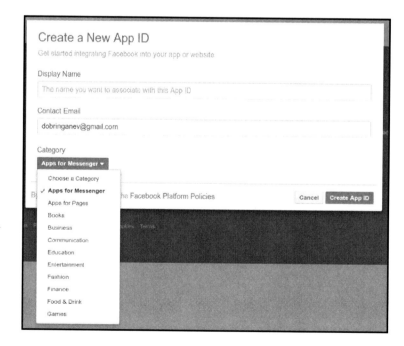

When the app is successfully created and our identity authenticated, we will be redirected to the dashboard of the app:

Here we need to do two things. Generate our **Page Access Token** and set up the **Webhooks**. Once we select a page from the drop-down, our token will be generated. Before we set up the **Webhooks**, we need to have our REST endpoints up and running in our Meteor app in order to talk with the Messenger and register our app.

In `server` folder in the Meteor app, create a folder called `fb_messages`. In that folder, we will add all the messaging logic. To keep the app a little bit more organized, create a file webhook.js, where we'll define the endpoint that Facebook needs.

For example, a typical REST endpoint looks like `http://localhost:3000/webhook`, which is basically a URL that accepts requests from the client. To expose that location to the client, we need to route it to the server in a similar way we did many times before using a client-side routing. For handling routing on the server, we can use a pretty simple-to-use package `meteor/meteorhacks:picker`:

```
>> meteor add meteorhacks:picker
```

To parse the body of each incoming request to a JSON object, we can use a middleware `body-parser`:

```
>> npm install body-parser
```

In `webhook.js` file, define the following function:

```
import {Picker} from 'meteor/meteorhacks:picker';
import bodyParser from 'body-parser';

const webhook = () => {
  Picker.middleware(bodyParser.json());
  const getRoutes = Picker.filter(function (req, res) {
    return req.method = "GET";
  });
  getRoutes.route('/webhook', (params, req, res, next) => {
    if (params.query['hub.verify_token'] ===
      'meteor_token_chatbot') {
      return res.end(params.query['hub.challenge']);
    }
  res.end('Validation failed, Verify token mismatch');
  });
}
export default webhook;
```

From top to bottom, we have imported `Picker` and added `bodyParser` middleware. To get this endpoint to accept only GET requests, we can filter the incoming requests using the Picker.filter function, where we can specify the method type in the callback.

In the next line, we will define our route as /webhook, which will make that endpoint available as `http://localhost:3000/webhook` on the client. In the body of the router function, we compare a token sent from Facebook with our token; if they match, we send back a response with the value of the parameter `hub.challenge`. If they don't match, we respond with an error message.

Create an `index.js` file in the `fb_messages` folder, and import/export the `webhook.js` module. Then, import it in our `main.js` module:

```
import {Meteor} from 'meteor/meteor';
import {webhook} from './fb_messages'
Meteor.startup(() => {
webhook();
});
```

If everything compiles correctly, browsing the `http://localhost:3000/webhook` should return the response (**Validation failed, Verify token mismatch**) from the server, which means the endpoint is alive but the request didn't come from the right source.

The next thing we need is to register our **webhook** URL and the
token (`meteor_token_chatbot`) in our Facebook app. You can and you should have
your own token that only your Meteor app and the Facebook app know about.

Going back to the Facebook app dashboard, let's set up the webhook:

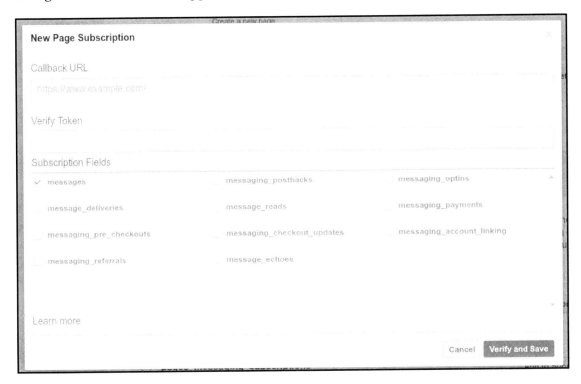

We serve our app locally and localhost or IP with a port will not work. We need to provide
a webhook URL as a secure HTTP which is HTTPS. To keep developing and prototyping
without having our app hosted somewhere with HTTPS, we can tunnel our localhost to
HTTPS address using a handy tool, **ngrok.**

You can download it from `https://ngrok.com/`. Once you've downloaded it, unzip it in
any location and open the terminal in that location. To start the tunnel, execute the
following command:

```
>> ./ngrok http 3000
```

Since our Meteor app runs on port 3000, it will create a tunnel on that port. You should see something like this in your terminal:

```
ngrok by @inconshreveable                                              (Ctrl+C to quit)

Session Status                online
Version                       2.1.18
Region                        United States (us)
Web Interface                 http://127.0.0.1:4040
Forwarding                    http://2dc40bc0.ngrok.io -> localhost:3000
Forwarding                    https://2dc40bc0.ngrok.io -> localhost:3000

Connections                   ttl     opn     rt1     rt5     p50     p90
                              6       1       0.02    0.01    126.32  126.77

HTTP Requests
-------------

GET /app/105605e340215f065547d888ee0cc2c5816eb8a7.map    200 OK
GET /packages/8024f6bce97bd768bcff7fc9d76449e74f051e36.m 200 OK
GET /packages/9651dba61aa212828975b89e7c889af540c6a5da.m 200 OK
GET /packages/8645fc685d558a15e6207c847f5709d20f6a14d9.m 200 OK
GET /packages/90f037f47abee1e74ba80360e6b3f3dbaa792260.m 200 OK
GET /packages/a3be1ee923a6fc933f063c7f8de3e15243e12f47.m 200 OK
GET /sockjs/939/bvwfs7hk/websocket                       101 Switching Protocols
GET /favicon.ico                                         404 Not Found
GET /sockjs/info                                         200 OK
```

This tool comes with a very nice web interface at http://127.0.0.1:4040, where we can see all kinds of information of the requests made in and out in our app.

Our HTTPS tunneling to our localhost:3000 should look something like this:

```
Forwarding https://2dc40bc0.ngrok.io -> localhost:3000
```

It is randomly generated, and your URL will be different from the preceding.

Going back to the webhook setup page, enter the
endpoint `https://2dc40bc0.ngrok.io/webhook` in the **Callback URL** field and the
token from our Meteor app **meteor_token_chatbot**. For the **Subscription Fields**, select
messages:

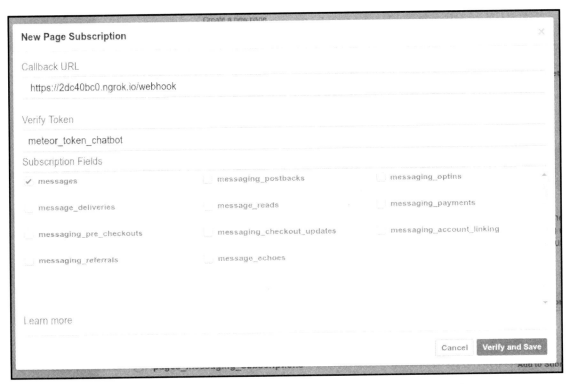

If everything is correctly added, clicking on the `Verify and Save` button should close that
form, if not an error message will be shown on the first field. If you get an error, try
verifying the endpoint and the token and keep in mind that your Meteor app and ngrok
should be both running, and if you restart ngrok, a new tunnel with a new HTTPS URL will
be created.

You can also go to ngrok's web interface, and check the request made by Facebook:

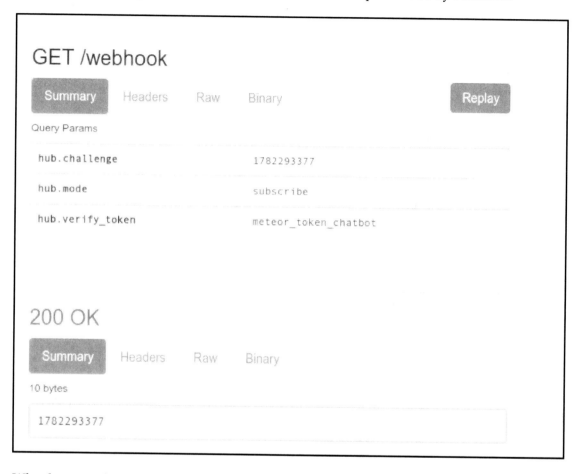

What happened is that Facebook sent us both the challenge (hb.challenge) and the token that we specified in the form. When we sent back the challenge, the Facebook app validated it and verified our webhook.

One last step we need to do is to subscribe the webhook to our page events:

In the **Webhooks** panel on the dashboard, select your page from the drop-down and click on **Subscribe**.

The next thing we need is to verify that we can receive the messages from the Messenger in our Meteor app. We will receive the messages as posts (POST). The way Facebook posts them is not compatible with our Picker post filter, and we need to use it directly without a filter. In the same webhook.js file, let's add that endpoint:

```
Picker.route('/webhook/', (params, req, res, next) => {
    console.log(req.body);
res.statusCode = 200;
res.end('200 test');
});
```

Note here that we need to respond with **200 OK HTTP**, otherwise the webhook will be unsubscribed from the platform. To test it go to your personal Facebook page and message to the page that we just created. The response should look something like that in the ngrok web UI:

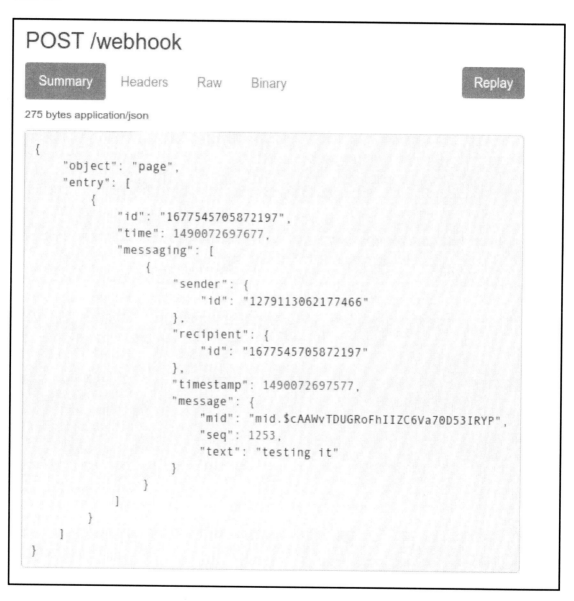

```
POST /webhook

  Summary    Headers    Raw    Binary                          Replay

275 bytes application/json

{
    "object": "page",
    "entry": [
        {
            "id": "1677545705872197",
            "time": 1490072697677,
            "messaging": [
                {
                    "sender": {
                        "id": "1279113062177466"
                    },
                    "recipient": {
                        "id": "1677545705872197"
                    },
                    "timestamp": 1490072697577,
                    "message": {
                        "mid": "mid.$cAAWvTDUGRoFhIIZC6Va70D53IRYP",
                        "seq": 1253,
                        "text": "testing it"
                    }
                }
            ]
        }
    ]
}
```

Now, we can receive the messages; the next thing we want to do is send some data back to the sender. For that, we need two things--a way to post messages from the backend of our app and also have the **Page Access Token** as a parameter passed with the post.

For the HTTP requests API, you can use any library that can do XMLHttpRequest from the server. For this demo, we can post the requests with a newer library node-fetch and also with one of the most popular one, request; let's try both of them:

```
>> npm install node-fetch --save
>> npm install request --save
```

To post messages from our Meteor app, we need to pass the following four parameters in our request:

- We need the REST endpoint with which we will accept our requests.
- A Facebook Page Token, that is, the token that our Facebook App will use to authenticate from where the request is coming.
- We need a recipient in our request. There can be many users chatting with our chatbot, and we need to respond to the sender only.
- The actual message that we want to send. It will be an object message with a key text and the actual text of the message as the value.

From the incoming messages, we can get the sender ID (the ID of the person who sent us the message), which will be our recipient in our post request:

```
"messaging": [
{
"sender": {
    "id": "1279113062177466"
  },
    "recipient": {
    "id": "1677545705872197"
  },
   "timestamp": 1490160662463,
  "message": {
      "mid": "mid.$cAAWvTDUGRoFhJcR_v1a9H83ZJMRd",
      "seq": 1480,
  "text": "Hello"
        }
    }
 ]
```

Here is the request in the following code:

```
Picker.route('/webhook/', (params, req, res, next) => {
    let sender_id =
      req.body.entry[0].messaging[0].sender.id
      request({
  url:
            'https://graph.facebook.com/v2.6/me/messages',
  qs: {
  access_token: process.env.FB_PAGE_TOKEN
            },
    method: 'POST',
    json: {
  recipient: {
          id: sender_id
        },
    message: {
        text: 'Hello from Meteor app'
        }
      }
    }, (error, response) => {
        res.statusCode = 200;
  res.end('200')
            });
    });
```

The first thing we need is to get the sender ID, which we parse from `entry` array. Then, we add the endpoint URL (`https://graph.facebook.com/v2.6/me/messages`) to our request, and for the **query string (qs)**, we pass our Facebook Page Token.

The best practice is to have all your secret tokens in an environment file, then export and load them when the server boots. For example, the tokens are declared in `env.js` file:

```
process.env['FB_PAGE_TOKEN'] ='your token...'
```

The token can be loaded in `main.js` with `require('./env')`, which will make it available as `process.env.FB_PAGE_TOKEN`.

The next thing we specify is the type of the request (method `POST`); for the recipient, we have our sender's ID, and for the `message` object, we add a simple test value to the key `text`.

Now, our Meteor app will respond with `Hello from Meteor app` to anyone who sends a message to our Facebook Page.

We can do the previous request in a very similar way with a node-fetch module:

```
const body = JSON.stringify({
  recipient: {
    id: sender_id
  },
  message: {
    text: 'Hello from Meteor App'
  }
});
const qs = 'access_token=' +
encodeURIComponent(process.env.FB_PAGE_TOKEN);
fetch('https://graph.facebook.com/me/messages?' + qs, {
    method: 'POST',
    headers: {
      'Content-Type': 'application/json'
    },
  body
}).then(() => {
    res.statusCode = 200;
    res.end('200')
})
```

We create a body of the request (**stringified JSON**) with the recipient and the message. The qs is almost the same as the previous example; at the end, we call the method fetch with all the parameters.

Facebook recommends our endpoints to return, as soon as possible, a response **200 OK**. Even before sending the message, we can post another request with an action instead of a message.

Try posting another request just before sending the message with this action sender_action: 'typing_on'. This will appear in the chat window like our app is typing the response:

```
const body = JSON.stringify({
  recipient: {
    id: sender_id
  },
    sender_action: 'typing_on'
});
```

Now, we have the messages in and out from the Messenger and our Meteor app; the next thing we need is to add the chatbot API to handle the conversation.

Once you log in to Wit.ai, you can go to `https://wit.ai/apps/new` and create an app:

When the app is created, the browser will redirect you to the main app dashboard. Clicking on the settings button will load the app settings. In there, you can find the **API Details** and your **Server Access Token**:

API Details

You can use the tokens below to start making API requests from your app. Learn more through the quickstart guide, or contact us at anytime. We look forward to what you create :)

App ID	58d35b52-c95b-4ed1-9c08-96e238029861
Server Access Token	S5BVJJZXG2A67KMFBWC7WHYNTA3PY3CZ
Client Access Token	
Allowed domains	</> Add a new domain name to this app...

No items!

Copy that token and create it in your `env.js` file as another token key, `process.env['WIT_TOKEN'] = 'wit  token..'`.

Training the bot

How will this bot know what to respond to our users?

There are two main types of machine learning algorithms, supervised, and unsupervised. The most common one is the supervised machine learning. It means that **we** feed a learning algorithm with sets of questions and answers, and after some type of learning processing, the algorithm will produce a trained model that will be able to predict the best possible answers for any unique questions that we ask.

Here is a very basic example that describes the idea of supervised learning:

Let's say we have a dataset of houses that have the size of the house in sqft for a question and the price of every house for an answer. If you plot the data on the x and y axis, it may look something like this:

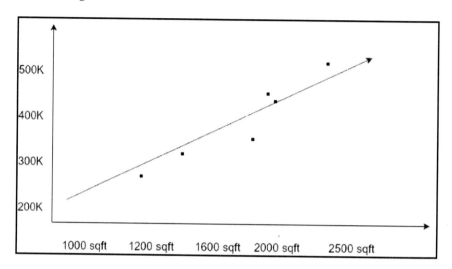

What we are trying to do is draw that third line that represents the trend of the data. If a new question is asked, for example, **How much would be the cost of a house if it is 2300 sqft?** (2300 sqft is not in our dataset). Of course, this is a very simple question to answer by just looking at the graph, and we don't really need a learning algorithm to predict that value. In real life, estimating house prices will require way more data than just the size. For example, location, number of bedrooms/bathrooms, condition, age, current sales of similar properties, and so on. The data becomes multidimensional (we can't plot it on the x and y axis only), and we need to implement sophisticated algorithms and let the machines do the heavy computations and build models from the training data provided by us.

To train our chatbot, we will do a very similar thing. We will add examples (questions) of conversations and we will validate them (giving the answers) to the algorithm. Open the dashboard in our Wit.ai app, and click on the **Understanding** tab:

To start a simple training of the chatbot, let's enter some samples and try mocking up a conversation between a buyer and an online store that sells flowers. In **User says...** field, enter the following example:

Wit.ai comes with many predefined entities, but for now, we need a specific entity called intent. Enter `intent` in the **Add a new entity** field. You can double-click on the word **bouquet**, and the value of the intent will be populated automatically. The final result should look something like this:

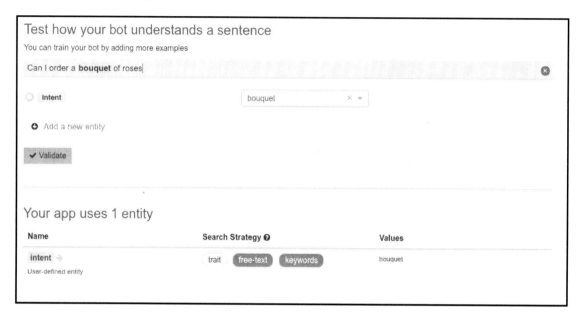

Now, we have the **intent** of the user as a **bouquet**; from here, we can add types of bouquets that we may have in the store. The sentence already has roses as a type. Let's see how we can add more keywords to the bouquet intent:

In the **Add a new entity** field, add the word `bouquet`, and add `roses` for the value:

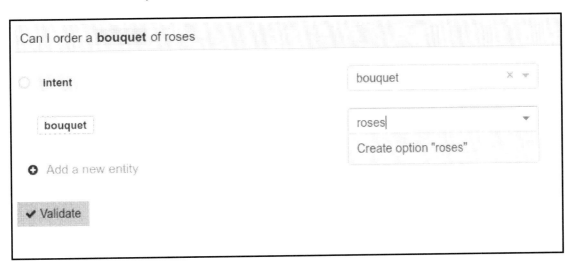

To improve the understanding of the chatbot, we need to provide as many questions and answers. For example, the user can say **A bouquet of roses please.** If you try that, you will see that after a search, we will find the correct intent bouquet and the correct entity **bouquet** with the value **roses**. By clicking on **Validate**, we add more variation to our dataset and make our bot understand more.

Now, we have only one type of bouquet, that is, **roses**:

Clicking on 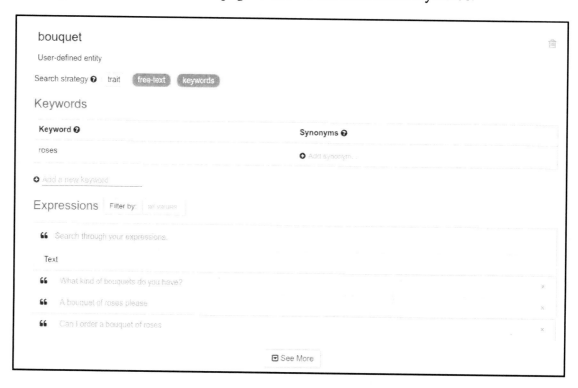 bouquet will load a page where we can enter more **keywords**:

bouquet

User-defined entity

Search strategy ❓   trait   free-text   keywords

Keywords

Keyword ❓	Synonyms ❓
roses	➕ Add synonym...

➕ Add a new keyword

Expressions   Filter by: all values

❝   Search through your expressions.

Text

❝   What kind of bouquets do you have?   ×

❝   A bouquet of roses please   ×

❝   Can I order a bouquet of roses   ×

⊡ See More

For a search strategy, select **free-text** and **keywords**, and for testing, we can add a few more keywords such as `tulips` and `lilies`. After we enter the new keywords, we can go back to **Understanding** tab and start asking a different variety of questions and validating the responses.

To make it a little more realistic, our bot should ask a question and persist the answers from the user. For example, our store can have different sizes of bouquets: `classic`, `deluxe`, and `grand`.

By repeating the previous steps, create a new entity `bouquetSize` with the three keywords, that is, `classic`, `deluxe`, and `grand`. It should look as in the following screenshot:

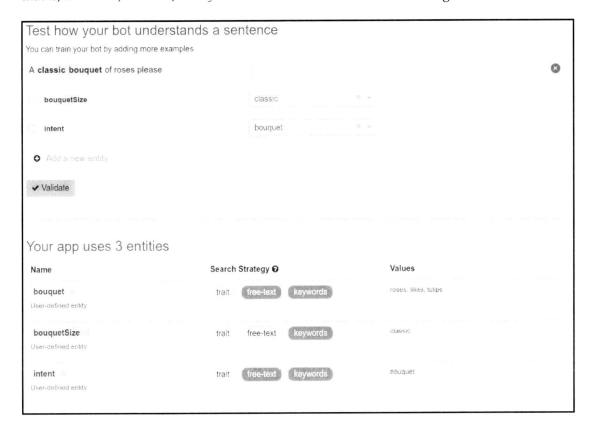

The next thing we need is to create a **story** and train the chatbot with different scenarios of **User says** and what the bot will reply, **Bot sends**. We can also execute functions based on the user response with **Bot Executes**. Click on the **stories** tab and then click on the **Create a story** button. For the **User says**, you can have something like **Can I order a bouquet** and for the bot sends, something like **We have roses, lilies, and tulips. Which bouquet would you like to order?**

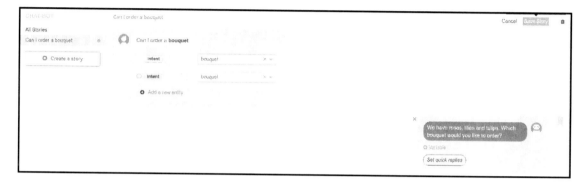

On the bot's reply, we can also set a **quick replies** button, so the user can just click on them instead of typing a response, which can reduce the typos and make the handling of responses easier:

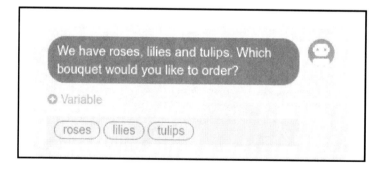

Note that the responses should match our keywords. The next step is the response from the user:

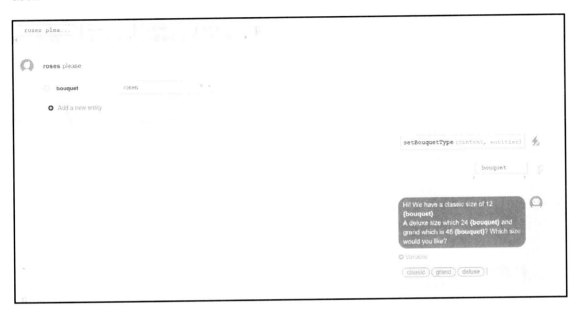

Going back to the bot reply, we can execute an action before the actual reply. Click on the **Bot executes** icon to create a function:

If we want to persist the user response, we can create a `setBouquetType` function (we will see how we can use it later in our Meteor app) that can map the context with the key bouquet with one of the keywords, `roses`, `lilies`, or `tulips`.

After we persisted the response, we reply with the following message:

Hi! We have a classic size of 12 {bouquet}. A deluxe size which is 24 {bouquet} and grand which is 48 {bouquet}? Which size would you like?

With the curly bracket notation { }, we can add variables to our response. You can type them or click on the **+Variable** button, which can add a variable in the template.

To recap the last step, we have set the type of the bouquet (adding a function that the bot will execute) and responded with a question of what size of bouquet the user wants. In the next step, we will do exactly the same thing; we will have the response from the user, then the bot will execute a function to persist that response and will respond back:

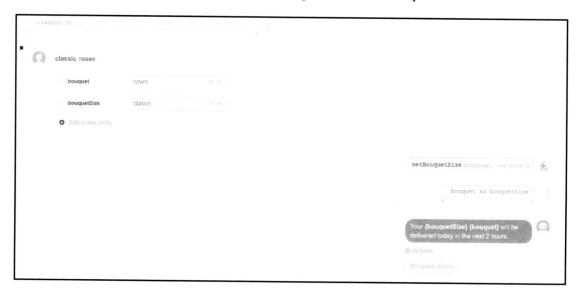

We create a `setBouquetSize` function, which will persist the size of the bouquet and also the type of the bouquet. Note that we are setting a `bouquet && bouquetSize` condition, which means both values should be provided by the user's response. This also means that if the user does not provide both values, the bot will not continue until this condition is met. If they type `classic roses` as shown in the preceding screenshot, we will persist both keys, `bouquet` and the `bouquetSize`, with the corresponded values.

To test all of the preceding actions, you can click on:

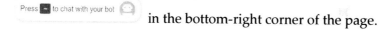 in the bottom-right corner of the page.

In the chat window, we can simulate the conversation by clicking and verifying the variables on all execution functions:

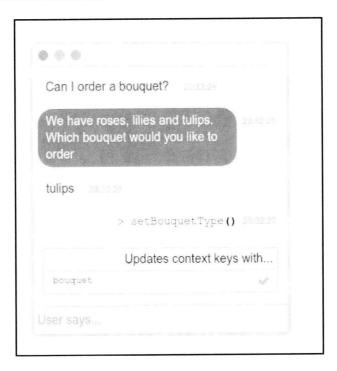

Our next step is to add this functionality in our Meteor app and have the bot respond to all incoming messages.

Moving the chatbot to the Meteor app

There is Node.js SDK with an npm module for Wit.ai app that we need to install:

```
>> npm install --save node-wit
```

In the GitHub repository of the SDK, there are a few examples, and one of them is the usage of the API with the Messenger. What we can do is grab that example and use it as a base for our app. The link to the examples is https://github.com/wit-ai/node-wit/tree/master/examples.

On the server in the `fb_messages` folder, create `bot.js` and `fb_messages.js` files:

Let's start from the `fb_message.js` file. We will create a simple function that will get the id of the recipient for parameters and the text we want to send. It is almost identical to the function we used to send direct messages from Meteor to Messenger:

```
import fetch from 'node-fetch'
 export const fb_message = (id, text) => {
    const body = JSON.stringify({recipient: {
        id
        }, message: {
            text
    }});
        const qs = 'access_token=' +
encodeURIComponent(process.env.FB_PAGE_TOKEN);
        return fetch('https://graph.facebook.com/me/messages?' + qs, {
        method: 'POST',
       headers: {
            'Content-Type': 'application/json'
        },
       body
    })
    .then(rsp => rsp.json())
    .then(json => {
     if (json.error && json.error.message) {
        throw new Error(json.error.message);
      }
     return json;
    });
  };
```

In our `bot.js` file, let's start with the definition of the webhook endpoint:

```
Picker.route('/webhook/', (params, req, res, next) => {
    const data = req.body;
    if (data.object === 'page') {
        data.entry.forEach(entry => {
            entry.messaging.forEach(event => {
                if (event.message && !event.message.is_echo) {
    const sender = event.sender.id;
const sessionId =
                    findOrCreateSession(sender);
    const {text, attachments} =
                    event.message;
            if (attachments) {
                fb_message(sender, 'Sorry I can only
                    process text messages for
                    now.').catch(console.error);
} else if (text) {
wit.runActions(sessionId, text,
        sessions[sessionId].context)
            .then((context) => {
                console.log('Waiting for next user
                    messages');
                sessions[sessionId].context = context;
            }).catch((err) => {
                console.error('Oops! Got an error from Wit: ',
                    err);
            })
        }
        } else {
        console.log('received event',
            JSON.stringify(event));
        }
        });
    });
    }
    res.statusCode = 200;
    res.end('200 OK');
});
```

From the body of the request, we get entry and the messaging, which are both arrays. We will loop through both of them to get every Sender-ID and the text message. We also check for attachments, and if the user sent us an attachment, we respond with some generic error message. The findOrCreateSession function does exactly what the name of the function says. If there is a new user, we persist it in an object session; if there is an already persisted user, we return that session ID. Here is the function:

```
const findOrCreateSession = (fbid) => {
  let sessionId;
    Object.keys(sessions).forEach(k => {
        if (sessions[k].fbid === fbid) {
            sessionId = k;
          }
      });
    if (!sessionId) {
        sessionId = new Date().toISOString();
        sessions[sessionId] = {
        fbid: fbid,
        context: {}
      };
    }
  return sessionId;
};
```

Once we have a user ID and the text of the message, we execute the wit.runActions function:

```
wit.runActions(sessionId, text, sessions[sessionId].context).then((context)
=> {
    sessions[sessionId].context = context;
})
```

In that function, we pass the session ID, the text message, and the context. When the function executes, we will resolve a new context that we persist in our sessions object.

The last thing we need is to configure the SDK to talk with our Wit.ai application:

```
const Wit = require('node-wit').Wit;

const actions = {
send(request, response) {
      const {sessionId} = request;
      const {text, quickreplies} = response;
      const recipientId = sessions[sessionId].fbid;
    if (recipientId) {
      return fb_message(recipientId, text).then(() =>
        null).catch((err) => {
```

```
                console.error(err.stack || err);
          });
        } else {
          return Promise.resolve()
        }
    },
  setBouquetType({context, entities}) {
        return new Promise((resolve, reject) => {
    return resolve(context);
        });
    },
  setBouquetSize({context, entities}) {
          return new Promise((resolve, reject) => {
      return resolve(context);
        });
    }
  };
  const wit = new Wit({accessToken: process.env.WIT_TOKEN,
      actions});
```

To configure Wit, we provide the Server Access Token (which we defined in the env.js file) and object actions. In actions, we have three methods, send, setBouquetType, and setBouquetSize. Both setBouquetType and setBouquetSize are defined by us when we create the story.

The setBouquetType in our story is as shown in the following figure:

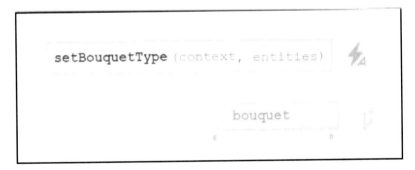

And the `setBouquetSize` is as shown in the following figure:

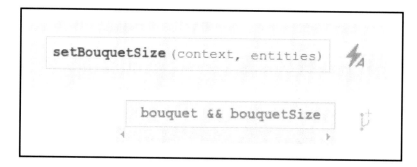

The `send()` method takes two parameters, the request and the response, both injected by the `wit.runActions` execution. When the recipient is found in the sessions object, we send a message by calling the `fb_message` function; if there is no recipient, we just resolve the `Promise`.

That is all we need to have a chatbot responding to our users.

Test it out and improve it!

A lot can be done on the chatbot side. We can add more variety of training data and make it a lot smarter than it is now. Keep in mind that we are not completely training the algorithm from scratch, and it is probably already pre-trained, and we may not need to provide thousands of data samples in order to get good results.

On the Meteor side, we can create a better session store than holding the user ID in an object, we can use more robust and scalable solutions, such as a **Redis**. Also, we can send messages with the quick replies buttons that we have defined in the story. We can add them in `message` object:

```
    const body = JSON.stringify({recipient: {
            id
        }, message: {
            text,
    quick_replies
        }
      }
);
```

The format of the object looks like this:

```
"quick_replies":[
    {
      "content_type":"text",
      "title":"classic",
      "payload":"some payload"
    },
    {
     "content_type":"text",
     "title":"deluxe",
     "payload":"some payload"
    }
  ...
  ]
```

Also, we could have a simple function that could build the buttons in a loop:

```
const quick_replies = (quickreplies) => {
    let q_replies = [];
        for (let i = 0; i < quickreplies.length; i++) {
            q_replies.push({"content_type": "text", "title": quickreplies[i],
"payload": 'none'})
        }
    return q_replies;
}
```

The next step is to persist all the messages in the Cassandra database.

Adding Cassandra to our stack

Apache Cassandra is another technology developed by Facebook and open sourced in 2008. It is known as one of the most performant distributed databases in the world. It is also a NoSQL database, like MongoDB, but very different in every aspect. The data is stored in columns and rows rather than JSON documents. Columns can be dynamically added, removed, or renamed, and by default, we can have up to 2 billion columns per row (also referred to as wide column store database). Another big difference with MongoDB is that Cassandra has no single point of failure. It means that it is masterless by architecture. The data can be distributed across many machines, and if one machine goes down, it will not affect the availability of the data.

To install Cassandra, open your terminal and execute the following commands:

```
>> echo "deb http://www.apache.org/dist/cassandra/debian 310x main" | sudo
tee -a /etc/apt/sources.list.d/cassandra.sources.list

>> curl https://www.apache.org/dist/cassandra/KEYS | sudo apt-key add -
>> sudo apt-get update
>> sudo apt-get install cassandra
```

Cassandra is installed as a service, and we can verify that it is running with the following command:

```
>> sudo service cassandra status
```

To execute queries against the database, Cassandra has its own query language called **Cassandra Query Language** (CQL). It is very close to the classic SQL, and if you have some basic SQL skills, learning CQL should be a non-trivial task. It also comes with a shell where we can execute the queries. Open the terminal and launch the shell:

```
>> cd /bin
>> cqlsh
```

Once the shell is started, you should see something like this:

```
Connected to Test Cluster at 127.0.0.1:9042.
[cqlsh 5.0.1 | Cassandra 3.10 | CQL spec 3.4.4 | Native protocol v4]
Use HELP for help.
cqlsh>
```

By default, it listens on localhost on port `9042`.

 Note that it internally uses more ports than the shown previously.

In Cassandra, the databases are called **keyspaces**. To see all keyspaces, execute the `describe` command:

```
sqlsh> describe keyspaces;
```

Usually, we will have one keyspace (one database) for the entire application. Let's create one called `fb_messages`:

```
sqlsh> create keyspace fb_messages
with replication = { 'class' : 'SimpleStrategy', 'replication_factor' : 3
};
```

We are running Cassandra on a single node, and for now, creating a keyspace with the previous replication settings will suffice for our demo. If we move our app to production and distribute it on multiple servers, we will have to use a proper replication strategy.

Contrary to **Relational Database Management Systems (RDBMS)**, Cassandra does not support table joins, and data modeling can be tricky to understand at first and it's out of the scope of this book. Without going into too much detail, we can layout the following statements to understand the basics needed for our app:

In Cassandra, we store the data in tables and every table must have a unique primary key.

The primary key can be as simple as one column or as complex as consisting of two or more columns.

To visualize the preceding statements, we can describe our table like this:

```
CREATE TABLE messages (
recipient_id text,
timestamp timestamp,
 message text,
 bot_response text,
 PRIMARY KEY (recipient_id, timestamp)
);
```

Here, we created a table called messages with four columns recipient_id (the user id), timestamp (a field to guarantee the uniqueness of each insert), message (the actual text of the message), and the response from the chatbot as bot_response. For the primary key, we have two parameters, recipient_id and timestamp. The first parameter is called a partition key, and it's extremely important in Cassandra. It has a lot of complex logic behind it, and it is all related to the location of that particular record. The second column, timestamp, is something called clustering column, and it's related to the order of the data in that location. What makes Cassandra extremely fast is that we know exactly where the data is by querying by the partition key. That said, to achieve the highest performance, we need to provide the partition key in all our queries, otherwise we will scan the entire table to find the result. This, in distributed database, means scanning every node in the cluster.

Let's create our table and perform some queries to see how querying data works. To switch to a certain keyspace, we use the following command:

```
sqlsh> use fb_messages;
```

Once we switch to the `fb_messages` keyspace, we can copy and paste the `create table` statement and execute it.

Let's insert some test data and perform basic queries:

```
INSERT INTO messages(recipient_id,timestamp, message, bot_response)
VALUES ('1677545705872197','1490574231364','can I order a bouquet of
roses','We have roses, lilies and tulips. Which bouquet would you like to
order');
```

Simply, select queries as shown in the following code:

```
select * from messages;
select * from messages where recipient_id
  ='1677545705872197';
select * from messages where recipient_id
  ='1677545705872197' and timestamp = '1490574231364';
select * from messages where timestamp = '1490574231364' ALLOW FILTERING;
select * from messages where timestamp = '1490574231364' ALLOW FILTERING;
select * from messages where message = 'can I order a
  bouquet of roses' ALLOW FILTERING;
```

In the last three queries, we didn't provide the partition key `recipient_id` and that resulted in filtering all the data. If we don't add the `ALLOW FILTERING` statement, the query will return an error, which is pretty self-explanatory:

```
InvalidRequest: Error from server: code=2200 [Invalid query]
message="Cannot execute this query as it might involve data filtering and
thus may have unpredictable performance. If you want to execute this query
despite the performance unpredictability, use ALLOW FILTERING"
```

The next step is to connect to Cassandra from our Meteor app. As with any modern database, it has an official well-supported Node.js driver:

```
>> npm install cassandra-driver --save
```

In the server folder, create a folder `cassandra` with the `index.js` file:

In the `index.js` file, add the following code:

```
const cassandra = require('cassandra-driver');
const client = new cassandra.Client({contactPoints: ['127.0.0.1'],
keyspace: 'fb_messages'});

const query = 'select * from messages where recipient_id
  =?';
client.execute(query, ['1677545705872197']).then(result =>
  console.log(result.rows));
```

We imported the driver and created a client pool, which will manage all the connections to the database for us. In the config of the client pool, we specified `contactPoints` parameter, an array of IPs of all Cassandra nodes (ours has only one and runs on localhost) and the keyspace is the database to which we want to connect.

With a question mark, **?**, in the qs, we can map the parameters of the query. To execute them, we use `client.execute`, a function that returns `Promise` that we resolve with the returned result from the query.

In the same file, we can create a simple function that can insert messages from the user and the chatbot:

```
export const insert_message = (params) => {
  const {recipient_id, timestamp, message, bot_response} = params;
  const query = `insert into messages
                  (recipient_id, timestamp, message,
                    bot_response)
                  values (?,?,?,?);`;
  client.execute(query, [recipient_id, timestamp,
      message, bot_response])
          .then(result => console.log(result))
          .catch(err => {
          console.log(err)
  });
};
```

In `bot.js` file, we import `insert_message` function and execute it in `send()` method defined in the Wit.ai app actions:

```
send(request, response) {
   const {sessionId} = request;
   const {text, quickreplies} = response;
   const recipientId = sessions[sessionId].fbid;
   if (recipientId) {
     return fb_message(recipientId, text,
       quickreplies).then(() =>
       insert_message({ recipient_id:recipientId,
```

```
                timestamp: new Date(),
                    message: request.text,
   bot_response:text}))).catch((err) => {
                console.error(err);
           });
       } else {
          return Promise.resolve()
       }
   },
```

From `request` parameter, we get the user's message and the chatbot message from `response`, then on the callback of `fb_message` (the message was sent without errors), we insert them into the database.

That is all we need to have all our messages persisted in Cassandra. Our next step is to add GraphQL to our stack and fetch all the data from the client.

Adding GraphQL to the stack

We need to add two components to import GraphQL into our app. We need a client GraphQL library and a GraphQL server. Although it is a pretty new technology, there are quite a few options for GraphQL server and client already. There is a list of JavaScript client and server libraries at `https://github.com/chentsulin/awesome-graphql#lib-js`. For this demo, we will use Apollo client. Apollo is an open source GraphQL client and server developed by the Meteor team (Meteor Development Group).

To install all the libraries, we need to execute the following commands:

```
>> meteor add apollo
>> npm install apollo-client --save
>> npm install graphql-server-express --save
>> npm install express --save
>> npm install graphql --save
>> npm install graphql-tools --save
```

The main component of GraphQL is the schema. The schema is the description of the data model as it is in every database, and as in every database schema, we specify the type of each field. With GraphQL, we have a lot of flexibility for expressing our model using basic types (scalars) as `int`, `string`, `float`, `boolean`, `id`, and also user-defined custom JSON-like objects. The most important type of the schema is the Query type, and every GraphQL schema **must** include a Query type.

To get an idea of how all this works, let's create a GraphQL schema by mocking our Cassandra table. Once we have done the schema definition, we can perform simple queries from the client (browser).

Create a folder on the server called **api** with a file schema.js:

The first thing we need is to define the fields and their types:

```
export const typDefs = [`
  type User {
  ricepient_id: String
  timestamp: String
  message:String
  bot_response: String
  }
  type Query {
    messages(ricepient_id: String): User
  }
  schema {
  query: Query
  }
`];
```

In the schema, we defined two types, the Query and User type. The User object is a custom type, which is basically a copy of the fields of our Cassandra table (messages). All fields in the User type are defined as strings. Currently, GraphQL does not have Date type or timestamp and we defined timestamp as String.

In Query type, we specify a function messages, which is a special function called resolver. Each Query must have resolver function to all the fields that we need to query. In our case, the resolver messages will resolve to User type, which has all the fields that we need to return to the client. The last thing we specify in the schema definition is the schema object with the key query and Query type for value.

Now, we have defined the schema and the types; the next thing we need is to define at least one Query with resolver function:

```
export const resolvers = {
  Query: {
    messages: (obj, args, context, info) => {
      return {
recipient_id: args.recipient_id,
        timestamp: '1490574231364',
        message: 'can I order a bouquet of roses',
        bot_response: 'We have roses, lilies and tulips. Which bouquet
would you like to order'
};
      }
    }
  }
```

In resolvers object, we define a Query object with messages function. One thing to remember is that parameters of every resolver are positioned and args is the second one. For now, to quickly test the queries, we can just return hardcoded data to the client.

The next step is to wire up the Apollo server with the schema and the resolvers that we just defined.

In main.js file, import the required packages and create the Apollo server:

```
import {createApolloServer} from 'meteor/apollo';
import {makeExecutableSchema} from 'graphql-tools';
import {typeDefs, resolvers} from './api/schema';
const schema = makeExecutableSchema({typeDefs, resolvers});
createApolloServer({schema});
```

That is all we need to have GraphQL server running in our Meteor app. At this point, even without having the client side of the app ready, we can do queries directly from the browser using a very useful in-browser IDE. To launch the editor, go to `http://localhost:3000/graphiql`. Note that the link is with character (i) GraphIQL. The editor has three columns, a query input, a result (the middle pane), and a Documentation Explorer:

In the first window, enter the following query:

```
query{
messages(recipient_id: "1279113062177466") {
      ricepient_id
      timestamp
      message
      bot_response
   }
}
```

To execute the query, we call the resolver function `messages` by passing the recipient ID as an argument. In the body of the query, we specify the fields that we want the query to return.

From the previous steps, we know how we can create a schema, a custom types, and resolver functions; our next step is to see how we can have multiple resolvers getting data from different sources.

To make it a little bit more realistic, we can have two resolvers called asynchronously. First, let's create another type called `UserAccount`, which will return user account information:

```
type UserAccount {
    recipient_id: String
    email: String
    address: String
    credit_card_info: String
}
type Query {
    messages(recipient_id: String): User
    user_account(recipient_id: String): UserAccount
}
```

In `UserAccount`, we defined a few account-related fields (`recipient_id`, e-mail, address, `credit_card_info`). In the Query type, we added another resolver `user_account`, which resolves to `UserAccount` type.

In the same file, let's create two async functions that will resolve our mock-up data:

```
const get_messages = (recipient_id) => {
    return new Promise(resolve => {
        setTimeout(() => resolve({
recipient_id: recipient_id,
timestamp: '1490574231364',
message: 'can I order a bouquet of roses',
bot_response: 'We have roses, lilies and tulips.
        Which bouquet would you like to order'}), 2000);
    });
}
const get_user_account = (recipient_id) => {
    return new Promise(resolve => {
        setTimeout(() => resolve({
recipient_id: recipient_id,
email: 'user@gmail.com',
address: 'street one',
credit_card_info: 'some card number'}), 1000);
    });
}
```

To mock up the idea of getting a data from two sources in one round trip to the server, we set up different timeouts on both functions. The first one will be resolved after 2 seconds and the second one after 1 second.

In the resolver functions, we return those async functions:

```
Query: {
        messages: (obj, args, context, info) => {
          return get_messages(args.recipient_id).then((res) => res);
      },
        user_account: (obj, args, context, info) => {
          return get_user_account(args.recipient_id).then((res) =>
  res);
      }
  }
```

In the IDE, our query and result should look like this:

The next step is to query Cassandra and get the data from the database. In the database, we will have many messages per user. Currently, our schema and the resolver return a single object User. To convert that to an array, all we have to do is define the type of the resolver as an array **[User]**:

```
user_messages(recipient_id: String): [User]
```

In the `cassandra` folder on the server, in `index.js` file, let's create a function that will query the database by the recipient ID:

```
export const get_messages_by_id = (params) => {
    const {recipient_id} = params;
    const query = 'select * from messages where recipient_
      id =?';
    return new Promise(resolve => {
        client.execute(query, [recipient_id]).then(result =
          > resolve(result.rows)); });
  }
```

The function is pretty simple since we already know how to query the database with the **client** (pool) object and we already tested that query.

In our schema, we can import and call that function like this:

```
import {get_messages_by_id} from '../cassandra'
  const get_messages = (recipient_id) => {
    return new Promise(resolve => {
        get_messages_by_id({recipient_id: recipient_id}).then((r
    esult) => {
            resolve(result)
        })
    })
  }
```

Cassandra will return an array of rows, which will match our GraphQL schema and we don't need to convert the result or do any extra steps. Note that you need to provide an existing in the database recipient_id.

Our second data source will be MongoDB. Let's open the Mongo shell and create a simple collection with one document to hold the user account data:

```
meteor:PRIMARY> db.createCollection('user_account')
meteor:PRIMARY> db.user_account.insert({recipient_id: '1279113062177466', e
mail: 'user@gmail.com', address: 'street one', credit_card_info: 'some card
 number'})
```

The next step is to simply query the collection and resolve the result in get_user_account function:

```
const UserAccount = new Mongo.Collection('user_account');
const get_user_account = (recipient_id) => {
    return new Promise(resolve => {
        const account_data = UserAccount.find({recipient_id: recip
  ient_id}).fetch();
resolve(account_data[0])
        });
}
```

The query returns an array, and again the fields of the schema are matched with the collection; all we need is to resolve the first item of the array. Now, if you execute both resolver functions in the query, you will get the data from both databases. That is what makes GraphQL an extremely powerful technology. Our last step is to have the actual application client to query the server. Apollo has full support for Angular 2, and this is the required package:

```
>> npm install apollo-angular --save
```

The first thing we need is to set up Apollo client. In the app folder, create a file `client.ts` with the following content:

```
import {ApolloClient, createNetworkInterface} from 'apollo-client';
 const client = new ApolloClient({
    networkInterface: createNetworkInterface({
        uri: '/graphql',
        opts: {
            credentials: 'same-origin'
        }
    })
});
export function getClient() : ApolloClient {return client;}
```

The next step is to import it in `app.module.ts` and add it to the rest of the modules in `imports` array:

```
import {getClient} from './client';
  @NgModule({
  declarations: [
    AppComponent, ListComponent],
    providers: [],
    imports: [BrowserModule, FormsModule, HttpModule, ApolloM
odule.withClient(getClient)],
    bootstrap: [AppComponent]
})
```

Adding it to the app root module will make Apollo available across the entire application.

In the app, we have created a list component when we were exploring Angular at the beginning of the chapter. Let's populate that list with the messages from the Cassandra database.

The first thing we need is to define the GraphQL query with all the fields that we need from the server. It is very similar to what we did in the in-browser IDE:

```
import {Apollo} from 'apollo-angular';
import {gql} from 'graphql-tag';

const getMessages = gql `
  query getMessages($recipient_id: String)  {
    user_account (recipient_id:$recipient_id){
      recipient_id
      email
      address
      credit_card_info
  }
```

```
        messages(recipient_id:$recipient_id){
          recipient_id
          timestamp
          message
          bot_response
      }
  }`;
```

From the top to bottom, we imported two packages, `apollo-angular` and `graphql-tag`. Then, we declared a `getMessages` constant assigned to our query. The only difference from the browser IDE queries is that we wrapped our query in the function query `getMessages` with an argument `$recipient_id` of type `String` in the definition, that argument(s) can be passed to all resolvers.

Here is the entire `ListComponent` as shown in the following code:

```
@Component({selector: 'list', template})
export class ListComponent implements OnInit {
    constructor(private apollo : Apollo) {}
        list : Array <String>;
        recipient_id : String;
        email : String;
        address : String;
        credit_card_info : String;
    ngOnInit() {
      this.apollo.watchQuery({
          query: getMessages,
          variables: {
              recipient_id: "1279113062177466"
          }
      }).subscribe(({data}) => {
          this.recipient_id = data.user_account.recipient_id;
          this.email = data.user_account.email;
          this.address = data.user_account.address;
          this.credit_card_info = data.user_account.credit_card_info;
          this.list = data.messages;
      });
    }
}
```

We imported and injected Apollo service in `constructor` and created a private variable `apollo`. After that, we defined class properties, which will hold the user information and the list of messages. With `apollo.watchQuery`, we are not actually executing the query. We are creating `ObservableQuery` with two options, `query` (the actual query) and `variables` (the parameters we need to pass). The `ObservableQuery` will cache the fetched result into a store, and if other parts of the application request the same query, it will skip the trip to the server and resolve it on the client.

The last part is to subscribe to the query, and when the data is returned, we assign it to the class properties.

Now, we can modify `list.component.html` template to render the data:

```
<p>Account Info</p>
<p>{{recipient_id}}</p>
<p>{{email}}</p>
<p>{{address}}<p>
<p>{{credit_card_info}}</p>
<ul>
    <li *ngFor="let item of list">
      <span>User: {{ item.message }}</span></br>
      <span>Bot:{{ item.bot_response }} </span>
    </li>
</ul>
```

Summary

In this chapter, we explored a few new technologies by building a simple Messenger chatbot. First, we started by adding Angular 2 as our view layer and overviewed the basics of the platform, such as modules, components, data binding, and DI.

After that, we moved to building the chatbot by setting up all required webhook endpoints and tokens. We then created a Wit.ai application and trained the chatbot with questions and answers data.

After we implemented the chatbot in our Meteor app, we installed and briefly overviewed Cassandra database.

The last addition to the stack was GraphQL. We created a schema and explored how we can query data from different sources (Cassandra and MongoDB) with only one round-trip to the server.

What have you learned and what can be your next steps?

On the frontend, you can add Redux to Angular 2 and have Redux to manage the state of the application.

Cassandra is an extremely powerful database, and with GraphQL we really have no problem adding it to any of our Meteor apps.

A lot can be explored and done with GraphQL. For example, we didn't insert any records from the client; these inserts can be defined as **mutations**. The following is a very handy cheat sheet that you can use for reference:

```
https://raw.githubusercontent.com/sogko/graphql-shorthand-notation-cheat-she
et/master/graphql-shorthand-notation-cheat-sheet.png
```

In the next chapter, we will build an IoT Meteor application that will connect to an **embedded** Node.js server, which will generate data in real time. With that application, we will take the opportunity to explore a **Remote Procedure Call (RPC)** from Google called gRPC.

9
Build Internet of Things Platform

Introduction

All the apps we've built so far were typical web applications with a frontend UI (accessible through a browser) and a server (backend) that serves the data and the UI content to a user, and the user interacts with the UI and sends data back to the server. That was pretty much the workflow so far.

In this chapter, we will build something different. We will add another communication layer to our stack, called **gRPC**, and we'll explore another scenario where we have machines exchanging data with other machines over the network without human assistance.

Internet of Things or **IoT** has become a buzzword recently due to the growth of devices connected to the Internet. Nowadays, there's nothing new in having a fridge, a doorbell, a thermostat, all connected to the network controlling the energy settings or security of your house. Today, almost every major car company invests heavily in the development of autonomous (self-driving) vehicles, and startups are popping up every day with all kinds of solutions, from real-time drone mapping and LIDAR sensing, smart cameras using deep learning for object recognition, and everything that you can think of that can automate our lives.

How does the Meteor platform fit into these kind of solutions? Meteor is a *web application framework* consisting of prepackaged modules that speed up the development and build process. That said, Meteor is a JavaScript framework, and we can run JavaScript in almost any environment. As for databases, while MongoDB is built into Meteor, we already started breaking the black box by abstracting our data sources with the GraphQL query language. In `Chapter 8`, *Build a Chatbot with Facebook's Messenger Platform*, we added Cassandra to the stack by simply installing it and connecting to it with Cassandra's Node.js driver.

Essentially, with the full integration of npm in Meteor, we can install any third-party application packages that we need.

In this chapter, we will have a Meteor app connected to a mock-up of our IoT platform, which will be generating data continuously; the data will be pulled into Meteor and served on the web.

Here's a diagram of what we will build:

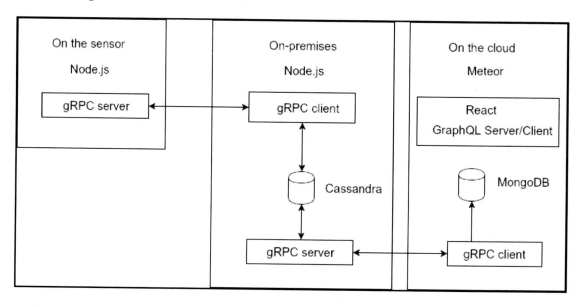

In the preceding diagram, we have three applications with three different deployment options. Let's say that the web app (the Meteor app) will be deployed on the cloud. The two other apps will be backends only (without any UI), and they can be deployed somewhere on the enterprise. When we say *On-premises*, it means that the software is deployed on the company's private machines/servers or any other type of devices. The third app is the embedded app that can be installed on hardware that can have a very specific role, for example, a board with a sensor that can read the temperature and pressure of some equipment. We will build and run all three apps on a local machine, but you can move them around on different platforms/hardware and experiment further.

There will be a few new concepts that we will learn by building these apps: connecting devices in remote environments with low bandwidth and unreliable Internet connection, storing the data from the sensor(s) as a time series in a database, pushing data to a cloud app, and visualizing the result on the web using GraphQL with React. We can start by exploring what gRPC is and what benefits we are getting by adding it to our stack.

What is gRPC?

With Meteor, we have DDP, so why do we need another RPC?

An open source Remote Procedure Call framework, gRPC uses HTTP/2 for the transport layer initially developed by Google based on their internal RPC framework.
The transport layer is one of the key components in gRPC. HTTP/2 is the major upgrade of HTTP/1.1, and it was standardized by the **Internet Engineering Steering Group (IESG)** in 2015. Every technology that is standardized on the web tends to survive for many years because we, the developers, all accept and agree with that standard primarily because the technology is not owned by a single company that decides its future. JavaScript is a great example of that.
On the other hand, Meteor's **DDP (Distributed Data Protocol)** uses WebSockets for transport format; the WebSockets protocol did not get standardized, which is one important consideration that may drive its future.
The second component of gRPC is the data format. The current industry standard is JSON over HTTP, DDP is also using JSON on the WebSockets; in contrast, gRPC uses **Protocol Buffers** (also developed by Google) to serialize the data. Here are some advantages of using Protocol Buffers over other formats:

- **Protocol Buffers is a strongly typed format**: JSON is a weakly typed key/value format, and we always have to take care of all the parsing and type checking of the data. The way Protocol Buffers work is that we define service contracts in one common format that can be consumed by many languages; in other words, it's a language neutral or polyglot. We can easily have our Meteor app talking to Java and C# backends, for example.
- **The size of the data**: Protocol Buffers encode the data in a binary format and this makes it extremely compact on the wire. Mobile phones and devices at remote locations (on the edge) are examples of having low bandwidth and unreliable internet connection at times. The data usage and the battery life all depend on the size of the data that is moved up and down to the servers.

The communication of DDP is bidirectional (due to the WebSockets nature); HTTP/2 is also bidirectional, and it has one big advantage over DDP.

WebSockets are opening a new connection for every stream. HTTP/2 uses a single TCP connection that can handle parallel requests without blocking each other. This is known as multiplexing. To understand how gRPC works, let's build a simple client-server app and see how we can transfer data between client and server.

For package manager, this time we will use Yarn instead of npm. Many great things can be said about Yarn: performance, security, better module versioning. Go ahead and install it if you haven't done so already:

```
curl -sS https://dl.yarnpkg.com/debian/pubkey.gpg | sudo apt-key add -
echo "deb https://dl.yarnpkg.com/debian/ stable main" | sudo tee
etc/apt/sources.list.d/yarn.list

>> sudo apt-get update && sudo apt-get install yarn
```

Now, let's create the app folder and install the `grpc` package:

```
>> mkdir grpc_intro
>> cd grpc_intro
>> yarn init
>> yarn add grpc
```

`yarn init` will generate a `package.json` file and the `yarn add grpc` command will install the package.

The demo will demonstrate a simple *client to server request* and *server to client response*. Here's the project structure:

Two things we need to have in gRPC service are a **message definition** and a **service**, both of which we define in a `.proto` file. In the `message.proto` file, we define them like this:

```
syntax = "proto3";
package messages;

service Messages {
  rpc SendMessage(ClientRequest) returns (ServerResponse) {}
}

message ClientRequest {
  int64 client_id = 1;
```

```
}
message ServerResponse {
  string message = 1;
  bool received = 2;
  bytes server_time = 3;
  int64 client_id = 4;
}
```

The first line in the file is to specify the `proto` syntax; it has to be on the first line and, if we do not include it, it will default to an older `proto2` syntax. Then, we have a package definition called `messages`; the package is needed during the loading of the `.proto` file. In the next line, we have our service definition, a service called `Messages` and in the body, we define an RPC method called `SendMessage`, which gets the client request (`ClientRequest`) and returns the response from the server (`ServerResponse`). This is the signature of the service and the messages:

```
service ServiceName{
  rpc MethodName(RequestFromClient) returns (ResponseFromServer) {}
  ... other rpc methods
}
message RequestFromClient{
  properties
  ...
}
message ResponseFromServer{
  properties
  ....
}
```

In the body of both the messages (`ClientRequest` and `ServerResponse`), we specify the type and name of each message field, and then we assign a **unique numbered tag** (used to identify the messages in the binary format) to each one.

Before moving to the client and the server, there are a few things you need to know.
The Protocol Buffers style guide recommends the following:

- Message definitions should be CamelCase
- The service name and the RPC methods should be CamelCase starting with a capital letter
- The unique numbered tags (example: string message = 1;) can be from smallest--1--to the largest--536,870,91; the numbers from 19,000 through 19,999 are reserved and cannot be used
- All other scalar types can be found at https://developers.google.com/protocol-buffers/docs/proto3#scalar

Before jumping to writing the server and client code, let's visualize the communication between them:

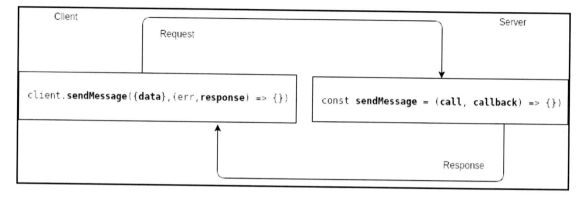

The client calls a gRPC method--**sendMessage**--by passing two arguments: the **data** (the message) and a **callback** function. That is the simplest way of communicating between the server and the client.

Let's start with the server; in the `server.js` file, paste the following code:

```
const grpc = require('grpc');
const PROTO_PATH = __dirname + '/messages.proto';
const messages_proto = grpc.load(PROTO_PATH).messages;

const sendMessage = (call, callback) => {
 let buf = Buffer.from(new Date().toString(), 'utf8')
   callback(null, {
              message: 'Message from server',
              received: true,
              server_time: buf,
              client_id: call.request.client_id
   });
}
const init_server = () => {
 const server = new grpc.Server();
     server.addProtoService(messages_proto.Messages.service, {
       sendMessage: sendMessage,
     });
     server.bind('0.0.0.0:50051', grpc.ServerCredentials.createInsecure());
     server.start();
}
init_server();
```

The first thing we do is import the `grpc` module, and then we load our `.proto` file with the `load().messages` method. The name of our package in the `.proto` file (package messages => `grpc.load(PROTO_PATH).messages`) is `messages`.

In the `init_server()` function, we created a new instance of the grpc server and with the `addProtoService` method, we add the service that we just loaded from the `.proto` file. This is the signature of the method:

```
server.addProtoService(service, { methodName:
methodFunction, anotherMethod:anotherFunciton});
```

Once we have loaded the proto service and added it to the server, we bind the server to a port and start it with the `server.start()` method. That's all we need to have gRPC server up and running.

When the client calls the `sendMessage` RPC method, the `sendMessage` function will be called, and we will get a request object that will contain the message (the data) and the callback function as arguments. When we want to respond to the client, we call the callback function with two arguments: the error and the data.
Let's see how we can send messages from the client:

```
const grpc = require('grpc');
const PROTO_PATH = __dirname + '/messages.proto';
const messages_proto = grpc.load(PROTO_PATH).messages;

const init_client = () => {
  const client = new messages_proto.Messages('localhost:50051',
grpc.credentials.createInsecure());
    client.sendMessage({
      client_id: 1234
    }, (err, response) => {
      console.log(response);
    });
}
init_client();
```

On the client, we import `grpc` and load the `.proto` file exactly the same way we did on the server. To connect to the server, we create a client stub by specifying the address of the server and the port.

Once we have the client connected to the server, we can start calling the server methods and receive the response from the callback.

At the time of writing, the methods are all callback-based and, if you want to use ES6 Promises, you have to use a third-party library.

To test it, open two terminals, change the directory to the root of the app, and execute the `server.js` and the `client.js` files:

```
//terminal one
>> node server.js

//terminal two
>> node client.js
```

There are four ways to pass data between the client and the server. The first one is the way we just did. We called an RPC method from the client by passing the message and a `callback` function and the server just executed the callback with the data.
Here are all the possibilities:

- Client calls a method with a request, and the server calls a callback function with the data
- Client streams data to the server and the server responds by calling the callback function
- Client calls a method with a request and the server streams the data to the client
- The client streams the data to the server, and the server streams the data back to the client

We can put all the preceding options in a table:

Client	Server
Request	Callback
Stream	Callback
Request	Streams
Streams	Streams

We have created the client request with the server callback; now let's see how we can implement the other three options, starting from the Client Stream and Server Callback.

In our `Messages` service in the `messages.proto` file, we can define another RPC method, called `ClientStream`:

```
service Messages{
    ...
    rpc ClientStream (stream Request) returns (Response) {}
}
message Request {
  int64 client_id = 1;
}
message Response {
  int64 client_id = 1;
  bytes stream = 2;
}
```

We specify who is streaming by adding the `stream` keyword before the name of the `(stream Request)` message; in this case, the client will stream but the server will not, since we have added the `stream` keyword to the client only.

In the `server.js` file, let's add another method and function to the proto service:

```
server.addProtoService(messages_proto.Messages.service, {
    sendMessage: sendMessage,
    clientStream: clientStream
});
```

The `clientStream` function looks like this:

```
const clientStream = (call, callback) => {
  let buf = Buffer.from(new Date().toString(), 'utf8')
  let client_id;
  call.on('data', (data) => {
      client_id = data.client_id
  });
  call.on('end', () => {
      callback(null, {
        stream: buf,
        client_id: client_id
    });
  });
}
```

Here's the difference from the preceding example--instead of getting the client request on the server, we are getting a readable stream in which we hook up a few event listeners. When the messages are incoming, the `call.on('data')` event will keep firing until all the messages are transferred from the client. After that, the `call.on('end')` event will fire, and this is the place where we can call our server `callback` function and send the data to the client.

Let's see how we call this method from the client. In the `client.js` file, add the following function:

```
const clientStream = (client) => {
    const call = client.clientStream((err, response) => {
      console.log(response)
    });
    call.write({client_id: 1234});
    call.end();
}
```

Since the client streams the data, we get a writable stream instead of readable and, once we have done writing to the stream, we can call the `call.end()` method, which will notify the server that we are done sending messages. On the other end, `call.on('end')` will be fired, and we can execute the callback function.

To clear up what we just did, we can visualize it through a diagram:

The next way of communicating is that the client will call a method with a request and the server will stream the data back to the client.

Let's define it on the service definition in the `.proto` file:

```
service Messages {
  rpc SendMessage(ClientRequest) returns (ServerResponse) {}
  rpc ClientStream (stream Request) returns (Response) {}
  rpc ServerStream (Request) returns (stream Response) {}
}
```

In the `server.js` file, the function of writing to the stream is pretty much the same as we did on the client:

```
server.addProtoService(messages_proto.Messages.service, {
    ...
    serverStream: serverStream,
  });
...
const serverStream = (call) => {
  let buf = Buffer.from(new Date().toString(), 'utf8')
    call.write({stream: buf, client_id: call.request.client_id});
    call.end();
}
```

Also, we can call the RPC method on the client, as shown:

```
const serverStream = (client) => {
const call = client.serverStream({client_id: 1234});
    call.on('data', (response) => {
      console.log(response);
  });
    call.on('end', () =>{
        console.log('all data was transmitted from the server');
  });
}
```

Visually, this is as follows:

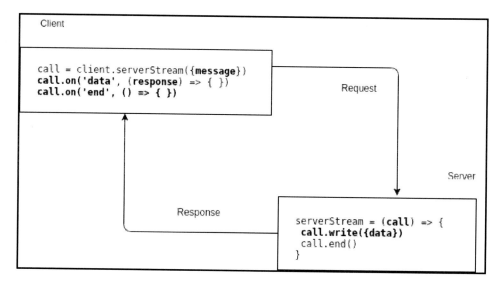

In the last option, we have both the server and the client streaming, which is bidirectional communication. Basically, we have both the readable and the writable stream on the client and on the server:

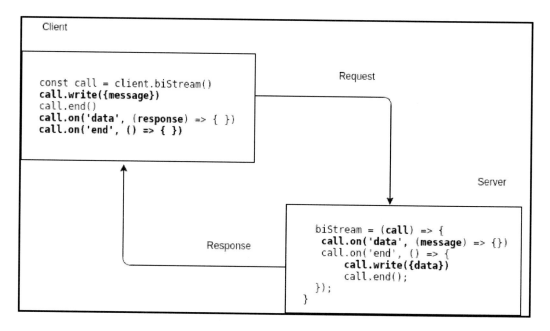

In the `.proto` file, let's define the bidirectional RPC method:

```
service Messages {
    rpc SendMessage(ClientRequest) returns (ServerResponse) {}
    rpc ClientStream (stream Request) returns (Response) {}
    rpc ServerStream (Request) returns (stream Response) {}
    rpc BiStream (stream Request) returns (stream Response) {}
}
```

Also, the `biStream` function is to be defined on the server:

```
const biStream = (call) => {
    let buf = Buffer.from(new Date().toString(), 'utf8')
    let client_id;
    call.on('data', (data) => {
client_id = data.client_id
    });
    call.on('end', () => {
      call.write({stream: buf, client_id: client_id});
      call.end();
    });
}
```

When all the messages are received from the client, the `call.on('end')` event will fire, and we can start writing to the stream after we are done with `call.end()`.
On the client, we can call for data like this:

```
const biStream = (client) => {
  const call = client.biStream();
  call.on('data', (response) => {
      console.log(response);
  });
call.on('end',() =>{
    // server is done sending messages.
  })
  call.write({client_id: 1234});
  call.end();
}
```

Test it out!

We have full control over the data flow between the client and the server. Also, the data is very efficient on the wire, which makes this technology very powerful. You can explore it more by creating more methods with different types. For example, we can specify enumeration types as shown:

```
message Response {
  int64 client_id = 1;
  bytes stream = 2;
  enum DayOfWeek {
    MONDAY = 0;
    TUESDAY = 1;
    WEDNESDAY = 2;
    THURSDAY = 3;
    FRIDAY = 4;
    SATURDAY = 5;
    SUNDAY = 6;
  }
  DayOfWeek daysOfWeek = 3;
}

//on the server.js
 call.write({stream: buf, client_id: call.request.client_id, daysOfWeek:
0});
```

Building the apps

We can start from the embedded app, which will be very close to what we just did. Before we start writing the code, we need to figure out the data flow between the machines. See the following diagram:

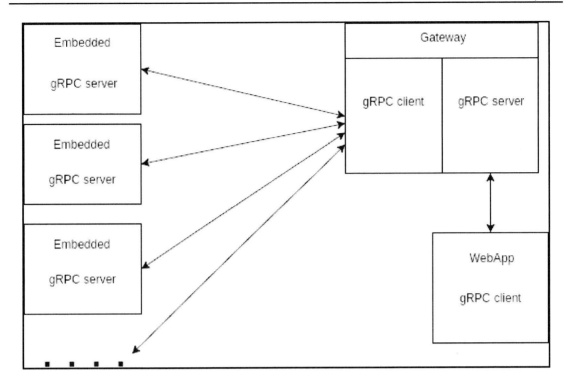

You probably already noticed that the embedded devices are gRPC servers instead of clients and our middle app, the **Gateway** between the sensors and the cloud is a gRPC client and a server. The other way around is probably the easiest and the least complicated setup where all the sensors are clients that connect to one **gRPC server** (the Gateway). There is one reason this setup may not work in some cases and all depends on the IT rules and the infrastructure of the company.

For example, if this is a residential home with wired sensors to the home network, it makes perfect sense to have them as gRPC clients who connect directly to a Gateway machine or even directly to the cloud. In the enterprise often it is not that simple. Usually, these devices will be sitting behind a firewall, and they may not be able to establish connections to outside networks but the Gateway machine, which may sit in a corporate office, can reach them. How all this is set up completely depends on what we are trying to build and for whom we'll be building it for.

The embedded app will be a very simple gRPC server that will return a temperature measurement any time a gRPC client requests it.

Let's start by creating a folder and installing the `grpc` package:

```
>> mkdir grpc_embedded
>> cd grpc_embedded
>> yarn add grpc
```

Here are the two files we need to create, the `server.js` and `temperature.proto`:

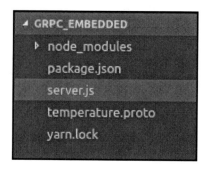

In the **temperature.proto**, we can define our gRPC service like this:

```
syntax = "proto3";
package temperature;

service TemperatureService {
  rpc Temperature (TemperatureRequest) returns (TemperatureReplay) {}
}
message TemperatureRequest {
  string security_key = 1;
}
message TemperatureReplay {
  int64 temperature = 1;
  string sensor_id = 2;
}
```

In the preceding code, we created a simple `TemperatureService` with one RPC method, called `Temperature`, with two messages: `TemperatureRequest` and `TemperatureReplay`. In the client message, we have one field--`security_key`--which will be passed by the client request.

On the server response (`TemperatureReplay`), we have the `temperature` and a `sensor_id` (a simple ID of the sensor).

The next part is to load the `.proto` file and build the server:

```
const grpc = require('grpc');
const PROTO_PATH = __dirname + '/temperature.proto';
const temperature_proto = grpc.load(PROTO_PATH).temperature;

const getRandomInt = (min, max) => {
   return Math.floor(Math.random() * (max - min)) + min;
}

const getTemperature = (call, callback) => {
 console.log(call.request.security_key) //you can use this to auth the
client
let readings = {
     temperature: getRandomInt(20, 25),
     sensor_id: '12345'
   }
callback(null, readings);
}

const init_server = () => {
   const server = new grpc.Server();
   server.addProtoService(temperature_proto.TemperatureService.service,
   {temperature: getTemperature});
   server.bind('0.0.0.0:50051', grpc.ServerCredentials.createInsecure());
   server.start();
}
init_server();
```

Here, we have a gRPC server almost identical to our earlier examples. The client calls the RPC method `temperature` and our server will call a function `getTemperature` which will execute a callback function with the data. In this demo, we are mocking the temperature readings by generating random values on every request, in real world applications, the access to the sensor will depend on the hardware specific API.

Note about security:

With this setup, the server is not secure and any client can call the `temperature` method and get the readings of the sensor. The first step of securing it is to add an SSL certificate to the server. The signature of adding it looks like this:

```
const credentials = grpc.ServerCredentials.createSsl(ssl_certs);
server.bind('0.0.0.0:50051', credentials);
```

When the client calls for data, we can authenticate it against the security key which can be stored in a database. Of course, security keys, tokens, and passwords should be encrypted and not stored as plain text in the database. Here is a very popular and well-supported encryption library that you could use for encryption `https://github.com/kelektiv/node bcrypt.js`.

Another consideration is the performance. If the client calls for data at a very high rate, you can place some type of caching of the credentials instead of authenticating the client on every call.

Now we have the server, let's build the client.

Our middle app (the Gateway) will have a gRPC client and a server. The client will be able to connect to one or many servers (sensors) and ask for data (let's say, once every minute); on the other end, the cloud app will connect to the Gateway server to query the latest data. Let's start by creating the app and installing the packages that we need:

```
>> mkdir grpc_gateway
>> cd grpc_gateway
>> yarn add grpc
>> yarn add cassandra-driver
>> yarn add --dev babel-cli
>> yarn add --dev babel-preset-es2015
>> yarn add --dev babel-preset-stage-2
>> echo { "presets": ["es2015", "stage-2"] } > .babelrc
```

This is a screenshot of the project folder structure:

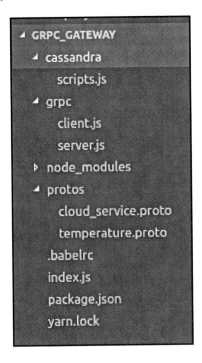

We have `index.js`, which will be our entry file of the app. We also have the `cassandra` folder, where we will define all our scripts in a `scripts.js` file. In the `grpc` folder, we will have the grpc client that will connect to the embedded app and the grpc server the cloud app will connect to.

If you skipped `Chapter 8`, *Build a Chatbot with Facebook's Messenger Platform*, and you don't have the Cassandra database installed, here are the scripts that can install it:

```
>> echo "deb http://www.apache.org/dist/cassandra/debian 310x main" | sudo
tee -a /etc/apt/sources.list.d/cassandra.sources.list

>> curl https://www.apache.org/dist/cassandra/KEYS | sudo apt-key add -
>> sudo apt-get update
>> sudo apt-get install cassandra
```

To verify your installation, run the following script:

```
>> sudo service cassandra status
```

Let's start by creating the database scripts that will create the keyspace (an equivalent of a database) and the table. We will run these scripts each time the server starts:

```
export const keyspace_query = `CREATE KEYSPACE IF NOT EXISTS iot WITH
REPLICATION = { 'class' : 'SimpleStrategy', 'replication_factor' : 1 };`;

export const use_keyspace = `use iot`;

export const table_query = `CREATE TABLE IF NOT EXISTS temperature (
sensor_id text,
date text,
event_time timestamp,
temperature text,
PRIMARY KEY ((sensor_id,date),event_time)
) WITH CLUSTERING ORDER BY (event_time DESC);`;
```

With the preceding code, we create (when executed) a keyspace called `iot` with the `IF NOT EXISTS` clause, and we give it replication strategy options suitable for a local development. As we are creating the keyspace in the code, we use another query to switch to that keyspace (this is similar to the MongoDB command `--use db_name`).

The next thing is the table, which is an interesting part of the database. Cassandra is a perfect database for storing data that continuously occurs over a period of time. When we call our sensors for the temperature readings, we will store the ID of the sensor and the date and time of the insert. Cassandra is a wide row database, which means that we can add up to 2 billion columns dynamically in a single row. Having a compound `PRIMARY KEY` as `((sensor_id,date),event_time)`, it means that we will create a new row with a number of columns depending on the amount of the inserts over the time for each day. For example, if we insert `temperature` data in the table *every second* from a sensor (with `sensor_id` 12345) using today's date for the field `date`, we will have one row with 86400 columns (`event_time`) since there are that many seconds per day. When the date changes (on the next day), data will be stored in the next row with another 86400 columns.

That may seem confusing at first, especially if you are coming from relational databases, but once you understand the concept, you will see the incredible power of this type of data store. You can get a lot more information from the official commercial-grade Apache Cassandra distributor, DataStax. Here are a few links where you can get started with time series data modeling:

- https://academy.datastax.com/resources/getting-started-time-series-data-modeling
- http://www.datastax.com/dev/blog/advanced-time-series-with-cassandra

We have the queries; now we can create a simple function that will execute them:

```
export const execute_query = (params) => {
  const {client, query} = params;
    return new Promise((resolve, reject) => {
      client.execute(query).then(result => resolve(result)).catch(err => {
        reject(err)
      });
    });
}
```

When we boot the app, we will call that `execute_query` function by passing all the queries. The order of the execution of each query matters, and it should be as follows:

1. Create a keyspace. We can't have any other queries before we create the keyspace; again, keyspace is an equivalent of a database.
2. Switch to the just created keyspace.
3. Create a table(s) or execute other queries.

Since the `execute_query` function is async and we need to execute them in the preceding order (in a synchronous fashion), we need to somehow control the order. This time, instead of calling each function when the preceding one is resolved, we will use an `async function`. In the `index.js` file, paste the following code:

```
import {execute_query, keyspace_query, use_keyspace_query, table_query } from
'./cassandra/scripts'
import cassandra from 'cassandra-driver';
const client = new cassandra.Client({contactPoints: ['127.0.0.1']});

async function cassandra_schema(client) {
    await execute_query({client: client, query:keyspace_query}); //pauses
until is resolved
    await execute_query({client: client, query:use_keyspace_query}); //pauses
until is resolved
    await execute_query({client: client, query:table_query}); //pauses until
is resolved
  };
cassandra_schema(client);
```

Once we have imported the scripts, we create a client connection to our database, and then we define an `async function`, called `cassandra_schema`. The way async functions work is pretty simple.

Async functions return a Promise and, in the body of the async function, we can call a function that returns Promise by adding the `await` keyword before the function's name (`await execute_query`). What `await` does is that it pauses the execution until the function is resolved, and then we can again put the next function on pause using the `await` keyword. This is a very nice new feature that makes the language syntax cleaner when dealing with nested Promises.

Our next step is to connect to the sensor, get the data, and insert it in the `temperature` table. In the `protos` folder, we have the exact same service file that we have on the server app (the `grpc_embedded` app):

```
syntax = "proto3";
package temperature;
service TemperatureService {
    rpc Temperature (TemperatureRequest) returns (TemperatureReplay) {}
}
message TemperatureRequest {
 string security_key = 1;
}
message TemperatureReplay {
 int64 temperature = 1;
 string sensor_id = 2;
}
```

From the preceding code, you can see that neither the client nor the server will stream their data. Instead, the server will reply to the client by calling a callback function. Now we have the proto definition; next, we can initialize our client and connect it to the server. In the `grpc` folder, create a file called `client.js` with the following content:

```
import grpc from 'grpc';
const PROTO_PATH = __dirname + '/../protos/temperature.proto';
import {insert_temperature} from '../cassandra/scripts';

const temperature_proto = grpc.load(PROTO_PATH).temperature;

export const init_client = (params) => {
  const {cassandra_client} = params;
  const client = new
temperature_proto.TemperatureService('localhost:50051',
grpc.credentials.createInsecure());

  setInterval(() => {
    client.temperature({
      security_key: 'qwertyui'
      }, (err, response) => {
    if (response) {
```

```
        const dt = new Date();
        const date = dt.getFullYear() + '-' + (dt.getMonth() + 1) + '-' +
dt.getDate();
    insert_temperature({
        client: cassandra_client,
sensor_id: response.sensor_id,
date: date,
event_time: new Date(),
temperature: response.temperature})
      }
  });
}, 60000); //every minute
}
```

In the preceding code from top to bottom, we imported the `grpc` module and from the `cassandra/scripts` directory, we imported a `insert_temperature` function (we will define it later). The next thing we do is load the proto definition file with the `load()` function.

Then, in the `init_client` function, we connect to the server on port 50051, and we call the RPC server method `temperature` every minute (using the `setInterval` function). When we receive the message on the callback, we insert it into the Cassandra table. The message from the sensor contains the `sensor_id` and the `temperature`; for the `date` field, we create a more readable date format as year-month-day (2017-4-23), and for the `event_time`, which we defined as Cassandra `timestamp` type, we use the built-in JavaScript `Date()` function.

Now, we need to add the `insert_temperature` function to our database scripts:

```
const insert_query = `insert into temperature
  (sensor_id, date, event_time, temperature)
    values (?,?,?,?);`;

export const insert_temperature = (params) => {
  const {client, sensor_id, date, event_time, temperature} = params;
  client.execute(insert_query, [sensor_id, date, event_time, temperature])
    .then(result => console.log('inserted in db'))
    .catch(err => {
      console.log(err)
  });
}
```

The insert query looks pretty much like a standard SQL query and, to map the values to the parameters, we use a question mark syntax(?). (?,?,?,?), [`sensor_id, date, event_time, temperature`].

The last step is to load our grpc client when the server boots. In the `index.js` file, add it to the `cassandra_schema`:

```
async function cassandra_schema(client) {
    await execute_query({client: client,query:keyspace_query});
    await execute_query({client: client,query:use_keyspace_query});
    await execute_query({client: client,query:table_query});
    init_client({cassandra_client: client});
}
```

Test it out!

Run it and see how the data gets injected every minute. You can also change the rate of the requests to any number you'd like. Note that Cassandra is an extremely high-performance database, and it has been proven that it can easily handle a million writes per second.

Our last app is the cloud app, which will be a Meteor app with React as a view on the frontend and GraphQL with Apollo client for querying the data from the server. It will also have a grpc client that will continuously fetch data from our Gateway app.

Let's create the Meteor app and install all the required dependencies:

```
>> meteor create cloud_app
>> meteor add apollo
>> npm install react --save
>> npm install react-dom --save
>> npm install react-apollo --save
>> npm install apollo-client --save
>> npm install graphql --save
>> npm install graphql-server-express --save
>> npm install graphql-tools --save
>> npm install express --save
>> npm install body-parser --save
>> meteor npm install grpc --save
>> npm install recharts --save
```

Throughout the book, we've been using strait `npm install` commands for installing packages. For the majority of the packages, this will work just fine. However, some npm packages may execute high-performance C or C++ libraries underneath and, in a case like that, we need to use `meteor npm install package_name` to prevent version mismatch with Meteor; gRPC is one of those packages, and we need to bundle it with Meteor.

Starting from the backend, create the following folders and files:

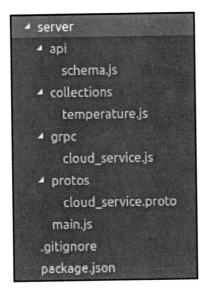

Let's start from the gRPC part by defining the shared file between the cloud app and the Gateway, which is the `cloud_service.proto`:

```
syntax = "proto3";
package cloud_service;

service CloudService {
    rpc Temperature (TemperatureRequest) returns (stream TemperatureReplay)
{}
}

message TemperatureRequest {
  string security_key = 1;
  string sensor_id = 2;
  string date = 3;
  string event_time = 4;
}
message TemperatureReplay {
```

```
    string sensor_id = 1;
    string date = 2;
    string event_time = 3;
    int64 temperature= 4;
  }
```

Nothing is really new here. We create a service called `CloudService` with one RPC method--`Temperature`--and two messages: `TemperatureRequest` and `TemperatureReplay`. It is not recommended to push a large size of data in a single message; here's a good example where we can use a stream instead of a callback. When the client calls for data, it will not know how many rows the table will return and the best thing we can do is write each row to the stream.

The data will be inserted into MongoDB; let's define a simple collection in the `collections` folder:

```
    import { Mongo } from 'meteor/mongo';
    export const Temperature = new Mongo.Collection('temperature');
```

We have the service and the collection, and we can now build our gRPC client and start messaging the server for data.

In the `cloud_service.js` file, copy and paste the following code:

```
    import grpc from 'grpc';
    const PROTO_PATH = process.env.PWD + '/server/protos/cloud_service.proto';
    import { Meteor } from 'meteor/meteor';
    import {Temperature} from '../collections/temperature';
    const temperature_proto = grpc.load(PROTO_PATH).cloud_service;

    const serverStream = (params) => {
     const {rpc_client, event_time,date} = params;
     const call = rpc_client.temperature({
       security_key: 'qwertyui',
       sensor_id: '12345',
       date: date,
       event_time: event_time});

       call.on('data', Meteor.bindEnvironment(response => {
           let last = Temperature.find({event_time:
    response.event_time}).fetch();
           if(last.length < 1){
               Temperature.insert(response)
           }
     }));
     call.on('end', ()=>{});
    }
```

```
export const init_client = (params) => {
 const client = new temperature_proto.CloudService('localhost:50052',
grpc.credentials.createInsecure());
  Meteor.setInterval(() => {
     let last = Temperature.find({}, {sort: {event_time: -1}, limit:
1}).fetch().pop();
     const dt = new Date();
     const date = dt.getFullYear() + '-' + (dt.getMonth() + 1) + '-' +
dt.getDate();
       if(!last){
         let now = new Date();
         now.setHours(0);
         now.setMinutes(0);
         serverStream({rpc_client:client, event_time: now.toString(),
date:date });
       }else{
         serverStream({rpc_client:client, event_time: last.event_time,
date:last.date });
    }
  }, 60000)//every minute
}
```

When the server boots, we will call the `init_client` function and, similar to what we already did a couple of times, we will connect to the server and call the RPC method (in this case, we will call for data every minute). To avoid any data duplication, we can simply query the collection and see whether the data already exists in the collection. If we don't have any records in our collection, we will ask the server for all the records since the beginning of the day:

```
if(!last){
  let now = new Date();
  now.setHours(0);
  now.setMinutes(0);
  now.setSeconds(0); // Sun Apr 30 2017 00:00:00 GMT-0600 (MDT)
    serverStream({rpc_client:client, event_time: now.toString(), date:date
});
```

The actual query on the server looks like this:

```
const select_from_temperature = `select * from temperature where sensor_id
= ? AND date = ? AND event_time > ? `;
```

Let's simplify the preceding statement by describing it in simple words. For this `date` (2017-4-30), our latest record (in the MongoDB collection) has this timestamp (`event_time` 2017-04-30 20:11:42.287000+0000), and returns all the records (if any) that are greater than our latest timestamp.

Now that we have the client, we can go back to the Gateway app and build our server part. On a diagram, the connection looks like this:

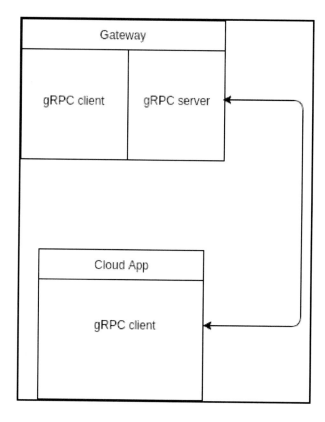

In the Gateway app, we need to add two files, as shown in this screenshot:

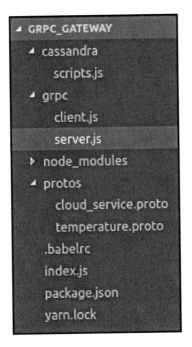

In the `grpc` folder, create the `server.js` file and in the `protos` folder, copy and paste the `cloud_service.proto` file from the `cloud_app` that we just created.

The gRPC server is pretty simple. When the client calls for data, we will query the database and get the result as an array of rows. Then, we will write each row to the stream and when we are done writing all the rows, we will close the stream by calling the `call.end()` function:

```
import grpc from 'grpc';
const PROTO_PATH = __dirname + '/../protos/cloud_service.proto';
import {select_temperature} from '../cassandra/scripts';
let db_client;
const cloud_service_proto = grpc.load(PROTO_PATH).cloud_service;

const getData = (call) => {
 select_temperature({
      client: db_client,
sensor_id: call.request.sensor_id,
date: call.request.date,
      event_time: new Date(call.request.event_time) }).then(result => {
   result.rows.map(res => {
   call.write({sensor_id: res.sensor_id,
```

```
                        date: res.date,
                        event_time: res.event_time.toString(),
                        temperature: res.temperature});
                        });
                call.end();
            });
    }
    export const init_server = (params) => {
        const {cassandra_client} = params;
        db_client = cassandra_client;
        const server = new grpc.Server();
            server.addProtoService(cloud_service_proto.CloudService.service,
        {temperature: getData});                server.bind('0.0.0.0:50052',
        grpc.ServerCredentials.createInsecure());
        server.start();
    }
```

The only thing left is to add the query to the Cassandra scripts and initialize the gRPC
server when we boot our app. In the `cassandra/scripts.js` file, add the following query
and function:

```
const select_from_temperature = `select * from temperature where sensor_id
= ?
    AND date = ? AND event_time > ? `;

export const select_temperature = (params) => {
    const {client, sensor_id, date, event_time} = params;
            return new Promise((resolve, reject) => {
                client.execute(select_from_temperature, [sensor_id, date,
    event_time])
                .then(result => resolve(result))
                .catch(err => {
                    reject(err)
            });
        });
    }
```

In `index.js`, we add it to the `cassandra_schema` function:

```
async function cassandra_schema(client) {
    await execute_query({client: client,query:keyspace_query});
    await execute_query({client: client,query:use_keyspace_query});
    await execute_query({client: client,query:table_query});
        init_client({cassandra_client: client});
        init_server({cassandra_client: client});
};
```

Test it out!

If you have the three apps, running the data should be automatically moved from the embedded app to the Gateway and eventually to the cloud. Even if you change the interval of the queries, the data should always be synced between the Gateway and the Cloud app.

One very useful feature of Cassandra is the **Time To Live** (TTL) property. In our example, the database in the Gateway app will accumulate a lot of data over time and, since we moved it to the cloud, we may want to delete it at some point. We can do that automatically by specifying TTL (in seconds) on each insert. In the following example, the record will automatically be deleted after one day:

```
insert into temperature (sensor_id, date, event_time, temperature)
   values (?,?,?,?) USING TTL 86400;
```

The last step is to build the frontend and visualize the data from the MongoDB collection.

Starting from the client, create the folders and files from this screenshot:

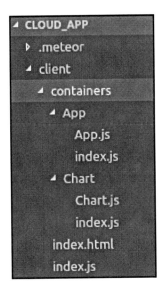

It will be a pretty basic app that will query the server (using GraphQL) and display all the results in a chart. Since the data is in time series format, we can easily plot it on the x and y axes.

In the `App.js` file, let's create our main/root component:

```
import React, {Component} from 'react';
import ApolloClient, {createNetworkInterface} from 'apollo-client';
import {ApolloProvider} from 'react-apollo';
import Chart from '../Chart';

const client = new ApolloClient({
  networkInterface : createNetworkInterface({uri: '/graphql'});
});

const dt = new Date();
const date = dt.getFullYear() + '-' + (dt.getMonth() + 1) + '-' +
dt.getDate();
const sensor_id = '12345';

class App extends Component {
  render() {
    return (
       <ApolloProvider client={client}>
          <Chart date ={date} sensor_id = {sensor_id}/>
       </ApolloProvider>
    );
  }
}
export default App;
```

Setting up the Apollo client is pretty easy. We create a new instance of `ApolloClient` by providing a network interface object. The `{uri: '/graphql'}`means that the endpoint of the GraphQL server will be on the localhost (`localhost:3000/graphql`). Next, we import specific-to-React **HOC (Higher Order Component)**, called `ApolloProvider`, which is similar to the Redux's **Provider** that we used to pass the store down to our components. `ApolloProvider` will enhance all our components with the ability to query the GraphQL server with the `graphql()` function. The query will simply be getting all the readings of today's date by `sensor_id`. We pass both the query parameters to the `Chart` component as props `<Chart date ={date} sensor_id = {sensor_id}/>`

Before we move to the `Chart` component, we need to have our GraphQL server up and running. On the server side in the `api` folder, create a file--`schema.js`--with the following content:

```
import { Meteor } from 'meteor/meteor';
import {Temperature} from '../collections/temperature';

const get_temperature = (sensor_id, date) => {
  return new Promise(resolve => {
```

```
      const data = Temperature.find({sensor_id: sensor_id, date:
date}).fetch();
      resolve(data);
  });
}

export const typeDefs = [`

type Temperature {
  sensor_id: String
  date: String
  event_time: String
  temperature: Int
}

type Query {
  temperature(sensor_id:String, date:String): [Temperature]
}
 schema {
   query: Query
   }
`];

export const resolvers = {
  Query: {
      temperature: (obj, args, context, info) => {
          return get_temperature(args.sensor_id, args.date).then((res) =>
res);
      }
    }
}
```

At the beginning of the code, we create a get_temperature function, which queries the collection temperature by sensor_id and date fields.

Then, in the type definitions, we specify two types: Query and Temperature. The Temperature type is our custom type reflecting our MongoDB's **temperature** collection. In the Query type, we specify a resolver function called temperature, which takes two arguments--the sensor_id and a date--and resolves an array of the Temperature type. At last, we define and export the resolvers object.

Now that we have the types and resolvers, we can build the schema and boot the GraphQL server. In the `main.js` file, add the following code:

```
import {createApolloServer} from 'meteor/apollo';
import {makeExecutableSchema} from 'graphql-tools';
import {typeDefs, resolvers} from './api/schema';

const schema = makeExecutableSchema({typeDefs, resolvers});
createApolloServer({schema});
```

To create the schema, we call the `makeExecutableSchema()` function by passing both objects--the `typeDefs` and `resolvers`--as arguments. After we have the schema, we boot our GraphQL server by passing it to the `createApolloServer()` function.

To verify that the server is up and running and returns the expected results, browse the GraphQL web IDE--`http://localhost:3000/graphiql`--and run a simple test query (your date variable will be different from the following one):

```
{
  temperature(sensor_id:"12345", date:"2017-4-30"){
      sensor_id
      date
      event_time
      temperature
    }
}
```

Now that we verified that the server returns the expected results, the last step is to execute the preceding query on the client and visualize the results in a simple line chart.

In the `Chart.js` file, paste the following code:

```
import React, {Component, PropTypes} from 'react';
import {gql, graphql} from 'react-apollo';
import
{ResponsiveContainer,LineChart,Line,XAxis,YAxis,Tooltip,CartesianGrid,Legen
d}
from 'recharts';

const ChartQuery = gql `
  query temperature($sensor_id: String, $date: String) {
      temperature(sensor_id:$sensor_id, date:$date){
          sensor_id,
          date,
          event_time,
          temperature
```

```
    }
}`;
class Chart extends Component {
render(){
  return (
    <ResponsiveContainer minWidth={1000} minHeight={500}>
      <LineChart data={this.props.temperature}
       margin={{ top: 20, right: 50, left: 20, bottom: 5 }}>
        <XAxis dataKey="event_time"/> <YAxis/>
        <CartesianGrid strokeDasharray="3 3"/>
        <Tooltip/>
        <Legend/>
        <Line type="monotone" dataKey="temperature" stroke="#82ca9d"/>
      </LineChart>
    </ResponsiveContainer>
  )
 }
}
export default graphql(ChartQuery, {
 options: (props) => ({
   variables: { sensor_id:props.sensor_id, date: props.date }
  }),
 props: ({ data: { temperature } }) => ({
    temperature: temperature
  }),
}) (Chart);
```

Apollo client is built on top of Redux, and we do almost the same steps of connecting our components to the store. The graphql function is an HOC that returns another function, which takes a React component as an argument (Chart in our case).

The signature of the component looks like this:

```
graphql(query,config={key:value,key:value})(ReactComponent)
```

The query is the first argument, and it is not optional. The second one is the config object where we can specify different configuration objects. We specify the first key options that have a value function, which returns the props passed to the Chart component:

```
<Chart date ={date} sensor_id={sensor_id}/>
```

Then, we set the variables object to the values of the props that get passed to the query. Apollo will do the data fetching and persist the result to its built-in Redux store. If the props change, say we pass a different sensor_id to our Chart component, Apollo will automatically refetch the data and re-render the component.

The next key is the `props`, which will return the `data` prop from Apollo that will contain the result from the query. This is very useful when we want to specify what props with what data we want to pass to the child components.

If everything compiles without errors, the final result should look something like this:

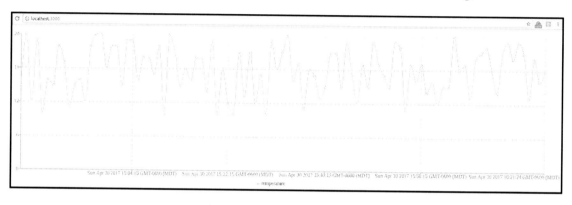

Test it and improve it!

Unlimited functionalities can be added to these three apps. You can flip the roles of who is a gRPC server and who is a client. You can also switch the databases by having MongoDB on the Gateway and adding Cassandra to the Meteor stack. Install the embedded app on a Raspberry PI (or similar board) with Cassandra, and let the data automatically sync with the Gateway by distributing Cassandra in a cluster. You configure Cassandra by modifying the `cassandra.yaml` file located in `etc/cassandra/cassandra.yaml`:

```
seed_provider:
  # Addresses of hosts that are deemed contact points.
  # Cassandra nodes use this list of hosts to find each other and learn
  # the topology of the ring. You must change this if you are running
  # multiple nodes!
  - class_name: org.apache.cassandra.locator.SimpleSeedProvider
  parameters:
  # seeds is actually a comma-delimited list of addresses.
  # Ex: "<ip1>,<ip2>,<ip3>"
  - seeds: "127.0.0.1"
```

Summary

In this chapter, we added a different communication layer--gRPC. We learned how we can build and connect grpc servers and clients, and we also learned how we can control the data flow from using simple callbacks to bidirectional streams. On the client, we briefly overviewed the `apollo-react` package from the Apollo client.

Index

A

Action Creators 122, 160
actions 116
Angular 2
  about 271
  URL, for cheat sheet 283
app
  bot, training 301
  building 118
  Cassandra, adding to stack 317
  chatbot, enhancing 316
  chatbot, shifting to Meteor app 311
  chatbot, testing 316
  components, creating 129
  data, obtaining from collection 125
  folder structure client 120
application components
  building 39
  CartContainer 44, 48
  functionality 41
  ProductsContainer 40, 43
  ProTypes 44
application
  router, adding 50, 53
async actions
  in Redux 127
Atom
  reference 12

B

books
  BooksContainer.js 56
Bootstrap
  and Meteor 80, 82
bounding box
  reference link 144

C

callback hell 218
canDrop method 153
card 94
Cart page
  URL 53
cart
  item quantity, removing 59
  item, removing 59
  method, creating for total price calculation 61
Cascading Style Sheets (CSS) 69
Cassandra Query Language (CQL) 318
chatbot
  building 284
  enhancing 316
  shifting, to Meteor app 311
  testing 316
  training 301
clustering column 319
command line interface (CLI) 11
considerations, scalability
  basic server validations 63
  defaults 66
  schema, defining 64
container components 36
contents, Meteor
  atmosphere 8
  communication 7
  databases 7
  frontend UI frameworks 7
  server 7
create, read, update, and delete (CRUD) 33, 147
CSS modules
  using, with, Meteor 82, 85

D

data container
   types 55
data
   obtaining, from collection 125
dataset
   reference 232
DDP (Distributed Data Protocol) 335
Dependency Injection (DI) 280
development environment
   setting up 8, 10
drag method
   testing 158
DragDropContext 149
DragSource 149
drop method
   about 153
   testing 158
DropTarget 149

E

embedded apps
   building 346
   testing 356

F

Facebook
   app, creating 288
   URL 287, 288
fibers
   reference 218
Filter components 133
Filter container 132
Filter functionality 132
Filters 112
folder structure client 120

G

Gateway 347
geographic information systems (GIS) 229
GraphQL
   about 271
   adding, to stack 322
grid

columns 71
container 71
rows 71
gRPC 333, 335, 347

H

Higher Order Component (HOC)
   about 147, 364
   building 187, 190
   testing 191
hover method 153

I

impure function 114
insecure default packages 58
Internet Engineering Steering Group (IESG) 335
Internet of Things (IoT) 333
Interpolation 278

J

JavaScript XML (JSX) 14

K

Kanban app
   building 158, 167
keyspaces 318

M

Material Design Lite (MDL)
   grid 103, 106
   used, for styling shopping cart 102
Meteor app
   building 11
   chatbot, shifting 311
   creating 271
Meteor Method 216
Meteor shell
   MongoDB, exploring 27
Meteor
   atmosphere packages, adding 22
   atmosphere packages, removing 22, 25, 26
   CSS modules, using 82, 84
   methods 58
   Publishing and Subscribing messaging pattern

28, 30
  reference 8
  using, with React 22
  with Redux 114
methods 58
Minimongo
  about 117
mobile devices
  apps, designing 70, 74
  making friendly 74
Modal app
  building 173, 185, 186
modular CSS
  using, with LESS 74, 77
  using, with Syntactically Awesome StyleSheets
  (Sass) 78
monetization 235
MongoDB
  about 271
  data, importing to 194
  reference 193
  search functionality, exploring 204

N

Natural Language Processing (NLP) 144
ngrok
  URL 291
node twitter
  reference link 142
node.bcrypt.js
  reference 350
Nuclide 12

O

object spread syntax 116

P

panel 94
presentational components 36
Products Route
  URL 53
Protocol Buffers
  advantages 335
Provider, Redux 364
Publishing and Subscribing messaging pattern,

Meteor
  about 28, 30
  improvements, in current code 30
pure functions 114

Q

query string (qs) 298
quick replies button 308

R

react-meteor-data 33
react-router 50
React
  about 271
  component state 16
  drag 148
  drop 149
  front-end 13, 15
  inheritance, versus composition 18
  integrating, with Meteor's reactive data system
  26
  state, adding to component 19, 21
  state, adding to stateless function component 16
reactive data system
  integrating, with React 26
real-time maps
  building 240, 252, 264
  server side 264, 270
real-time search application
  building 205, 232
Redis 316
reducer function 116, 167, 173
Redux store, connecting with React components
  about 129
  components, of app 132
  containers, of app 132
  Filter component 133
  improving 144
  on the server 142
  Sentiment component 139
  testing 144
  Tweets component 138
Redux
  about 114
  async actions 126

components 116
meteor 114
using, on client 117
Relational Database Management Systems
    (RDBMS) 319
router
adding, to application 50, 53
App.js 54
data containers 55
MusicContainer.js 56
ProductComponent.js 54
RPC
testing 346

S

scalability
considerations 63
scalar types
reference 337
Sentiment component
about 112, 139
reference link 142
server-side
index.js file 36
insertData.js file 36
shopping cart
structure, creating 33, 36
styling 86, 91

styling, Material Design Lite (MDL) used 102
Single Page Applications (SPA) 50, 240
stringified JSON 299
supervised learning 302
Syntactically Awesome StyleSheets (Sass)
about 78
Modular CSS, using 79

T

text field
indexing 195
time series data modeling
reference 352
Time To Live (TTL) property 363
Tweets component 112, 138
Twitter
application structure 112
streaming 109
URL, for creating account 110

U

unique numbered tag 337
user account's functionality
maintaining, example cases 235

W

webhook 291
webpack 86